PR

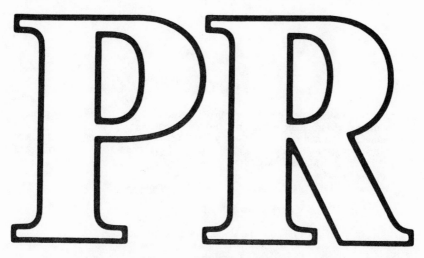

PR

HOW THE PUBLIC RELATIONS INDUSTRY WRITES THE NEWS

JEFF & MARIE BLYSKAL

William Morrow and Company, Inc.   New York

ABU 2063 - 3/1

To Paul and Dorothy—
the best inspiration any writers could have

Library of Congress Catalog Card Number: 85-80602

ISBN: 0-688-04788-2

Printed in the United States of America

First Edition

1 2 3 4 5 6 7 8 9 10

BOOK DESIGN BY JAYE ZIMET

Contents

one

The Communications Elite

PUBLIC RELATIONS' RISING NEW INFLUENCE AND POWER

With public sentiment, nothing can fail; without it, nothing can succeed. Consequently, he who molds public sentiment goes deeper than he who enacts statutes or pronounces decisions.

—ABRAHAM LINCOLN, July 31, 1858

WASHINGTON, OCTOBER 24, 1983. The unpretentious silver automobile rumbles away from the Pentagon, then swings out into the night of Highway 110 North. The trip across the Arlington Memorial Bridge, past the Lincoln Memorial and down Twenty-third Street to the State Department, might take seven minutes.

Inside, the news executive contemplates tomorrow's front page news. He prides himself on the extent of his empire—400 radio and television stations worldwide, two daily newspapers, two magazines, a motion picture studio in Hollywood. "I have the largest media conglomerate in the world," he has boasted more than once. The executive is not talking about ABC, CBS, or NBC News. He is not referring to the New York Times Company or the Washington Post Company.

Assistant Secretary of Defense for Public Affairs Michael Burch—the news executive riding in the silver automobile—is talking about his 1,000-man, $100-million-a-year worldwide public relations operation at the Defense Department.

It is not stretching the truth to call Burch a news executive, because that's exactly what much of his job is. While there are regular exceptions, in the normal course of the day it is often not the scores of Pentagon correspondents who decide what will make the day's Defense news; they have neither the worldwide Defense Department omnipresence nor the far-reaching access to military personnel and affairs.

Michael Burch, however, does. And while he can do little to control a Blue Angels jet crash, a test site accident, or the murder of more than 241 Marines in a Lebanese barracks—which happened the morning before—he holds a tight, careful reign on other news that he can control and even design to his needs and specifications. Are the Russians overtaking us in the arms race? Burch can tell you and will probably offer the services of military spy satellites or intelligence agents to vividly illustrate his story. Is morale rising or falling in the Army? Burch will be there with the story. Are we holding war games or naval maneuvers near one of the Soviet puppet states? Burch will give your TV cameramen notice well in advance and even see that the necessary transportation and facilities are provided free of charge. After all, Michael Burch is a news executive with "the world's largest media conglomerate."

If the name "news executive" makes you just a bit too nervous, call him one of The Communications Elite, an increasingly powerful group with a potent blend of news and public relations talent. Their business is what Lincoln recognized almost 130 years ago as more important than the power of government itself: the molding of public opinion.

Perhaps at no time in Burch's career had his talent been more important than on that night, Monday, October 24, 1983, the eve of the U.S. invasion of a tiny island in the Caribbean called Grenada.

For the next several days and beyond, Burch and the government's other PR people would help shape the news about the military action. Again, while they could not control all the events of the battle, they would exert a frightening degree of control over the news coverage. By influencing the media, the government's PR machinery helped create a favorable public opinion toward the Grenada affair, the military, and President Reagan.

Burch's car pulled up at the State Department. He stepped out and briskly proceeded to the office of Langhorne Motley, assistant secretary of state for inter-American affairs. There he sat down at an 11 P.M. meeting with John Hughes, assistant secretary of state for public affairs; Motley and his assistant Craig Johnston; Navy captain Robert Sims, press officer for the National Security Council; Alan Romberg, deputy assistant secretary of state for public affairs; and representatives of the Joint Chiefs of Staff and the United States Information Agency, the propaganda arm of the U.S. aimed overseas.

In that office, behind closed doors, The Communications Elite mapped out their strategy.

Much of what went on behind those closed doors for the next hour and a half remains a secret, for, in order to work effectively in the business of molding public opinion, government PR people must operate in the shadows. To protect the secrecy of the government PR behind "Operation Urgent Fury," the military's code name for the Grenada invasion, the State Department and the National Security Council refused to release documents concerning this strategy session.

Nevertheless, history, involved parties, documents obtained from the Department of Defense and USIA, and a careful analysis of the subtleties of the Grenada PR reveal much of the strategy that evolved at the State Department and other meetings in the shadows.

Of course, history had already primed the public for a daring U.S. military action anywhere. The demoralizing military and political setbacks of Vietnam, Watergate, the Iranian hostage crisis, and the death of the U.S. Marines in Lebanon at the hands of terrorists had prepared the public for acceptance of the Grenada invasion, and the struggle for power on Grenada between Prime Minister Maurice Bishop and his "friends" had laid its groundwork.

Nonetheless, proper government PR handling of an issue as potentially volatile as war waged by a "trigger-happy" President is necessary to prevent presidential gold from turning into dross. Anyone who buys the line advanced by many of the government PR people involved—that the PR's main job in Grenada was to "provide as much information as possible," especially in light of the restrictions on the press—is naive. The government's PR machinery, both successfully and unsuccessfully, does not close up shop when a "crisis" like Grenada is sprung upon it. It works overtime.

Many members of the press have said Grenada was a "public relations disaster" for the White House—primarily because of the news blackout. They do not understand the sophisticated nature of modern government PR players. These people are not the stereotypical Hollywood press agents or corporate flacks in plaid jackets. They are less conspicuous because "politics" and public relations are so intertwined. Michael Deaver, former deputy White House chief of staff, is a PR man, but so is President Reagan himself part of the time. A major responsibility of every politician is public relations, because he needs public support to keep his job. Closer examination of the Grenada PR in this light reveals that indeed it was not a disaster; in fact, it was a PR coup.

The government PR successfully pushed the idea that this was a hastily put-together operation with little time for planning and strategizing. President Reagan described "an urgent, formal request" from the Organization of Eastern Caribbean States (OECS) on Sunday, October 23, at his October 25 press conference announcing the invasion. Secretary of State George Shultz, however, said later that the request came a day earlier, on Saturday, October 22, at 2:45 A.M. In fact, an informal request was made on October 20, according to John Compton, prime minister of St. Lucia, one of the OECS nations. Compton was one of the chief architects of the OECS/U.S. intervention in Grenada.

Compton says he spoke with Deputy Assistant Secretary of State for Caribbean Affairs Charles Anthony Gillespie on October 19, the day of Bishop's murder. "We talked about the situation in Grenada and I expressed our concern that we would have to do something," says Compton. "I informed the U.S. at four A.M. on October twentieth that . . . we intended to move militarily. No offer of assistance was made by the U.S." Later that morning, at the signing of a U.S. economic treaty in St. Lucia at about 10 A.M., Compton says, a "request [for assistance] was made informally to Gillespie."

Gillespie confirms that he spoke privately with Compton on the morning of the twentieth and the prime minister said,

"We're going to need help." Later that day in Barbados, Gillespie says he met with Prime Minister Eugenia Charles of Dominica and the late Prime Minister John Adams of Barbados, who also made an informal request for assistance.

Compton says he also talked to U.S. Ambassador Milan Bish "the day before Bishop's murder [October 18]. It wasn't just a conversation, obviously. It was an expression of concern. We hoped to start getting some sort of reaction. I was sending him a message—and I'd hoped they'd attune themselves to it."

Compton's messages apparently came across loud and clear. On October 20, Admiral Wesley L. McDonald, commander in chief of the U.S. Atlantic Command, diverted the USS *Independence Carrier Battle Group* and the *Amphibious Ready Group* of ships to Grenada. The group had been bound for Lebanon.

The U.S. was apparently involved even earlier than that. On Saturday, October 15, said Adams, a Barbadian military official "reported . . . that he had been tentatively approached by a United States official about the prospect of rescuing Maurice Bishop from his captors and had been made an offer of transport."[1]

Finally, according to testimony given by Admiral McDonald to the House Armed Services Committee in late January 1984— three months after the invasion—"We started preliminary planning for the evacuation of U.S. citizens after Prime Minister Bishop was arrested on 13 October, 1983. Detailed planning did not commence, however, until after he was killed on 19 October."

So the U.S. was laying plans for involvement, presumably military in nature, almost a week and a half before the "urgent" request for assistance came from the OECS.

Why then create the impression of extreme haste, when more than a week of earnest deliberation and diplomatic messages preceded the final decision? The implication was that the U.S. government had absolutely no premeditated plan to invade Grenada in order to oust an unfriendly government. Much better, from a public relations standpoint, to appear to act quickly and decisively to a request for aid that came from the blue. This was the first public relations step the U.S. took. It was subtle but very useful in building support for the invasion.

The urgent request from the OECS nations also took care of another PR problem: how could the Reagan administration get itself involved without appearing to be looking for trouble? Prime Minister Compton: "I wouldn't say the U.S. was spoiling for a fight, but . . . there was a regime the U.S. was uncomfortable with. . . . The U.S. knew that if it had an opportunity to intervene militarily in Grenada, it would have Caribbean support."

Of course, Caribbean support is one thing; Caribbean leadership is quite another. If the Caribbean nations, which had genuine vital interests in ousting the Soviet satellite government from the region, were to lead the charge, the U.S. would not be cast in the warmonger role but rather in that of a duty-bound ally.

Compton denies that the U.S., whose military was already laying plans for Grenada, tipped the OECS that the idea of an invasion should be made to look as if it came from the OECS first instead of the U.S. But Compton and the other OECS prime ministers are not naive about the workings of international relations and public relations.

Says Compton, "We knew we had to take the leading edge. We had to provide the grounds for U.S. intervention; we didn't expect them to go in by themselves. The U.S., diplomatically, had to play the 'support' role, even though militarily they took the lead. We set the stage for U.S. assistance."

There was another very good reason for this. "By the twenty-second, we knew we didn't have what we needed [militarily]," says Compton. "If the U.S. didn't get involved, there was nothing we could have done. We couldn't have beaten Grenada; many of the OECS nations don't even have armies. We would have gotten clobbered." But "by Saturday, I fully expected the U.S. to come in just from knowing the administration's stand. Once the request was there and [the U.S.] had the cover of legitimacy—the OECS treaty—[I knew] they would have moved.

"If there had been no invasion, I wouldn't be sitting here today," says Compton without a smile from his Forty-second Street consular office in New York.

So, from the start, the government Communications Elite anticipated the public relations difficulties of a U.S. invasion and created a setting that would inhibit those potential problems from becoming real problems. Lower-level government PR people mechanically implemented this strategy by making sure the "urgent" request and OECS/U.S. joint involvement was clearly stated at the top of press releases, guidance papers for public affairs spokesmen, press conferences, speeches, and media interviews.

The PR also drove home the point that the invasion was not the U.S.' idea by making sure Eugenia Charles, prime minister of Dominica and head of the OECS, was present at President Reagan's 9 A.M. news conference announcing the invasion. That seemingly minor but actually important detail kept "Warmonger" President Reagan off the front page and put Charles in first position flanked by "Dependable Ally" Ronald Reagan, instead.

The third major PR strategy involved the so-called press blackout, which was reportedly decided at the 11 P.M. State Department meeting on the eve of the invasion.[2]

Actually, this was not a true blackout, though that is what the press reported. Rather, the Pentagon PR operations simply refused to transport or help journalists get to Grenada and turned back huge press yachts or airplanes that were attempting to enter the war zone. The military made the job of reporting difficult for the press—but by no means impossible. More than a dozen journalists and photographers who did not depend on the Pentagon PR office got onto the island via small boats and covered the operation.

The fence around Grenada had holes in it just big enough for journalists traveling light to get through—if they tried seriously. The ones who didn't get through were the network TV crews, each of which required several people and a ton of bulky video equipment.

Note that point: print reporters and still photographers got in; network TV was kept out. That was no accident, for the point of the no-assistance press policy by the Pentagon was to specifically "keep TV out." Says the State Department's Hughes: "The military has a prejudice against TV. They were sensitive to the idea of people sitting down to dinner while watching the evening news with horror footage from Grenada. The military feels it got burned in Vietnam [by TV]."

All PR people know that the effects of TV coverage and print coverage are dramatically different. A television account of war is immediate, alive, real, graphic, bloody—and, most important, TV is an emotional medium.

A print account or still photo of the very same story is less "real." The very medium places a safe barrier between the reader and the action that distances him; it also allows for a more intellectual, abstract understanding of the war, its causes and its meaning.

For the Communications Elite, placing the story in distancing print rather than on immediate TV lent an advantage. They could get their view of things across much more easily than could potentially critical television journalists wielding bloody videotape.

The White House pointed the finger of blame for the "blackout" on the military planners. Given the Reagan administration's record of careful PR planning, the White House assertion—to put it gently—lacks credibility. What that story says is, "What you saw about Grenada was not staged; it was real. After all, what do generals know about PR?"

To believe that, one would have to believe that President Reagan and his image makers would, without care, allow the single aggressive military action of his presidency to be sold to the public by the military—just a year before the presidential election. It is impossible to accept the suggestion that the most sophisticated PR president since John F. Kennedy, with the most talented group of PR people ever advising him, would allow that. We can only conclude that the so-called blackout was a carefully thought-out White House PR design made only after all the advantages and disadvantages were fully weighed.

That the press blackout was really a "no-assistance" PR policy is further demonstrated by the experience of members of the press who did take the trouble to get on the island. "We didn't stop reporters who were there from doing their job," says the Pentagon's Burch. The facts give Burch's statement credibility.

"A group of seven journalists . . . succeeded in reaching Grenada," said the *Washington Times* on October 27, adding incorrectly, "where they were immediately placed under house arrest, according to conflicting reports." In fact, the journalists had landed on the island in enemy territory, eventually crossed over to U.S. lines, and had free run of the island. Just read the detailed accounts by two of the reporters, the *Miami Herald*'s Don Bohning on October 28 and *Time*'s Bernard Diederich in the November 7 issue. Nor did the U.S. military hamper journalists on the island or hold them hostage, despite what many Americans read in the newspapers.

U.S. TROOPS REMOVE REPORTERS FROM ISLAND trumpeted the *Washington Post* erroneously on October 27. Said Bohning, "[*Washington Post* reporter Edward] Cody, *Newsday* correspondent Morris Thompson and I went looking for the Marines to see if they could help us file our stories." The reporters were then taken to the USS *Guam,* where they were unable to do so. Bohning had to hedge by saying that he and the other two journalists were held "more or less captive." But again, the journalists didn't run into interference from the military until they asked the military to help them perform their jobs.

A journalist in another group of reporters that got to the island, Charles Lachman of the *New York Post,* also reports they received no resistance from military personnel. Even when they got to Marine checkpoints, they were allowed to pass through after showing their press credentials. The Sygma News Agency, which managed to get three still photographers and even one video camerawoman to Grenada, also says its people were not prevented from doing their job. Nor were they kept out of areas or away from the action, taken off the island, or disturbed in any way by the military.

The fourth major piece of the PR puzzle involved the "rescue" of the students at St. George's University School of Medicine in Grenada.

The students may have been in a potentially dangerous situation; whether they would have actually been taken hostage à la Iran is pure speculation. A State Department survey reportedly taken of 500 students showed that 320—64 percent—had wanted to leave the island. Astonishingly, considering the danger they had supposedly been in, most of the remaining 36 percent of students had been undecided about leaving.[3]

Also, the students apparently didn't see many of the enemy soldiers who were supposed to be a threat to them during the invasion. "No one saw the other troops," says Jeff Geller, who was at the True Blue campus near the Point Salines airfield.

"We saw Americans firing back at something, but we never saw what."

Nor were any of the students injured or taken hostage, even though the True Blue campus was not secured until around 9 A.M. on October 25, almost four hours after the invasion began: the Grand Anse campus was not secured until 4 P.M. on October 26, thirty-five hours after the invasion began.

The job of PR was to make sure the more publically acceptable "rescue of students" was pushed to the front of the list of justifications for the invasion. Trying to justify U.S. imperialism or the imposition of a friendly government on another country—two other reasons for our invading Grenada—might have eroded support for the action.

It was thus PR that made sure the students were front and center. "We have taken this decisive action for three reasons," said Reagan at his October 25 press conference. "First, and of overriding importance, to protect innocent lives, including up to 1,000 Americans whose personal safety is, of course, my paramount concern."

That theme was stressed in virtually all guidance papers to government public affairs officers. "The central U.S. concerns throughout the events in Grenada have been the safety of American citizens . . ." explained one limited-official-use telegram on PR guidance from USIA to public affairs officers at U.S. embassies around the world. Explained a classified State Department cable on "Grenada Public Diplomacy Themes": "The brutal behavior and record of members of the RMC [Revolutionary Military Council] . . . led to grave concern about the safety of nearly 1,000 Americans and other foreigners in Grenada. Our concerns for safety of U.S. citizens were heightened by a shoot-on-sight twenty-four-hour curfew. . . ."

One government PR man close to the situation admits the students furnished a point for the government PR to emphasize: "How much danger were the students in? That was a judgment call. Whether you call it a rescue mission or an invasion has an effect on public opinion. We emphasized the students, not the unfriendly U.S./Grenada relations."

But the day of the invasion a very credible-sounding voice was raising doubt about the danger the students were in. The school's chancellor, Charles Modica, who had been in contact with the campus via telex, charged that he thought Reagan was "very wrong" in saying American lives were in danger.[4]

The Communications Elite knew this voice had to be silenced, and acted swiftly to do so. They invited Modica to a private briefing at State on the twenty-sixth. There, Modica says, he was shown captured documents which lent support to the hostage theory. "I saw contingency plans for taking the students hostage. The plan was made by a person associated with the Bishop government, the New Jewel Movement," says Modica. "Nothing I saw said they would be taken hostage on a certain day, but an element of danger was at least present. The question of degree is open to interpretation."

Modica says he "expected to be bulldozed" when he was invited, but when he left, "I was convinced the [documents] were genuine and I'm still convinced."

After the State Department briefing, Modica reversed himself and said ". . . President Reagan was justified in ordering the invasion," according to the *New York Times* account.[5] That killed the issue, and, because Modica didn't go into detail about what he had seen, the public was undoubtedly left with the impression that real evidence existed that proved the students had been in danger.

Meanwhile, on the *Today* show, Secretary of Defense Caspar Weinberger was carefully sidestepping a question from host Bryant Gumbel.

GUMBEL: Mr. Secretary . . . can you give us any hard evidence those Americans were in any real danger?
WEINBERGER: Well, when you're in a twenty-four hour curfew and you're told that if you're found on the street you'll be shot . . . I would classify that as at least pretty uncomfortable conditions. Also, in those circumstances you always have to be worried about hostages being taken. . . .

Why didn't Weinberger point to the solid evidence of the contingency plans that Modica was being shown in private the very same day? Could it be that the documents never existed?

The next day, government PR "leaked" a story in the *New York Times* which began:

U.S. REPORTS EVIDENCE OF ISLAND HOSTAGE PLAN
By PHILIP TAUBMAN

WASHINGTON, October 27—Reagan Administration officials said today that United States invasion forces in Grenada had found evidence that the Grenadian government, in conjunction with Cuban advisers, had been considering a plan to hold United States citizens hostage in the near future. . . .

"It is clear from these documents and other information we now have that serious consideration was being given to seizing Americans as hostages and holding them for reasons that are not entirely clear, but seem to involve an effort to embarrass the United States and, more immediately, to forestall American military action in Grenada," one senior official said.

Another senior official said, "It appears we got there just in time to prevent a tragedy." The official declined to describe the documents in detail or to discuss specific information about the potential seizure of hostages.[6]

Taubman's article shows why reporters should not always rely on leaks, which are often PR devices. The *Times* story and the papers Modica saw were part of the PR strategy to build confidence in the students-as-hostages story and to shut up a noisy opponent in the crucial early stages when public opinion about the invasion was being formed.

The *Times* article marks the last time we've seen these documents cited. No other government officials mentioned them. Important as they were to establishing credibility for the pretext of the U.S. involvement, they were not released with the "treasure trove" of documentary evidence released the week of November 6. They are not even mentioned in "Grenada, a Preliminary Report," a twenty-five-page booklet released by the Department of State and Department of Defense; they are not mentioned in "Grenada: Background and Facts," another booklet released by the United States Information Agency; they do not appear in "Grenada Documents, an Overview and Selection," a two-inch-thick compilation of the documents from Grenada published by the Defense Department and Department of State a year after the invasion; they remain untold in *Grenada: The Untold Story,* a 1984 book by Gregory Sandford, a foreign service officer in the State Department who did an extensive examination of the captured papers, and Richard Vigilante, a Washington-based journalist. Numerous State Department officials who should know about such important documents, including Gillespie, confess ignorance about the existence of them.

Finally, says one informed State Department source who asked not to be identified, "This was frankly discussed as one of the reasons for the invasion. But I've never seen a piece of paper that described such a plan. We don't know of any specific document like that—we'd love to find one, though—and it's a major enough document for me to know about if it did exist."

Adds Prime Minister Compton, another man who should know, "There was no evidence the students were in danger. The students were used—the question of the students' safety was a secondary reason for the invasion. . . . This was a regime the U.S. was uncomfortable with."

These were, of course, only the major building blocks of the White House/Defense Department/State Department PR strategy for Grenada. Numerous other PR techniques designed to help build public support were implemented throughout the period:

INFORMATION CONTROL: To exert maximum control of the news content and to roadblock the more than 400 news people covering the Grenada story from "on the scene" in Barbados, Defense Department PR made sure all the news came from Washington. "Having one source of information is a standard public affairs principle," says Navy captain Owen Resweber, public affairs officer for the United States Atlantic fleet in Norfolk. "All information came out of the Assistant Secretary of Defense for Public Affairs' [Michael Burch's] office."

PHOTO OPPORTUNITIES: On October 26, television news and the rest of the press were alerted in ample time to set up their equipment to cover the arrival of student evacuees aboard two C-141 Starlifter transports at Charleston Air Force Base in South Carolina. At that photo opportunity, student Jeff Geller made his famous gesture of kissing the ground, which provided the administration with all the "evidence" it needed that the students thought the invasion was justified. Geller's move was *not* arranged by government PR. It was actually more a joke than a political/emotional statement of relief. "I wanted my friend to take a picture of me because of a running joke we had during the tense ten days before the invasion," says Geller. "I had said then, 'If I ever get off this rock, I'll kiss the blankety-blank ground.'" Hungry for the emotional and visual content the artificial event seemed to provide, most of the media never questioned the motive or sincerity of the gesture—an unexpected bonus for Grenada's PR masterminds, and an indicator of press preference for drama over accuracy.

NEWS TIMING: Weinberger and General John Vessey, Jr., chairman of the Joint Chiefs of Staff, gave an upbeat report on the progress of the invasion in a televised press conference from the Pentagon commencing at 4:30 P.M., October 26. Just as the conference was winding down, network television coverage switched live to Charleston Air Force Base and the arriving students. The students gave credibility to the upbeat press conference. "We didn't plan that at all," protests Burch, but in fact the 5 P.M. student landing, described in a press advisory earlier in the day, and the 4:30 press conference were both timed by Defense public affairs for maximum effectiveness.

By contrast, arrival of another C-141 Starlifter transport—this one carrying the bodies of U.S. Marines killed in the Beirut bombing—was arranged to take place at Dover Air Force Base at 3 A.M. October 29, when no television would broadcast the media event live.

DAMAGE CONTROL: When word reached the press that U.S. planes had bombed a mental hospital on Grenada, killing perhaps fifty people, Pentagon PR people leaped into action. Apparently without much information to go on, a Defense press release posted at 1:15 P.M., October 31, said, "Preliminary indications are that casualties are substantially, repeat substantially lower than being reported in various media." Later that day, the Pentagon dug up a director of the hospital, a Dr. Clement Gabrial, and reported in a press release that twelve bodies were recovered from the rubble. Despite the brouhaha over war coverage by press release, the *New York Times* chose to believe the Pentagon

PR and downplay the on-scene journalists who broke the story. U.S. CONCEDES BOMBING HOSPITAL IN GRENADA, KILLING AT LEAST 12, read the page-one headline. That evening, a Defense Department video of an interview with a hospital administrator was flown via S-3 aircraft from the deck of the USS *Independence* to Andrews Air Force Base outside of Washington.

PUBLICITY: The Defense Department and White House made sure plenty of officials were put in front of the cameras to push the administration's views that the students were in danger, that U.S. intervention was legal, that troops would be out "as soon as possible," and that the situation in Grenada before the invasion was volatile and dangerous. "The administration can be more effective by filling interview requests," says Gergen. That way the administration "story" gets coverage. So Weinberger was on the *Today* show, the *CBS Morning News,* and *Good Morning America.* In addition, White House PR sought coverage outside the national press. "You blitz," says Gergen. "They call us, we call them. We put people on local call-in shows."

PUBLICITY: Admiral McDonald, commander in chief of the Atlantic fleet and head of the Urgent Fury invasion, left the battlefield to hold a press conference at a Pentagon studio on October 28—after two days of fighting. "He recognizes the importance of communicating with the public," says Resweber, McDonald's PR man. "It's a necessary part of modern warfare."

The United States Information Agency christened its Euronet [now Worldnet] satellite press conference service with Grenada. United States Ambassador to the United Nations Jeane Kirkpatrick, St. Lucia's Compton, and Barbados' Adams were put on Euronet and were made available to journalists via satellite for simultaneous press conferences in London, Paris, Geneva, Brussels, Bonn, and Rome. That got the administration story out to the European media.

MEDIA EVENTS: The White House arranged to have the "rescued" students visit the White House to thank President Reagan for rescuing them. "We knew that was something the media would cover," says Gergen.

Captured materiel from Grenada was put on display at Andrews Air Force Base on November 10. "That was the President's idea," says Gergen. Once again, the objective was to push the credibility of the administration's story. One result was a UPI article which included the following: "Passing a table full of Soviet-bloc sidearms and machine guns, [Vice President George] Bush picked up a new Russian AK-47 assault rifle. He shook his head and said, 'I guess everything we heard is true. This is pretty stark evidence.'"

CONTROLLED NEWS: The Defense Department provided the media with several thousand feet of videotape and motion picture footage it said was uncensored except for two cases involving national security. Of course, the footage was "edited," in that the military chose what it wanted to film. In addition, some 200 still photos by Defense Department photographers were also provided to the press. The press used them. The PR "themes" these pictures supported were represented in one package of nine photos released showing Eugenia Charles conferring at the White House (demonstrating the OECS request); two photos involving the Caribbean forces (demonstrating that this was not just a U.S. invasion, but a joint effort); Geller kissing the ground; an American soldier with happily rescued students and students lining up to leave the island (demonstrating the relief of the students); captured materiel (demonstrating the arms buildup); and happy Grenadians welcoming the arrival of the multinational troops (demonstrating that the U.S. action was approved by the oppressed Grenadians).

All of this PR work translated into real political capital for President Reagan. According to a Gallup poll taken before the invasion of Grenada between September 30 and October 16, Reagan's approval rating stood at 46 percent. At the same time, 37 percent disapproved of his handling the job of President. On October 23, more than 225 U.S. Marines were massacred in Lebanon. Considering the U.S. negligence that helped make that massacre possible, Reagan's popularity would have surely suffered a devastating blow—had it not been for the big news of the Grenada invasion on October 25, which divided public attention and news resources between two major stories.

On October 26 and 27, a Gallup organization poll showed,

Reagan's popularity had risen to 48 percent approval with 39 percent disapproval. The lack of movement is not unusual; confronted with such significant, confusing, and incomplete information as that coming out of Beirut and Grenada, the public needed time to digest it and reassess its opinion, if warranted.

Finally, the poll that should have sent corks popping in the White House PR offices: between October 28 and November 13, Reagan's approval rating, according to Gallup, had risen 5 more points to 53 percent while his disapproval rating fell 8 points to 31 percent. The spread between the two had more than doubled to 22 points from 9 points.

One can easily imagine a much different result if the U.S. had barreled into Grenada without a nod to the OECS; if Reagan had come right out and said, "We're taking one domino back from the Soviets"; if network television had broadcast the daily body count in living color (Marine green and blood red); and if Congress had been able to take the lead in forming public opinion and had denounced Reagan as interfering in the affairs of sovereign nations just as the Soviets do.

No, Grenada was not a public relations disaster, it was a PR coup.

The sophisticated public relations management of the news media and public opinion surrounding the Grenada invasion is not unusual. Michael Burch, David Gergen, Michael Deaver, and the scores of other government PR people who "sold" Grenada to the public are only a fraction of more than 100,000 largely unseen public relations professionals tinkering behind the scenes with the day's news. Their objective is to orchestrate PR that in one way or another helps move inestimable billions of consumer, business, and government dollars from one set of pockets to another.

When the average person ticks off on his fingers the most powerful influences on public opinion, he's likely to recognize politicians, the news media, business leaders, the entertainment world, perhaps advertising. Public relations, on the other hand, is normally seen as the province of the inept and painfully transparent huckster.

Yet over the past three decades, PR has sprung up virtually unnoticed into an enormous shadow industry of persuasion that influences your choices in what you buy, the foods you eat, the books you read, the movies you watch, the issues you support, and the politicians you elect. It helps you decide where you'll live and, sometimes, where you'll die.

Most people think they know all about PR because they are aware of Hollywood press agents who are always dreaming up crazy publicity stunts to get their clients' names in the newspapers. This PR man is usually deemed "harmless."

Another PR man, the chief spokesman for the White House, is much more responsible for creating the public's sense of what PR people and public relations are all about. The White House spokesman is always on the evening news, often seemingly making one excuse after another for the President.

This kind of limited exposure to PR by the public has created a number of false images of the profession:

□ PR people are always lying.
□ The news media always "see through" the lies.
□ PR people are kicked around like dogs; they are humiliated, degraded servants to their master. (PR can thank Nixon press secretary Ron Ziegler for that.* Remember the incident in August 1973 when, with Watergate at full boil, a disgruntled Richard Nixon was being followed into a convention center by members of the press? Nixon suddenly stopped, spun around, grabbed Ziegler by the shoulders, and shoved him at the press. "I don't want the press with me," snarled Nixon. "You take care of it.")

These images add up to the conclusion that PR people are largely ineffective at their game of manipulation. Nothing, however, could be farther from the truth.

Since World War II, PR has grown from a one-dimensional "press agentry" function into a sophisticated communications network connecting the most powerful elements of our society. Through this network, corporations, unions, government, nonprofit organizations, and other interest groups attempt to influence the various "publics" with which they must deal all the time: consumers, employees, voters, investors, regulators, and other groups. Publicity messages sent along this network are carefully constructed to put the interest group, its goals or its

*Ironically, Ziegler's background was not PR, it was advertising.

products, in the best possible light, so that the specific "target publics" will think and behave in a manner beneficial to the special interest group.

For example, when the Internal Revenue Service (a special interest group) wants taxpayers (a specific target public) to fill out its tax forms as fully, accurately, and honestly as possible, it will swoop down on a couple of high-visibility tax cheats, just as April 15 approaches. A movie star charged with tax evasion or underreporting of earnings makes big news, and taxpayers hear about it loudly in newspapers and on television. The effect of this kind of publicity—which usually spotlights the tens of thousands the tax cheat owes in back taxes or penalties—is to scare the hell out of taxpayers so they will be sure not to cheat in a big way themselves, lest they be caught too.

That is PR manipulation of the public through use of the news media, because it creates the impression that the IRS always gets its cheater. In fact, the IRS is far too understaffed to catch the majority of cheaters. The estimated $90 billion yearly in unpaid tax due to nonfiling, underreporting of income, and phony deductions is ample evidence of that.[7] The IRS does not have the resources to uncover every phony deduction or every dollar of nonreported income. Nor can it audit everyone. So it needs PR to make people think the IRS is more of a Big Brother than it really is.

Chances are, in the past twenty-four hours, carefully designed PR communications like that one have pulled your opinion in several dozen different directions without your even knowing it.

And with the shrinking of Marshall McLuhan's global village; with the rise of consumerism/environmentalism; and with the public's growing awareness of Madison Avenue's highly polished, overtly manipulative advertising techniques, the future holds great promise for the continued growth of PR's silent influence on the public. PR's practitioners are becoming the new "hidden persuaders" of the eighties.

How have such lowly "flacks" achieved such lofty heights? Because, contrary to what the press usually tells you, the poorly regarded business of public relations actually works. Business and government and other interest groups have realized what Hollywood studios and astute politicians have known for years: PR gets results. And nothing attracts booming demand for a service more than success. In 1983 alone, revenues at the 50 largest PR firms grew almost 20 percent to more than $352 million, says the 1984 edition of *O'Dwyer's Directory of Public Relations Firms.*[8]

Public relations now sells movies, products, corporate images and goals, politicians and government programs by getting publicity in the media. But a news story in the *Washington Post* or on the *CBS Evening News* is not the ultimate goal of a PR person; that is only a means to an end. The end is getting some target public to do something as a result of the publicity seen in the media.

To get the news coverage they want, PR people have carefully studied what makes the media tick. They know what turns on a reporter's nose for news. They know how much time a journalist has before deadline—meaning they know how much time he has to check out all angles of the PR "story." PR people know that the media have to fill a certain number of pages or a certain number of minutes of air time. They know how a writer or news organization will "slant" a story. They know who's reading or watching what publications and news broadcasts.

Simply put, PR people know how the press thinks. Thus they are able to tailor their publicity so that journalists will listen and cover it.

As a result much of the news you read in newspapers and magazines or watch on television and hear on radio is heavily influenced and slanted by public relations people. Whole sections of the news are virtually owned by PR. According to some estimates, 45 percent–50 percent of the business news appearing in the *Wall Street Journal* is made up of press release rewrites or stories initiated by PR people. Newspaper food pages are a PR man's paradise, as are the entertainment, automotive, real estate, home improvement, and living sections.

Overall, maybe half of a newspaper's contents, including hard news as well as softer feature news, is initiated by a press release or by a PR man giving a story tip to a journalist.

Unfortunately "news" hatched by a PR person and journalist working together looks much like real news dug up by enterprising journalists working independently. The public thus does not know which news stories and journalists are playing servant to

PR. Some examples of PR stories that look like anything else you'd see in the press:

☐ When the movie *Jaws* was ready for release, Charles Powell, a former MGM/UA publicist, says he hired a Montauk, Long Island, shark hunter to find a great white shark. Whether the man actually saw a great white—the subject of the movie—or not is unknown, but the Sunday before the film's release, the shark hunter sure enough reported to the Associated Press, United Press International, and the New York press that one certainly had been spotted and almost caught off Long Island. Remember for a moment the fear of sharks and ocean swimming that swept America at that time and you will touch the power of PR.

☐ The front page of the February 4, 1985, *New York Post* was vintage tabloid: a third of the page was taken up by a photo of a shapely brunette romping in the surf in a sexy bathing suit. Readers were directed to the centerfold where no less than nine beauties in various slinky bathing suits took the entire two-page spread. Standard Murdoch fare when winter temperatures plunge, yes. But the pictorial was also PR for Gottex, the swimsuit maker. These comely models, readers learned, were wearing Gottex' summer 1985 line. While the *Post*'s photo department had initiated the photo story, it depended on Gottex PR for the pictures.

☐ PR played an important role in creating excitement for the debut of the Ford Mustang in 1964. Says Lee Iacocca, the "father" of the Mustang:

"Four days before the car was officially launched, a hundred members of the press participated in a giant seventy-car Mustang rally from New York to Dearborn. . . . The press recorded its enthusiasm in a massive and lyrical outpouring of words and photographs that appeared prominently in hundreds of magazines and newspapers. . . .

"The press played an important role in creating . . . excitement. Due to the tireless efforts of Walter Murphy in public relations, the Mustang was featured simultaneously on the covers of both *Time* and *Newsweek*. This was an astounding publicity coup for a new commercial project. Both magazines sensed we had a winner, and their added publicity during the very week of the

Mustang's introduction helped make their prediction a self-fulfilling prophecy. *I'm convinced that* Time *and* Newsweek *alone led to the sale of an extra 100,000 cars."* [Italics added.][9]

By the best available estimates, there are at least 100,000 public relations people in the U.S. But that number is probably a conservative one, for PR people do not always go by the moniker "Public Relations Person." PR people go by a wide variety of pseudonyms and euphemisms that serve to distance them from the disparaging stigma of "flack" or "press agent": spokespeople, directors of communications, investor relations officers, public affairs people, publicists, press liaisons, legislative affairs people, press secretaries, communications specialists, public relations counselors, directors of corporate affairs, media relations people, and—the latest buzzword—issues managers.

Politicians also qualify as PR people—at least part-time. So does an increasing number of lawyers, like Dan Burt (attorney for General William Westmoreland in his libel suit against CBS) and the flamboyant Melvin Belli; and corporate executives, like Chrysler's Lee Iacocca and Apple Computer's Steve Jobs. Trade associations, like the American Medical Association or the Truck Stop Operators of America, are also involved in doing public relations for the groups they represent. Political organizations like Greenpeace and the National Organization of Women are also partly public relations organizations that try to get favorable news coverage for whatever cause their members are advancing. Include these part-time spokespeople who have a keen sense of PR techniques and the 100,000 figure could easily double.

Complicating attempts to count PR people is the fact that there is little real structure to the profession. Still, only a handful of large public relations firms dominates the business. Burson-Marsteller, with $64 million in billings and more than 1,400 employees, is the largest PR firm; Hill & Knowlton, with $61 million in billings, is a close second.[10] Hundreds more smaller firms, ranging from one to dozens of employees, specialize in PR work.

Most of corporate America has in-house PR departments of varying size and effectiveness. Federal agencies, the White House and congressmen all have PR staffs. State and local politicians and agencies also have PR representatives. Stars and movies have their own PR people. Even news organizations like *Time, Newsweek,* the *New York Times, Forbes,* network and local television news departments have PR people.

As with any group, many PR people carry out their jobs as, well, jobs. They know most of the standard "tricks" of PR, they try to keep up with advances in the profession, and they collect their paychecks.

Above this group are the truly superb PR people, who understand the business inside out and who continually strive to do a better job at the business of manipulation. They are creative, intelligent, personable, confident, and powerful in what they can accomplish. These are The Communications Elite this book will be dealing with.

We will also be concerning ourselves with the very top of the pyramid. Here is the leading edge of PR that is advancing the profession closer and closer to near-perfect control of public opinion. These elite communicators are innovators, pioneers. They go by names that you have probably never heard of—because you're not supposed to: Michael Deaver, President Reagan's former PR man; Robert Gray, of Washington's Gray & Co.; Richard Cheney, of Hill & Knowlton; Harold Burson, of Burson-Marsteller; and Herbert Schmertz, of Mobil Corporation, to list only a few.

These people are continuing the evolution of PR by developing new techniques and using new technologies to manipulate and monitor public opinion, which is why they bear close watching. For there is a continuum of significance along which PR is traveling. On the first rung is entertainment PR, often seen as innocuous, innocent tomfoolery, and a fact of life as far as the press is concerned. PR literally generates entertainment news for the press.

Next comes the burgeoning field of product PR. Increasingly the press is letting business PR people manufacture "news" about new products, different products, old products, better products, weird products.

After this, the PR starts operating in more significant areas under the general heading of business PR. Image PR helps create a favorable public view of a corporation that helps that corporation do its job more easily and with as little interference—from stockholders and government regulators, say—as possible. *Ad hoc* PR solves individual business problems like getting the public to accept a new chemical plant in town or getting employees to accept a 20 percent wage cut. Crisis PR helps get companies through disasters and assaults on their reputations. It also protects companies and their managements from corporate takeovers.

At the highest levels of importance is political PR. The business of politics revolves around public support, and PR is playing an increasingly important role in this, from the White House to the swelling ranks of political activist groups. More and more, PR is becoming the game that gets things done.

But PR is still evolving. International PR is now in an embryonic stage. This is also perhaps the most significant PR because it involves such issues as U.S./Soviet relations and the nuclear arms race.

Crucial to the rise and influence of all public relations opinion molders, however, are the press and the media. They hold the keys to the massive communications machinery of this nation. Through that machinery PR people work their magic.

"The media set the agenda for public debate on every issue," says Henry Catto, former assistant secretary of defense for public affairs and now editor of the *Washington Journalism Review*.

But it is PR that often sets the agenda for the media. Says Michael J. Robinson, director of the Media Analysis Project at George Washington University, the media "keep the momentum going for an agenda set by the political leadership."[11]

Our examination of public relations implicates for the first time the press and media as partners in deception with PR manipulators. PR cannot influence public opinion without the blessings of the press. Contrary to the anti-PR image the press paints for itself, though, the press is presently and increasingly lending its weight to PR. Herein lies the irony. For the press, the only watchdog that can protect the public from manipulation, is in reality fast asleep.

two

Imitation News

THE PRESS AND PR, PART I

The American press—and by proxy the American public—has a huge problem on its hands: reporters, newswriters, editors, publishers, managing editors, photojournalists, anchorpeople, TV news cameramen, radio personalities, commentators, syndicated columnists, and broadcast news producers are falling down on the job.

The press is well aware that there is a problem. According to polls conducted by the National Opinion Research Center in Princeton, New Jersey, the percentage of Americans who have a great deal of confidence in the press fell from a post-Watergate high of 29 percent in 1976 to a distressingly meager 13.7 percent in 1983. Even bankers did better with 24.1 percent.

On December 12, 1983, *Time* magazine ran a long, introspective cover story about the press. Among the reasons people dislike the press, *Time* revealed, are that journalists appear too intrusive; they are often inaccurate and sometimes downright fabricate their stories; confrontation and ambush journalism is unfair to the news subject and distorts the facts; reporters have no shame in invading the privacy of individuals if the story warrants it; the press breaks a story regardless of the consequences; members of the press freely allow their own biases to find their way into stories that are supposed to be objective.[1]

Unfortunately, while this embarrassing record indeed re-

---

flects the confused environment in which the press today operates, *Time*'s soul-searching completely missed another major problem—one well hidden by its own complexity: that the press has grown frighteningly dependent on public relations people.

Outsiders—the reading and viewing public—would have a hard time discovering this on their own because the dependence on PR is part of behind-the-scenes press functioning. Where does the idea for a story come from? How does a story qualify as "news"? How much time does a reporter spend on a story? What questions didn't the reporter ask?

Meanwhile, like an alcoholic who can't believe he has a drinking problem, members of the press are too close to their own addiction to PR to realize there is anything wrong. In fact, the press, which has a seemingly inborn cynical, arrogant, down-the-nose view of public relations, seems sadly self-deceptive about the true press/PR relationship. While occasional problems are recognized, journalists almost without fail adopt an "It can't happen here" attitude. Says Seymour Topping, managing editor of the *New York Times:*

> Given some of the time pressures and encapsulated presentations, there does tend to be more susceptibility to puffery. But I wouldn't want to make any generalizations because news organizations run the whole gamut from irresponsible and inefficient to highly organized, sophisticated, and efficient. I think our reporters are really much too experienced to be taken in by high-pressure PR salesmen. We can see through that puffery.

Topping and others like him are, perhaps, a bit too confident.

In May 1984, President Reagan's reelection campaign wanted to get its message spread all over the country—for free. So Reagan's PR people put the media onto the "news story" about the release of the candidate's television commercials. *USA Today*, the *New York Post,* and the *New York Times,* along with papers all across the nation, carried this story. The hot news? Read about it in the *New York Times* account by Francis X. Clines:

> WASHINGTON, May 17—President Reagan's opening series of re-election television commercials, replete with enacted tableaux

of euphoric Americans, was unveiled today to broadcast the message that Mr. Reagan has revived both the national economy and the Presidency itself.[2]

News? In an increasingly PR-dependent press, sure!

Meanwhile the Democrats were at the same game too. ABC *World News Tonight* carried a story about how the Gary Hart campaign was planning to "sell" the Colorado senator, complete with exciting footage of the making of the Hart TV commercials. ABC anchorman Peter Jennings led into the piece this way: "Why do campaign strategists tell us how they're going to 'sell' their candidate? We don't know. . . ."

The answer to the riddle is that a story on ABC *World News Tonight* about the selling of a candidate is just one more way to get valuable exposure for the candidate to some 12 million viewers. Ditto for stories appearing in the print media. ABC is happy because it looks as if it has the "inside" scoop, and the PR people are happy because, while there may have been a few analytical barbs by the reporter, the candidate got two minutes of network airtime which probably would have cost him hundreds of thousands of dollars if he had had to pay for it.

The stories you read in your daily newspaper or monthly magazine, or the ones you watch on the evening news, fall into two distinctly different categories of quality. Like everything else, at the top there are a few superlative pieces—stories that are well thought out and well reported by a journalist who had the time to think, ask the right questions, and dig out all the hard-to-get facts. These are the handcrafted works of art.

Then there is the great bulk of stories that are the product of assembly-line factory journalism. They are produced by journalists following most of the basic rules of the profession. But, for any of a thousand reasons, the stories are throw-togethers with sloppy paint jobs, loose bolts, and missing engine parts. Not that the journalists didn't put in a full day's work—and more. But shortcuts have been taken:

□ Contradictory facts from one source, or from among several sources, were not recognized—or were ignored.

- Enough questions were not asked.
- Only the barest number of sources was contacted.
- Facts were not checked or double-checked.
- The writer didn't have enough knowledge about the subject to ask probing questions, so he or she played it safe and wrote a laudatory "puff piece."
- A source failed to provide crucial facts, and the reporter didn't press for them, or never suspected that something was left out.
- The reporter committed an error in reasoning.
- The reporter didn't feel like chasing down that one extra fact that might have changed the whole direction of the story.

We are not talking about the rare stories that are outright lies: the Pulitzer Prize-winning "Jimmy's World" about a preteen heroin addict, fabricated by *Washington Post* reporter Janet Cooke; or the fictitious and partially plagiarized report on Cambodia by free-lance writer Christopher Jones in the *New York Times Magazine.* We are talking about the great middle ground: minimum-quality journalism.

Why do journalists take shortcuts? Here are just seven reasons:

- The writer needs a "quickie" story to fill space in the magazine or newspaper.
- There is just not enough time to dig for all the facts because of deadlines or because the other network or paper might break the story first.
- The reporter—who may have a hot date tonight (reporters are people too)—already has the who, what, when, where, and why, and that's good enough.
- Forty-five seconds of air on the evening news does not allow much depth, so why bother getting the whole story?
- Informed, cynical speculation is a lot easier than digging around to prove or disprove a statement—and it sounds a lot better too.
- The reporter is not really interested in the story.
- The journalist is just plain lazy.

It really happens. In spring 1984, *Fortune,* the most prestigious of the major business magazines, ran a fairly positive, upbeat story about Robert Brennan, the rags-to-riches boy wonder who built his estimated $250 million fortune from a brokerage firm called First Jersey Securities. You may know Bob Brennan from his TV commercials aired during the 1984 Olympics and Super Bowl games and set in front of the Erie Canal, the Grand Coulee Dam, and the Capitol Building in Washington, D.C.

Three months later, Richard Stern, a hard-driving investigative reporter at *Forbes* Magazine, wrote about *his* five-month investigation of First Jersey salespeople and disappointed customers. *Forbes* examined reams of Securities and Exchange Commission material and company records obtained from former salesmen. The result was a stinging cover story on Brennan that alleged "a clever and apparently legal system for fobbing off shoddy and overpriced merchandise on a not very well informed public. A marriage of greed and gullibility." Brennan called the story "sheer nonsense" and denied the charges in an eight-page letter which *Forbes* refused to print.

Stern's work was a handcrafted masterpiece—the opposite of minimum quality journalism. While the *Fortune* and *Forbes* pieces about the same subject were apparently of decidedly different quality (*Fortune* writer Peter Nulty says he had only a week-and-a-half to do his story), both articles appeared equally impressive, equally authoritative. How are readers to know which respected publication to trust? The answer is, they can't—though the *Forbes* article later won a Loeb Award; the *Fortune* article did not. In November 1984, on allegations similar to those in the *Forbes* article, Brennan signed a permanent injunction by consent with the Securities and Exchange Commission agreeing not to violate one of the antifraud provisions of federal securities law which prohibits the purchase and sale of securities while at the same time engaging in the distribution of those same securities. By signing, Brennan neither admitted nor denied violating the law. As part of that agreement, a government consultant was appointed to examine the business operations and practices and sales practices of First Jersey.

The great differences in quality, such as that in the above case, and the public's inability to detect those differences creates an enormous opportunity for the public relations profession to infiltrate the media. And that's exactly what PR people do.

Let's go back to Grenada.

There, press dependence on PR to provide it with a story was exposed to the point of embarrassment. While a few journalists were busy getting to Grenada on their own, some 400 journalists from 170 news organizations around the world were back in Barbados virtually paralyzed and waiting for the news to come to them.

What was everyone else doing in Barbados? Here's one snapshot from a *Washington Post* story by Phil McCombs, who was in Barbados:

> "Seven days down here and it's been a bitch," said *Time* magazine photographer Michael Luongo, standing outside the old shambling airport building that has become the press center. "Press liaison has been nil. We've had no briefings to speak of."
>
> "Everybody in the press is outraged," said *Newsweek* correspondent Elaine Shannon in the air-conditioned restaurant at the airport, where she had sought a cheeseburger and respite from the heat. "I've never seen so much pent-up fury."[3]

"Very few actually tried to get to the island," says the *Washington Times* journalist Jay Malin, a thirty-year veteran who has covered eight wars. "We were trying to convince the Navy to let us go in and were waiting for orders to come through to let us in. We knew it was just a matter of time."

So why take any unnecessary chances? "They were rough seas," says Malin. And "we could get a boat, but it would take two, three, four days to get there, and we'd miss an awful lot of news in the meantime."

"We were sitting around the hotel talking about how to get there," says *USA Today* reporter David Bauman. "I flew to St. Vincent myself and almost got on a boat with five other journalists. But I decided not to go. In my judgment, these guys were crazy—but they made it. Then I heard that the military might let us go in, so I went back to Barbados."

Getting the Grenada story was just too hard for most of the press. The only way the press could deal with its own crushing weakness was to turn the focus elsewhere—by raising a censorship issue. Ridiculous attempts to "sneak" onto Grenada via huge journalist-laden yachts or press-chartered aircraft easily sighted by radar provided a good coverup excuse for why the press was not doing its job. Why not? Ronald Reagan's military censors made it "impossible."

Then the press got into the PR business—for itself. ABC correspondent Josh Mankiewicz, who expected to get past the naval armada in broad daylight in a huge chartered fishing boat, was stopped by a U.S. destroyer. "I got a good look at that gun on the foredeck and decided we were simply outclassed. I know *force majeure* when I see it," Mankiewicz told *Time.*

"Now the military—everyone's military—has a natural age-old aversion to independent reporting," explained Dan Rather on his daily CBS Radio Network commentary program. "That's understandable. They like to control information the way they like to control territory, completely and without question.

"But in this country there is a long tradition that has always overridden that antipathy, a tradition that puts the press in the battlefields so citizens at home can find out from independent reports what's happening."

But wait a minute. Let's see just how independent the press really is in time of war. In 1975 British journalist Phillip Knightley published his extensive award-winning examination of wartime press coverage, *The First Casualty—From the Crimea to Vietnam: The War Correspondent as Hero, Propagandist, and Myth Maker.* Knightley puts Dan Rather's "independent" eyes for the citizens back home in quite a different light.

Discussing World War II, Knightley draws a frightening picture of the press as a virtual PR arm of the government. "Public relations, of which war correspondents were considered a part, became another cog in the massive military machine the Americans constructed to defeat Hitler," says Knightley. "The supreme commander, General Eisenhower, spelled it out very clearly. 'Public opinion wins war,' he told a meeting of American newspaper editors. 'I have always considered as quasi-staff officers, correspondents accredited to my headquarters.'"[4]

The press went along with military PR people to glorify generals like Douglas MacArthur or to play up or play down military battles, according to military needs. It allowed the military PR people to hide the true level of devastation at Pearl Harbor for more than a year, and hide parts of the story until after the war.[5]

Charles Lynch, a Reuters correspondent during the war quoted by Knightley adds, "It's humiliating to look back at what we wrote during the war. It was crap—and I don't exclude the

Ernie Pyles or the Alan Moorheads. We were a propaganda arm of our governments. At the start the censors enforced that, but by the end we were our own censors. We were cheerleaders. I suppose there wasn't an alternative at the time. It was total war. But, for God's sake, let's not glorify our role. It wasn't good journalism. It wasn't journalism at all."[6]

Grenada, of course, was not all-out war. But the press was never "brought along" for the successful *Mayaguez* incident during the Ford administration when U.S. Marines took back a merchant container ship seized by Cambodia. Nor was the press along for the ride on the ill-fated Desert One raid to free the fifty-two American hostages in Iran during the Carter administration. No one raised a freedom-of-the-press question about those incidents. A comparison of the press accounts from those military actions and those from Grenada shows little difference. Why? Because in all three cases and in all war reporting, the press depends heavily on the Defense Department public affairs staff for information that independent journalists often cannot get on their own: casualty figures, overviews of the battle, progress of a military action.

The fact is that war today is not news to the press unless the warriors cooperate with the press and help serve up the story. Real reporting is much too difficult. There is the Soviet invasion of Afghanistan, where some 100,000 have been killed since 1978, but press coverage of that is minimal because the Soviets are not publicizing their actions and the press can't or won't do it on their own.

There is the significant war between Iran and Iraq, but press coverage again is minimal, except when one side or the other's PR interests are best served by it. For example, when the war escalated in February 1984, CBS's Erik Durschmied, NBC's Phil Bremen, and ABC's Bob Sirkin all got pictures from the Iraqi front, showing the military superiority of Iraq. The next month, ABC's Bill Redeker got a story out of Iran—reporting about Iraq's use of poison gas against Iran.[7]

There is war in Cambodia (4 million dead in the last ten years), Angola, Chad, and Indonesia (250,000 dead since 1965), but again, coverage is minimal.

In Grenada President Reagan and his PR strategists accomplished their PR goals and rubbed the press's nose in it to boot.

Most of the press, meanwhile, enjoyed playing the martyr, even though it had to use its own PR to draw attention away from its embarrassing dependence on military public affairs people.

As time goes on, the press will find it harder and harder to hide its cozy dealings with PR, because Grenada is not an exception; today, more than ever before, the press feels it needs PR people to get the news.

But does it really?

It was October 26, 1983, and the *New York Post* had now been shut out of the Grenada story for two days. Metropolitan Editor Steve Dunleavy would not stand for it anymore.

A tough, hard-driving Aussie, Dunleavy had no patience for anything less than aggressive pursuit of a story. He called over Charles Lachman, a general-assignment reporter, and told him to get to Grenada. And when Dunleavy said "Grenada," he meant exactly that. For almost every other newsman covering the story, "Grenada" meant Bridgetown, Barbados—160 miles northeast of Grenada—because of the government's PR-imposed "press blackout."

"I don't know what you can do," said Dunleavy, "but I'm hoping for a miracle. And don't wait for the PR people to come around. Get what you can on your own."

Next morning, Thursday, Lachman caught the half-empty 6 A.M. flight from JFK to Barbados. Three hours later, he was at the airport in beautifully balmy Bridgetown. It was a mob scene. Hundreds of reporters from around the world were here in what veteran *St. Louis Post-Dispatch* White House correspondent James Deakin (cynically) calls the milling-around area—that place reporters tend to gather while waiting to go where the news is. Barbados, as a sort of Washington, D.C., of the eastern Caribbean, was a bona fide news nerve-center, and few reporters wanted to leave. The airport was also the military staging point for the Grenada operation; supplies and troops flew in and out. The Pentagon and the Barbados government had set up their press centers in an empty terminal several hundred yards from the main terminal. However, with no high-ranking officials, they were useless, pathetic operations, Lachman found.

He threw his bags into a locker and wandered around. When Post photographer Michael Norcia arrived on a later flight, the pair began in earnest their search for a way to Grenada.

Money would not buy a pilot or plane; the airspace around Grenada was closed. Passage from Barbados by boat was out too. One hundred sixty miles by sea would cost too much in time and money. But if they could get closer and then hire a boat, perhaps they had a chance. Lachman and Norcia quickly checked their maps and found St. Vincent, another flyspeck island in the Windward chain. It was only sixty miles from Grenada. And there was air service to St. Vincent from Barbados. The two quickly booked seats on the next flight out, early Friday morning.

Once on the small island of St. Vincent and with no contacts, the *Post* reporters grabbed a cab. "We need to go someplace where we can get a boat," Lachman said. The cabbie nodded and sped off. At a dock where scuba equipment was rented to tourists, they found a boat—for a price. According to the darkly tanned blonde who served as "agent" for the boat's owner, a purported drug smuggler, the figure was nonnegotiable: $5,000.

Unfortunately, the Post had authorized only $2,000 for a boat. "If you have the five thousand, we'll do business," the woman insisted. "If not, it was nice meeting you." Frustrated, Lachman stormed outside. Meanwhile, a stream of journalists with expense authorizations of their own began showing up at the dock. By late afternoon, a deal agreeable to a number of them had been hammered out. Each reporter or photographer—Lachman, Norcia, Peter Goodspeed of the *Toronto Star*, Michael Posner of *MacLean's* and Paul McIsaac of National Public Radio—would pony up $1,200. Total: $6,000. (The price had risen with demand.) Lachman paid with his American Express green card.

The twenty-two-foot open Fiberglas boat was owned by "the kind of guy who looks like he'll take our money, take us out two miles, then blow our heads off," as Lachman confided to Norcia. The drug runner's mate, who spoke with a heavy West Indian accent, stationed himself at the rear to operate the 90-horsepower twin-engine outboard. The owner gave no name to the reporters and said almost nothing throughout the trip.

The journalists were given life jackets and packed their cameras in waterproof cans usually used to protect drugs. The boat set sail in calm seas at 8 P.M., under cover of darkness.

Before long, as the boat got farther out, the seas grew

rougher. Water began splashing in and the night temperatures dropped. In less than an hour everyone was wet and freezing cold. One of the reporters became terribly seasick, vomiting over the side of the boat. Lachman suddenly became acutely aware that he didn't know how to swim.

Shortly after 1 A.M., Lachman saw the pinpoints of light that were the U.S. naval armada stationed off Grenada. He thought about being stopped but did not consider the possibility he might encounter gunfire. And he never worried how the devil some night officer might figure out that this was a boatload of journalists—not a boat full of Cuban gunrunners.

The mate slipped through the flotilla of ships unseen. He then headed for shore at a point twenty-five miles north of St. George's, the island's capital city, to avoid landing on a beach full of U.S. Marines.

The boat landed near a rocky outcropping. "Jump out!" yelled the mate as he brought the bow around. Lachman and the others were startled. Jump? But they were not on shore yet. Because of the waves washing in, the boat could not get close enough to shore for a dry landing. It was either overboard or back to St. Vincent.

"Jump out!" said the mate again. The owner had taken the throttle and was getting ready to head back to sea; he didn't want his boat wrecked. McIsaac turned on his tape recorder and captured the wails of the wet journalists flailing their way toward land and clambering up the rocks.

It was 2 A.M. and the five journalists had done what most of their peers could not. They were on the forbidden island.

Meanwhile, back in New York, the huge printing presses of the *New York Times* on Forty-third Street were rumbling with the Saturday edition. Among the plentiful coverage of Grenada was a page 1 story about how the press was still being man-handled:

WASHINGTON, Oct. 28—Major news organizations across the country say that the Reagan Administration's restrictions on reporting in Grenada are preventing crucial information on military activity there from reaching the press and the public.

Three days after the United States and Caribbean invasion of Grenada, only small pools of reporters accompanied by military escorts are being allowed to visit the island, and they are on a set itinerary. No reporters are being allowed to remain on the island.[8]

The aggressive Lachman and company had not been "allowed" on Grenada either. But there they were.

After a short night, the reporters awoke and found themselves near a farm with a green van. The owner, Donald McQueen, a local bus driver, agreed to drive them to St. George's in exchange for payment. Stopping at the bullet-riddled transmitting facility of Radio Free Grenada, Lachman encountered a man who said he was a janitor at a mental hospital farther south.

"They bombed the crazy house," he told Lachman. "There were dozens of people killed and the crazy people are loose."

"Who bombed the crazy house?" Lachman asked. "The Cubans? The Marines? Who?"

"The Americans."

"This is the big scoop," Lachman thought to himself. "We've got to go there," he said to the driver.

Back on the road and several miles farther south, the van came upon an American marine checkpoint at a Texaco gas depot. "Great!" Lachman thought. "Just when we're getting to something, we're going to be stopped." Everyone produced his press credentials and the soldiers, much to everyone's surprise, waved the truck through.

The Richmond Hill Mental Hospital was nearby. More U.S. troops were stationed at the bottom of the hill. They too let the journalists through after checking their credentials. Lachman was not sure the soldiers were aware that a hospital had been bombed, or that there was any good reason to keep the press away from here, or even that there was supposed to be a news blackout. None of the journalists was going to ask about those issues either. They moved on up the hill.

There they found the rubble of the hospital. Norcia snapped more photographs and Lachman took notes. Workers were still sifting through the timber and bricks to reach victims. Survivors were huddled in a courtyard. Fifty people were feared dead from the accidental bombing by U.S. planes, Lachman learned.

But the nurses and other survivors did not seem bitter; they saw it as an accident of war.

Lachman and Norcia traveled around St. George's the rest of the day and saw the looted food stores and the Queen's Park soccer field, which had been turned into a military headquarters and prison. They also saw Bernard Coard, the deposed deputy prime minister and perhaps the most feared politician in Grenada, led away to a Navy helicopter. The crowd screamed for Coard's head.

Finally, Lachman and Norcia went to the American military headquarters and approached a corporal. "We're Americans, and we'd like to be evacuated from the island," Lachman said. Norcia's cameras were hidden in his bag; Lachman smartly failed to inform the corporal that he was a journalist. The pair boarded the next helicopter to Barbados.

Back at the airport Lachman raced to the first phone and dialed the *Post*. Dunleavy was ecstatic. His boys had done what no one else in the press could—brought back fresh, independent news right from the battlefield. "Charlie," he laughed, "I could kiss your ass in Macy's window!"

three

The Remote-Controlled Journalist

THE PRESS AND PR, PART II

The influence of PR is not limited to reports from the battlefield.

Earlier we showed how the press thinks it's too savvy to be fooled by PR. Actually, journalists seem to suffer from a kind of double-think fallacy. On the one hand, they find it easy to dismiss PR's influence as minimal. On the other hand, they admit to using PR—extensively.

Seymour Topping again:

> PR people do influence the news, but really more in a functional manner rather than in terms of giving new editorial direction. We get hundreds of press releases every day in each of our departments. We screen them very carefully for legitimate news, and very often there are legitimate news stories. Quite a lot of our business stories originate from press releases. It's impossible for us to cover all of these organizations ourselves.
>
> In New York City we get handouts from hundreds of organizations that range from church groups and charity organizations to the Red Cross, to every type of activity. Often the first hint of a newsworthy event is first heard of by us from a press release. There has been a tremendous increase in PR activity in the last ten years.

Topping will even go so far as to admit that PR is becoming a second news network behind the legitimate news media: a second network that feeds the real news media more and more of its news.

Now for the emergence of the second personality. "We're not dependent on that [PR]," says Topping. "Some of our best stories and most interesting material does not come from PR handouts." Therein, perhaps, lies a lesson.

It would, of course, be unfair to single out the *New York Times*—and not just because journalism's critics always attack the newspaper that is often thought to set the standard in the profession. It's true that the *Times* is an influential publication, partly because influential people read it. That reason alone should explain why it is a natural magnet for PR influence. But the rest of the media, up and down the scales of influence and quality, are equally dependent on PR.

"It's impossible to 'place' a story in the *Wall Street Journal*," maintains Charles Staebler, that paper's assistant managing editor. Now watch again for the second personality. "But we do get ideas from PR people, particularly from those who know what we're interested in. We look at press releases positively as a source of tips. They can alert us to things that are going on."

Staebler admits, however, that press releases are often more than just tipoffs. "For some stories, the press release has the entire story," he says.

The *Wall Street Journal* gets hundreds of press releases a day. These are routed to the appropriate editors or reporters. Like millions of sperm making their way to an unfertilized egg, the swarms of press releases have a high mortality rate. Many of them are thrown right into the wastebasket. That's the part of the story you usually hear from journalists.

What you almost never hear about are the press releases and phone-in story pitches by PR people that do survive. The survival rate as a percentage of the huge number of proposals that come in is not high. However, of all the stories that do make it into the newspaper, the percentage of them that have PR roots is shocking. Staebler estimates that perhaps 50 percent of the average *Journal*'s stories are spurred by a press release. He hastens to add, "In every case we *try* [emphasis ours] to go beyond the press release."

How does the *Journal* "go beyond the press release"?

Staebler is unspecific. "The reporter checks it out with the company involved," he says.

But here's how Hill & Knowlton, the world's second largest PR firm, which deals with the *Journal* every single day, sees the relationship:

> The *Wall Street Journal* and [the] Dow Jones [ticker] are two separate entities under the same umbrella. . . . Say your news release is in the field of banking. You read your story to the proper person at Dow Jones. It appears thereafter on the ticker. You then phone the banking editor of the *Journal* to let him know of the ticker story. He may ask you a few questions. In most instances he'll simply thank you and ask where you can be reached if there are any follow-up questions. Chances are fair your ticker story will be printed in some form by the *Journal*.[1]

The *Columbia Journalism Review* in 1980 looked more carefully at one typical issue of the *Journal*—October 4, 1979—then contacted the companies appearing in 111 *Journal* stories to obtain copies of the original press releases. Seventy companies responded. The result?

> In 53 cases—72 percent of our responses—news stories were based solely on press releases; in 32 of these examples, the releases were reprinted almost verbatim or in paraphrase, while in 21 other cases only the most perfunctory additional reporting had been done. Perhaps most troublesome, 20 of these stories (29 percent) carried the slug "By a *Wall Street Journal* Staff Reporter." Based on these returns, we project that 84 stories were based on press releases in the October 4 *Journal*—45 percent of the day's 188 news items and 27 percent of the paper's non-tabular news hole.[2]

Journal executive editor Frederick Taylor was quoted in the CJR article as saying that 90 percent of daily coverage is started by a company making an announcement.

Many of these stories are corporate announcements that have to be covered because they are of interest to shareholders. The *Journal,* in addition to being the nation's largest daily and one of the most respected, is also a newspaper of record—a trade paper. "We don't have people hanging around the treasurer's office of U.S. Steel waiting for the board to raise the dividend," remarks Staebler.

Staebler refutes the *Columbia Journalism Review* critique. "That story is a phony! It remains a mystery to us as to what they thought they discovered. A lot of the stories had to do with a quarterly earnings report, a new president, a stock split. . . . Talk to anyone who reads the *Journal*. They'd laugh at the idea that the *Wall Street Journal* just publishes handouts."

Perhaps. But one wonders how many investors would be laughing if they knew about PR's ability to influence the *Journal* in a matter involving Osborne Computer Corporation. Osborne, of course, produced the revolutionary Osborne 1 transportable computer, then collapsed into bankruptcy in the fall of 1983. Adam Osborne, the flamboyant company founder and a skilled user of PR techniques, admits he misled the *Wall Street Journal* about the health of his foundering company in the spring of 1983. Ironically this was no press release rewrite either; it was a bona fide bylined story on the *Journal*'s second front page.

Journal reporter Erik Larson was sniffing around interviewing computer vendors and dealers and getting perilously close to the truth that Osborne Computer was in serious financial trouble, recalls Osborne. "It was imperative to draw Larson away from the facts, thereby giving [Osborne Computer president and chief executive officer Robert] Jaunich the needed time to complete a planned private stock placement," says Osborne.

He continues:

> I therefore carefully devised a story that would sell. It was plausible in that it spoke of a month without income [and explained that the newly developed Osborne Executive computer] had been preannounced—so I said. The story made good copy by representing Adam Osborne as the brash hero-in-penitent-pose. Erik Larson bought it and ran a story. . . .[3]

The *Journal* story of July 13, 1983, concluded on an upbeat note:

> The company seems to be recovering, although its officials are less boastful than in the past and decline to discuss revenues or

---

earnings. Some dealers say the Executive is selling well. And Osborne recently reached an agreement with a unit of Harris Corp., Melbourne, Fla., to distribute the machine to big companies, a lucrative market that many computer makers are aiming at. "Osborne is still the top name in portables," says Computique's [Jeff] Margolis [director of marketing].[4]

Says Osborne: "The *Wall Street Journal* story was not true. It was, in fact, the single and only time I have ever deliberately lied to the press." The Executive had not in fact been prematurely announced before production could meet public demand; it had been announced on April 17, 1983, he says, and shipped the first week of May.

The *Journal*'s Larson refuses to confirm or refute Osborne's story. "As far as I'm concerned, the Osborne story is dead and buried," Larson says. "I don't want to get into a pissing match with a guy who has a better talent at pissing than I do. But, if the chief executive officer of a company lies to you in an interview, there's not much of a defense, is there? I don't know why anybody would do that."

The point, however, is not that PR has the ability to lie; it is that the press sometimes has an inability to detect a lie. Despite the post-Watergate journalism fanfare that the truth will always out, the fact is, the press can be fooled. That, of course, means the public can be fooled too.

In any case, most of the time PR people do not lie at all; they just give their point of view. But a reporter who thinks he hears a good and complete story may not bother to explore other possibilities, or other facts, or other directions that aren't contained in the PR client's spiel. PR people know this. That is why, to get their story into print in the so-called "free media," PR people are willing to risk giving up the control they could easily buy with an advertisement—the "paid media."

The PR industry makes it its business to know the weaknesses of the press and use those weaknesses to its own advantage. As a result, the press and PR are in bed together almost everywhere you turn. "It is a safe generalization to say that 40 percent of the news content in a typical newspaper originated with public relations press releases, story memos, or suggestions," says Scott M. Cutlip, retired dean of the Henry W. Grady

School of Journalism and Mass Communications at the University of Georgia. Cutlip's estimate is based on newspaper content studies he and his students conducted in the seventies. "And the *New York Times* is just as dependent on PR personnel as the *Madison* (Wis.) *Capital Times*," he says. "The bottom line is that newspapers and broadcasters couldn't operate without PR. The news media just do not have the manpower or expertise to cover today's broad spectrum of news."

Unfortunately, the public cannot be expected to detect a PR-sponsored story. So when the press and PR people get together to push a special interest group's product or idea—a de facto advertisement—the public's natural defenses against the surreptitious ad are down, if not completely absent. Adding to the confusion, not all members of the press use PR ideas to the same degree. For example, ABC News president Av Westin freely admits, "Quite a few of our story ideas come from PR people. All three of our programs, *20/20, Nightline,* and *World News Tonight,* use them." And Westin sees no problem with that.

NBC News seems more level-headed. "Any time we deal with PR people, we're cautious," says *NBC Nightly News* senior producer Bill Wheatley. "Our motive is to fully inform people; [PR's] motive is to inform the public about what's in the best interest of its client. We have to retain the reporter's independence."

Wheatley says that "very few" of NBC's stories originate from PR ideas, but "PR people are sources to us, like anyone else. For example, there's a PR outfit handling Nicaragua these days. Occasionally that firm has pointed out things to us that we thought were worth putting on the air."

While readers are completely unaware of it, whole sections of their daily newspaper are virtually PR's playground. The entertainment section is full of PR-originated stories. Often, gossip columns are "ghost-written," either in part or in full by PR people for celebrities, movies, or shows. Studio 54 co-owner Steve Rubell regularly fed items to columnists at *Women's Wear Daily,* the *Daily News,* the *Post,* and the *Soho Weekly News.* "There were many days," says former Studio 54 PR woman Michael Gifford, "when Steve would call me up and brag that he had fed Earl Wilson his entire column."[5]

Home improvement and living sections are likewise heavily dependent on PR people for material, as is the automobile section. Real estate sections are often turned over for wholesale rape by PR people. For example, this August 1984 story on the front page of the *New York Daily News* real estate section:

THE CAREFREE LIFE IN FLA.

Florida's ShadowWood Village proves that mobile-home community living is carefree living. . . .[6]

Or this piece appearing in the *New York Post* real estate section on the same day:

HOMES SELLING LIKE HOTCAKES

The first four sections of Meadowood Estates in Holmdel, N.J., have been completely sold out in a record-breaking eight weeks.[7]

Even the *New York Times* engages in this dirty business. "We place stories in the *New York Post, Daily News* and the *New York Times,*" says Barbara Fondeur, of Gerald Freeman PR across the river in New Jersey. "They're always looking for material."

Says *Times* real estate writer Alan Oser, "Press releases are one source of story ideas, in addition to reports, newsletters and real estate periodicals." Adds Kirk Johnson, another real estate writer at the *Times*. "PR firms send in a lot of press releases about real estate. We usually put them in a file and do the stories at an appropriate time, for example when the project goes on sale or when the last unit has been sold." The major New York area firms in real estate PR dealing with the *Times*, says Johnson, are Howard Rubenstein PR, David M. Grant, and Gerald Freeman PR.

These "articles" are printed and headlined just like every other article in the newspaper, and there is nothing to indicate that these are actually cleverly disguised advertisements. A journalist might easily spot this charade, but what about the average reader or an eager househunter looking for objective confirmation about the quality, value, and trustworthiness of a new housing development?

In another section of the news, Hill & Knowlton, the country's second largest public relations firm based in New York, is a huge supplier of material to newspaper and magazine food and travel sections. "We send color pages like this to newspapers," explains B. J. McCabe, head of H&K's food, wine, health, and entertainment unit, as she flips through a huge black book filled with clippings of her article placements for one client in scores of newspapers, including the *Beloit* (Wis.) *News, Seattle Times, Atlanta Journal, Chicago Tribune, Marysville* (Calif.) *Appeal-Democrat,* and *Amarillo* (Tex.) *Globe Times.* "If we offer them a whole camera-ready layout [of the article text, complete with pictures and recipes], they usually won't take the product name out," says McCabe.

Weekly newspaper placements also go out of McCabe's Lexington Avenue offices in camera-ready matte form, for reproduction exactly as is. Weeklies, like daily newspapers, eagerly eat up this PR-manufactured material. Food stories are not so easily planted as-is in magazines. But McCabe can show you the abundance of clips from her placements in scores of periodicals, including *Good Housekeeping, Ladies' Home Journal, Southern Living, Family Circle, Bon Appetit,* and *Coed.*

The trade press—which publishes periodicals for specific groups, such as accountants, steel company executives, the oil industry—is especially susceptible to PR's siren song. "Unfortunately, the trade press uses PR a lot," says Bob Heady, publisher of *Bank Advertising News,* in Miami. "There are two schools of thought in trade publishing. One is to identify the reader's needs and then provide the editorial content first to meet those needs. The second school first identifies the market the advertisers wish to reach, then creates an 'editorial product' to fill the publication with. There are a lot more trade publishers following the second school, which depends more heavily on PR for material. We think it's the responsibility of the journalist to dig out his own story, so we don't depend on PR for our content."

The military trade press, meanwhile, is often used as a conduit by Pentagon PR people. It is a tool of PR to influence the rest of the press. "The Pentagon," says James Doyle, former chief political writer for *Newsweek* and now assistant editorial director of *Army Times Publications,* "has the feeling that if they get the information to us, it will be rendered accurately to the general interest press. The people who are covering the Pentagon tend to use us as a tip sheet or source of information."[8]

Business news is another paradise for PR. The reason again is that the press has been caught short-staffed. The demand for business journalism has far outstripped the supply. Economic issues such as inflation, recession, recovery, unemployment, stagflation, import quotas, certificates of deposit, bank deregulation, money market funds, balance of trade, devaluation of the U.S. dollar, federal budget deficits, bankruptcies, federal bailouts, bank failures, the stock market (both bull and bear), oil stocks, petrodollars, baskets of currencies, windfall profits, gold prices, Federal Reserve policy, money supply, government fiscal and monetary management—or, rather, mismanagement—and the Third World debt crisis have become front-page news that affects everyone. Since 1970, newspapers from coast to coast have added business sections to meet the demand for business news, but also because they saw the phenomenal and lucrative success of the *Wall Street Journal,* now the largest-circulation daily newspaper in the nation with some 2 million readers.

Meanwhile, business magazines like *Fortune, Forbes, BusinessWeek, Inc., Money, Venture,* and *Dun's* have been booming in both circulation and advertising-page growth. Of the top ten national magazines in number of ad pages in 1983, three were business magazines—*BusinessWeek* (first), *Forbes* (fifth), and *Fortune* (sixth)—according to *Ad Age* magazine. While industrywide magazine revenues were up 15 percent in 1983, business magazine ad revenues were up 24 percent.

Between 1980 and 1985, the number of regional business magazines and newspapers jumped fivefold, to almost 100.[9] These publications, both old and new—*Crain's Chicago Business, Manhattan, inc., New England Business,* the *Kansas City Business Journal, Hawaii Business, City Business*—have been enjoying strong circulation and ad growth too.

Television has gotten into the act also. Network and local news programs are carrying more economic and business-related stories. Programs like Louis Rukeyser's *Wall Street Week* and

The Wall Street Journal Report draw respectable audiences, as does cable television's Financial News Network.

During this expansionary period, there has been a shortage of capable journalists who can handle the ins and outs of financial reporting. Not only must a business writer be able to understand what the chairman of a company or the head of a municipal loan corporation is saying, he must also translate it into language that the general reader can comprehend. Inexperienced financial writers can quickly and easily be intimidated into violating one of the first rules of journalism: don't write something if you don't understand what it is you're writing. This has spelled opportunity for PR. Many business journalists have had to depend on PR people as security blankets to reassure them that what they're writing is correct, as the PR person pulls the strings by "explaining" the meaning of the complicated details.

"We run into inexperienced business reporters all the time," says Lucien (Toney) File, head of H&K's business and financial media relations group. "I literally had to explain the meaning of the word 'profit' to the bureau chief of one newspaper. In another case, one of my clients was making a tender offer and I had to spend four hours on the telephone explaining it to a crime reporter from a major daily who was covering the story. I had to hold his hand all the way through. Most PR men would jump up and down for an opportunity like that and say, 'Boy, I've got him now!' But I worry. I want the reporter to get it correct."

Seasoned business journalists worry too. One senior editor at a major business magazine commented in disbelief about a new writer who did not know the meaning of the term "return on equity"—a measure of profitability that tells how much profit a company is making from the total equity dollars invested in the company. The managing editor of another business publication that had sought several big-name nonbusiness writers to do stories for it was disappointed upon receiving the finished material. "These guys don't know how to read a balance sheet!" the editor commented.

Because companies are essentially private entities that do not have to reveal all the information a reporter would like, a business journalist also has to have the skill to interpret the information that is released by the company. Annual reports, Securities and Exchange Commission filings, public statements, general industry and economic conditions and factors, and keen observation of what others in the industry are saying and doing tell a story—but the reporter has to know how to read that story. Does General Motors want import quotas to keep Japanese competitors out of the U.S. so American auto workers can keep their jobs? Or does GM really just want to keep competitors out so Americans have no choice but to buy overpriced cars from Detroit? You don't need a degree in business or economics to figure that one out, but there are many more business stories in which the real motives of business and government regulators are not so apparent. Was the government bailout of Continental Illinois Bank a good or bad idea? Should the U.S. sell the profitable ConRail?

PR also gets its foot into the door with experienced business journalists. For any publication, an increase in advertising pages means that more stories have to be produced to put between those ads. The writers have to fill space. Someone has to think up the ideas for all that copy. Editors and writers do some of that, but when PR people call up with decent story ideas, they are welcomed with open arms.

"*Fortune* is another cup of tea," says an H&K PR handbook for clients. ". . . in fact, *Fortune* has an associate editor whose sole responsibility is the development of stories from outside the magazine, mostly from public relations sources. . . . Said Carol Loomis, one of the magazine's editors at [a] 1972 [public relations] seminar, 'We think good management stories are hard to find; any ideas you've got, we'd like to have.'"[10]

"Contacts are not as important in getting a story placed as is a good idea," says H&K president Loet Velmans. "If I have lunch four times a week with [then-*BusinessWeek* editor-in-chief] Lewis Young, it doesn't matter. But if I have an important message, he'll have lunch with me tomorrow to hear it."

"If you want to sell a corporate strategy story to *Business-Week,* the best way to do it is to quote the boss setting his goals five years ago," says H&K's file. "Next paragraph of your pitch letter says, 'Here's what he did.'" Adds the H&K handbook: "Suffice it to say, you have a ready audience in the editors of *BusinessWeek.*"

What does *BusinessWeek* have to say about this? "I'd say Lew Young doesn't have lunch with a lot of PR people," says managing editor John A. Dierdorff. But he goes on to confirm everything H&K says. "Contacts made by PR people do figure in the eventual evolution of a number of *BusinessWeek* stories. I sometimes talk to PR people and tell them what we're looking for. I tell them, 'You can be helpful.' . . . Yeah, we're being used. The press and PR use each other—unethically at times. But [New York Mayor] Ed Koch is using the press too when he says this or that. There is certainly a symbiotic relationship that has developed between the press and PR, but we should never forget the adversary relationship."

This much ballyhooed adversary relationship is often just the window dressing that helps journalists rationalize their incestuous relationship with PR. When the press depends on PR, it can only lead to trouble. Take this classic true story at one national business magazine based in New York in the late seventies. One of the writers had a girl friend in Florida and was always looking for Florida feature stories so that he could visit her on reporting trips there. Along comes a Miami PR firm with—a story in Florida. Soon, this writer began doing stories on all of the PR firm's Florida-area clients. Meanwhile, other writers at the magazine, for various reasons, also wanted stories in Florida. The Miami PR firm was doing a booming business. One day a PR man from that firm boasted to the *Miami Herald* that this big New York magazine was in its pocket—which was true, in a sense. Back in New York, the editor of the magazine got wind of the story and ordered that no writers would ever deal with that PR firm again.

Sometimes the relationship between a news organization and its PR sources leads to legal trouble. On July 12, 1984, Chief Judge Aubrey E. Robinson, Jr., of the U.S. District Court in Washington, D.C., ruled that *Stock Market Magazine* had violated the antifraud provisions of the securities laws and failed to register as an investment adviser. He found that some of the magazine's features were written by the PR people of the companies profiled in the articles, and authors of some of the features were also paid fees by the companies they profiled.[11] The magazine, through its attorney Joe Sharlitt, denies the charges. *Stock Market Magazine* is presently appealing the decision, and another court has since stayed Robinson's decision, pending appeal.

PR is also influential when television covers business news. A classic example is the great oil profits case.

You remember when oil prices shot up in 1979–1980 and oil companies were suddenly accused of usurious profits as their earnings soared, in some instances up as much as 160 percent year to year. The leading PR mind in the oil business decided to attack the industry's image problem head-on. Herbert Schmertz, the outspoken vice president in charge of public affairs at Mobil Oil who has achieved a certain superstar status because of his flamboyant style and reported $300,000-a-year salary, led the charge. ABC's Westin lauds Schmertz for bringing "the public relations position of Mobil to us. He understands extremely well how a story develops, how a story is covered, and how within that mix a position should be forcefully presented," says Westin. Simply put, Schmertz knows that the same set of facts presented in two different ways can result in two decidedly different conclusions.

"It was certainly Mobil's efforts—and I'd attribute it to Schmertz's skills—that made us sensitive," continues Westin. "I remember a piece we did on *World News Tonight* in which [economics editor] Dan Cordtz didn't come in and say, 'Boy, those profits are obscene,' but he did a kind of comparison to say they were high in absolute terms, but percentagewise they were actually within an acceptable range when compared to businesses like [broadcasting]."

Cordtz disagrees with Westin's giving credit to Schmertz for making ABC sensitive to the oil industry side of the story, even though it was Mobil that called Cordtz and other journalists to a press conference, thus setting the agenda for the news coverage.

And the ABC News story seems to indicate Cordtz had indeed been sensitized into giving the oil industry the benefit of the doubt. Here's part of what Cordtz said in his report:

> . . . oil profits are not out of line with those of other industries. Over the past five years, major oil companies averaged about a 15 percent return on the money they had invested. The average for all U.S. industry was about 14 percent, and com-

panies in the highest profit business, radio and TV broadcasting, earned more than 20 percent on their investment.

Cordtz may have been too sensitive. If oil profits shot up only in the middle of 1979, including them in the previous five years' return on investment would automatically tend to dilute the impact of the gains. Cordtz's point was to show oil company profits over the longer term; but Schmertz's point was to blunt the impact of the immediate huge oil profits. Had Cordtz been able to jump a year ahead—to 1980—he would have seen a much different picture. According to *Forbes* magazine's annual industry roundup, the energy industry's average five-year return on investment of 19.3 percent as of 1980 ranked ninth among forty-nine industries, beating even the computer and electronics industries. For the year 1980 alone, the median return on investment for international oil companies like Mobil was an astounding 25.6 percent—making it the most profitable of forty-nine industries. (Mobil itself actually did better: 26.9 percent.)

Yes, we are Monday-morning quarterbacking, but the fact remains that PR successfully attempted to manipulate the public perception of the truth. Oil companies—even over the long term—were making money hand over fist. Critics had good reason to call profits outrageous.

Television is not just using PR for complex business stories. Its use of PR is rampant throughout local and network news, news magazines, and talk shows. "Local news especially is flagging things [for PR]," says Sy Pearlman, executive producer of NBC's short-lived *First Camera* news magazine. "Every celebrity that comes through town usually gets an interview on [New York City's local news program on WNBC-TV] *Live at Five*. It happens because there's just so much time to fill. There are two hours of local news now in most big markets."

Says Scott Cutlip, "Local radio and TV stations are more dependent on PR than newspapers because they have smaller staffs."

The 1984 Democratic presidential primary candidates depended heavily on local TV news appearances in their campaign, sometimes only landing at the airport for a quick press conference so they could also make the local news in another—or two more—nearby cities. Local newsmen ate it up because it gave them an intimate local angle on a big national story.

Local television talk shows also depend heavily on PR people to provide them with a steady stream of guests, as do the three network morning talk shows. Again, there's simply so much air time to fill.

The increasing use of feature news stories leaves a big opening for PR people to influence network television news. "Let me tell you," says Elmer Lower, president of ABC News from 1967 to 1978, "when ABC put *20/20* on the air, they felt they couldn't make it in prime time with only hard-hitting news. The theory is to throw in one frothy piece on entertainment or a star to compete with the prime time entertainment programming on the other two networks. Recently my son, a producer for ABC News in Paris, did a piece on James Bond. It ran twenty minutes as the lead item to get the people into the tent. It was tied in a few days after the movie *Octopussy* opened in theaters across the nation. They figured they'd capitalize on the interest people had in the movie."

20/20 managing editor Paul Dolan maintains that that particular feature was not initiated by PR people.

But PR has become such a normal accepted part of news development that the PR person often doesn't even have to push hard anymore to sell a story idea; TV journalists are recognizing the benefits they can reap from promoting movies, stars, books, and everything else. *20/20* is tacitly accepting an under-the-table "payment" in the form of ratings points—that will translate into ad revenues for ABC—in exchange for promotion that will translate into revenue dollars for the PR person's client.

Counters Westin: "We would not have gotten access to Sean Connery or Roger Moore or Cubby Broccoli if they weren't trying to raise the public's awareness of their new movie."

Is PR using the media or are the media using PR? Says Pearlman: "If the media are pandering to PR, they damn well know they're pandering; in fact they're not being used, they're users."

Call it what you will, *20/20*, like so many other news and entertainment shows, was promoting the latest flick in exchange for access to its stars. "They were playing off each other," says Lower. When journalists willingly barter away their news judgment to meet the requirements of PR people, that spells trouble. The journalist's primary goal is then no longer the truth, it is ratings and profits; and holding the key to those profits and life-sustaining ratings is the PR profession.

This is disturbing enough on the soft-feature side of news. But when PR gets its hands into influencing or creating the legitimate news sections of newspapers, magazines, television, and radio, the hidden "plug" is even more insidious. And the press has given up nearly as much control of the legitimate news department to PR as it has with the soft features. That makes the PR profession's influence on the American media complete.

Says James Deakin, twenty-five-year veteran White House correspondent for the *St. Louis Post-Dispatch,* in his book *Straight Stuff, The Reporters, The White House and The Truth*:

> Most of the governmental news in the American news media is furnished by . . . the government. A 1973 study by Leon V. Sigal showed that 58.2 percent of the news in the *New York Times* and the *Washington Post* came from press conferences, press releases, and other official sources. Another 25.8 percent came from interviews and other activities that in many cases served official purposes. The score thus was: government 84, victims 16. Lou Cannon of the *Washington Post* wrote that "this means that the two newspapers usually considered most skeptical, independent, and critical of government wound up printing pretty much what the executive branch of government gave out." Tom Wicker of the *New York Times* has said that the reliance on official sources for news is "the gravest professional and intellectual weakness of American journalism." . . . And Bill Moyers, who has worked for both government and the news media, has said: "Most of the news on television is unfortunately, whatever the government says is news."[12]

The press and PR depend heavily on each other for leaks and comments that are not for attribution or are on "deep background." Even though this information is in the guise of news, it is really publicity for some interest group—who, we do not know.

For example, when Henry Kissinger was secretary of state during the Nixon and Ford administrations, he regularly provided information to reporters, yet he was always quoted as "a senior State Department official," remembered ABC News's Ted Koppel on a *Nightline* program about leaks.

Explained Kissinger, "Everybody really knew that I was the senior official. The advantage of doing it in this manner was that it enabled foreign governments not to have to take a formal position about what I had said, and not to force me to take a formal position. Since everybody in the negotiations was, theoretically, pledged to secrecy, but at the same time, since everybody was giving a briefing on their own version, I felt it was important that the American version also be available, so we all played this complicated game."

ABC News's Sam Donaldson, however, points out the problem with that. "Dr. Kissinger is correct: sophisticated players like governments know who the senior official is aboard the secretary of state's plane. But the people who don't know are the American people out there in Oklahoma, out there in Texas, out there in Nevada. They aren't sophisticated, so when they hear reporters say, 'Officials said so and so,' they don't know who's talking. The business of doing it on background or deep background is just wrong."

Nevertheless, Donaldson gets background and deep background information every day in his capacity as White House correspondent. But what are guys like Donaldson to do? If they don't report what White House sources and insiders say, some competitor will. That's the conundrum the press lets itself in for when it becomes too dependent on PR.

That impotence is, perhaps, one reason the press doesn't want to look too closely at what PR does—and why the public should be concerned. If nothing can be done about the blatant PR manipulation in the hot spotlight on the White House, what's going on in the press/PR partnership that is not so visible? There, the press ignores the manipulation and takes credit itself for digging out the information provided by PR. That, in turn, makes the press look better, more omniscient than it really is, inflating the press's own PR image.

When Reverend Jesse Jackson returned victoriously after winning the release of captured Navy lieutenant Robert Goodman, he sat down in a private conversation with CBS News anchorman Dan Rather. After that interview, Rather gave the "inside" account on the *CBS Evening News* about how Jackson's wit and charm persuaded Syrian president Assad to release Goodman. The "inside" source for that story was clearly Jackson himself.[13] Good reporting? No, good PR.

Sometimes the press is not even aware of when it has been used by slick PR people intent on influencing the news. For example, during the 1984 Republican national convention in Dallas, a "rumor" circulated—and network and local newscasts helped spread it—that U.S. Ambassador to the United Nations Jeane Kirkpatrick, who was a Democrat, was going to use her convention address to announce she was switching parties.

But when the speech was done, Kirkpatrick had not switched parties. What went wrong? The "rumor" was the concoction of the GOP's PR brains. Purpose: to spotlight the fact that Kirkpatrick was a Democrat, which would lend more credibility to her speech attacking the Democrats. The possible party-switch angle was merely a vehicle to call attention to Kirkpatrick's party affiliation. The networks would not make a big deal about a "rumor" that Kirkpatrick was a Democrat. But they would gladly run with a rumored party switch.

Shortly after the speech, former President Gerald Ford even tipped the GOP hand. "It was a very tough speech—by a Democrat. And it's more effective because it comes from a Democrat." But even after Ford spoke, the press was still baffled. "Why doesn't Kirkpatrick join the Republican party?" asked ABC's David Brinkley. "I don't know, David," came the reply from Sander Vanocur on the convention floor. (Of course, much later Kirkpatrick really did switch parties.)

An even more frightening example of manipulation is the Hamilton Jordan cocaine case. You heard the story this way: President Carter's chief of staff Hamilton Jordan was charged with using cocaine in Studio 54, a New York nightclub (whose fame, curiously enough, was itself the creation of smart PR and an incestuous relationship between the club's owners and some in the New York press.) The charges were so credible that the FBI entered the case and began an investigation of Jordan. Later the attorney general entered the case and eventually appointed a special prosecutor.

The real story, according to an excellent examination of the particulars by journalist Henry Post in the *Columbia Journalism Review,* involved a PR squeeze play. At the time, Studio 54's owners were being indicted for tax evasion, conspiracy, and obstruction of justice. The Hamilton Jordan cocaine charge was invented by Studio 54's attorneys and hyped by Roy Cohn— attorney and PR man for Studio 54—to fuel a plea bargaining attempt according to the *Post*.[14]

The FBI, attorney general, and special prosecutor's office entered the investigation not because the charges were valid. Rather, they investigated because of a technicality in the 1978 Ethics in Government Act. "The Ethics in Government Act contained a provision that required the attorney general to investigate thoroughly any charge of criminal behavior made against any person on a list of 140 government officials, no matter how frivolous the accusation or how incredible its source," explains former Carter press secretary Jody Powell in his book, *The Other Side of the Story*. "If the investigation did not, within ninety days, show the charge to be without substance (if, in effect, the Justice Department was not able to prove that the accused was innocent), the attorney general had to appoint a special prosecutor."[15]

The law required that such preliminary investigations and the appointment of a special prosecutor remain confidential. Because of that, Studio 54's first plea-bargaining attempts didn't work: the government could not make a deal in exchange for Studio 54's silence on the Jordan allegations, because the law would not let the government ignore the charges.

However, if a special prosecutor could be appointed, explains Post, he might take over jurisdiction of the Studio 54 tax case to obtain Rubell's testimony against Jordan. Studio 54 thought it might be able to strike a better deal in its own case with the special prosecutor. How to get a special prosecutor hired? By publicizing the phony charges in the media. Cohn did just that. Said the *Columbia Journalism Review*:

> According to several reporters at the *New York Times*, and according to [Studio 54] co-counsel [Mitchell] Rogovin, on about August 20, Cohn called his good friend *New York Times* columnist William Safire to tell him about Jordan's alleged use of cocaine at Studio 54. Safire wrote up a short memo and passed it on to a number of *Times* reporters; to Bill Kovach, a *Times* Washington bureau editor; and to executive editor [Abe] Rosenthal.

The memo emphasized that drug use by a high government of-ficial was a grave and serious matter and described the source of the information as "a lawyer you and I both know."

Reporter Philip Taubman began checking out the story for the *Times*; meanwhile, information was also leaked to the *Washington Post*, where Charles Babcock started digging. The key evidence, aside from Rubell's testimony, was the [John (Johnny C)] Conaghan tape, which purportedly discussed Jordan's alleged cocaine use. At neither paper did reporters ever hear the actual tape; instead, it was "characterized" to them. Thus, in the end, the credibility of the cocaine charge depended on the credibility of one [self-interested] source: Roy Cohn.[16]

In a travesty of journalism, the *Times* page-one story described the source of the story as "sources close to the investigation," rather than what would have been more correct: "interested parties." The *Times*'s Rosenthal has "made no secret of his dislike for Jimmy Carter and his administration," says Powell. Safire, it should also be pointed out, is a former PR man himself.

This is what can happen when the press and PR enter into their hidden partnership. It will happen again. Because of the press and PR's very real mutual dependence, the weaknesses of the press, the ingenuity and intelligence of the PR business, and the ignorance of journalists and the public, the press/PR partnership grows closer each day. And as that happens, it is the PR business, not the subservient press, that gains increasing control.

But ultimately it is not the press that PR wants to control. Manipulating the media is only a necessary means to an end. You are the ultimate target.

four

Dramamine Screamers

HOW PR WORKS

Almost everyone is mistaken about just what this beast public relations is. The Nixon administration naively thought that good public relations was simply a matter of covering up the Watergate mess, then telling the world that it was doing everything possible to bring the facts to light. Hollywood producer Jack Warner, Jr., thought he had the goods on public relations; in a *Los Angeles Times* op-ed piece, he recounted how a PR man might have advised Abraham Lincoln on the Gettysburg Address. ("You tend to dwell too much on the word 'dead.' I wish you could manage . . . a more cheerful note.") And, of course, everyone in the press thinks the government's handling of Grenada was a "public relations disaster." As we have seen, Grenada was a superlative example of the power of PR to deftly mold public opinion.

Ironically, journalists in recent years have been fascinated about "manipulation" of the press—especially when it is the White House that they think they've caught with its pants down. But even these holier-than-thou examinations that totally ignore the press's own part in the game fail to get to the truth.

For example, the *Washington Journalism Review* thought it discovered the truth about "How Reagan Controls His Coverage," in a September 1984 article by David Hoffman, who covers the White House for the *Washington Post*. Among

Hoffman's "revelations": the Reagan image makers highlight the positive and play down the negative; plan "what he [Reagan] should say" on television news programs; offer "staged speeches, a blizzard of transcripts and written statements"; have the President talk "vaguely" about his proposals; float trial balloons and even announce injections of federal funds into geographic areas or industries at the best possible moment for Reagan.[1]

Considering the fact that these secrets have been used by politicians for decades, at least, Hoffman brings nothing new to the examination of how PR actually does manipulate the public.

So the questions still remain: just what is public relations, and how does it really work?

Start first with the question of what PR does.

The ultimate goal of PR is to *sell* products, services, reputations, projects, programs, people, politicians, beliefs, ideas, everything and anything.

Forget the dictionary definition—"the art or science of establishing a favorable relationship with the public." Forget the idea that PR is a device that innocently expresses an opinion or side of a story. Forget the oft-stated argument that PR people are simply exercising their First Amendment right to communicate ideas or points of view. You should even forget the press view that PR people are engaged in the narcissistic business of trying to make their clients "look good." Those explanations are part of the equation, but they are only a means to an end.

The ultimate goal of PR is to *sell*.

"Essentially, PR works with the opinion-formation process," says Harold Burson, the grandfatherly chairman of Burson-Marsteller, the nation's largest PR firm. "The real payoff, though, is getting people to buy a stock, support an issue, buy a product. A story in *Life* magazine—publicity in *Life*—has a tremendous impact. It translates into sales."

Thus the true definition of PR sounds a lot like advertising. While PR is the blood brother of advertising, it is much different. For starters, television and radio commercials and print ads specialize in two or three areas—products, services, maybe politicians. PR, too, excels in selling tangibles (products, services), but it also does a superb job pushing intangibles—corporate images, political programs, and social ideas. PR is a jack-of-all-trades in the selling game.

A second attraction of PR is that it does a relatively low-cost selling job compared to advertising. For example, Batten, Barton, Durstine & Osborne, the ad agency for PepsiCo, estimates that for the price of several PR staffers creating "news" about the Pepsi ad campaign featuring singer Michael Jackson, PepsiCo got TV coverage worth $2.75 million.[2]

And, of course, Madison Avenue has its problems these days, particularly with television advertising. Not only is the cost of air time getting prohibitive, but viewers are "zapping" out TV commercials with remote-control channel switchers and the fast-forward buttons on their video cassette recorders.

Finally, ever since Vance Packard and Wilson Bryan Key blew the whistle on how advertisers lie to and manipulate us, the public has become increasingly cynical about what they see in TV commercials and print ads.

How does PR overcome these obstacles? Edward L. Bernays, the universally acknowledged "father of public relations" who pioneered development of the profession in the thirties and forties, has a sobering phrase to describe the process: the engineering of consent.

"This phrase means, quite simply, the use of an engineering approach—that is, action based only on thorough knowledge of the situation and on the application of scientific principles and tried practices in the task of getting people to support ideas and programs," says Bernays.[3]

There are four main elements to the mechanics of public relations' carefully engineered manipulation: 1) the message to be transmitted; 2) an "independent" third-party endorser to transmit the message; 3) a target audience that, it is hoped, will be motivated to buy whatever is being sold; and 4) a medium through which the message is transmitted. Possibly the most crucial of these four elements is the independent third-party endorser. But let's start at the beginning of the list with the PR message.

There is a great deal of confusion about the credibility of PR people. In general, PR "flacks," as they are disparagingly called by the press, are seen as outright liars. In general, and especially for the upper reaches of the PR industry, that is a false assessment. PR people know they must deal with facts—and they do deal in facts. If they couldn't be trusted in the PR-journalist relationship, the press would always be double-checking what the PR people have to say. Neither party would like that: not the journalists, because it would mean twice the work for them (and, as we know, journalists often depend on PR people for shortcuts); and not the PR people, who seek to discourage the press from digging up other sides of a story.

If PR can be accused of lying at all, it would be found guilty of "lying" about the importance, "slant," or likely consequences of its "story." Good PR is rather like the placement of a fish-eye lens in front of the reporter. The facts the PR man wants the reporter to see front and center through the lens appear bigger than normal. Other facts, perhaps opposing ones, are pushed to the side by the PR fish-eye lens and appear crowded together, confused, obscured. The reporter's entire field of vision is distorted by the PR lens.

Hyping the importance of whatever story PR is trying to sell to the media is necessary to getting press coverage. What PR people really want is a free advertisement, but ostensibly the press is not in the advertising business. "Listen, the media get paid to cover news," says Washington PR man Michael Dowling matter-of-factly, "so you create news. Public relations sets up a situation where you literally know the news media will want to cover it."

PR thus dresses up an advertisement to look like something that in most cases it is not—news. That allows the press to run a free ad without its looking like an ad. And it gives the journalist his most valuable commodity—a story. One hand washes the other.

An excellent illustration of how advertisements become news is Burson-Marsteller's PR promotion of drug maker G. D. Searle's antinauseant Dramamine.

Dramamine is by far the leading antinausea drug, with an 87 percent share of the market. But at the beginning of the campaign there were two problems: 1) the market for this drug was mature, meaning everyone who wanted to buy it was already buying it; and 2) many people who might otherwise buy Dramamine to quell carsickness or seasickness hesitated because they viewed Dramamine as a "serious drug" that is more like blood pressure medicine, say, than aspirin. Searle, obviously, would like the public to think of Dramamine on the same level as aspirin. That would boost demand—and sales.

Sounds like a job for advertising, right? Maybe, but Searle felt PR could do a better job, and Burson-Marsteller dreamed up a media event sure to catch the eye of editors and producers around the country without its looking too much like an advertisement. "Since most nausea comes from motion sickness, we were looking for an event that would dramatize motion and tie it to the Dramamine name," says John Morrison, vice president of sales and marketing for Searle. Burson-Marsteller and Searle hired Gary Kyriazi, author of *The Great American Amusement Parks,* and two Hollywood stunt men. The gimmick: these dyed-in-the-wool roller-coaster fanatics would set out on the noble quest of finding the best damn roller coaster in the country from a field of seven contenders, including those at Great America in Santa Clara, California, Six Flags Over Georgia in Atlanta, and Astroland Park on Coney Island.

Was the press "taken in" by the Dramamine Screamers contest? "The press coverage was phenomenal," says Jan Norton, director of consumer marketing at Burson-Marsteller. "After Coney Island, the story went national thirteen different ways. We even made the *International Herald Tribune.*"

Media outlets across the nation were indeed taken in by the story, and we don't just mean small, story-hungry papers like the Toms River (N.J.) *Times-Observer,* the Tulare (Calif.) *Advance-Register,* or the Lubbock (Texas) *Evening Avalanche-Journal,* all of which carried the AP and UPI accounts of the story. Some of the more prominent news organizations through which Searle broadcast its message were *USA Today, People* magazine, the *Village Voice, PBS Nightly Business Report, St. Louis Post-Dispatch, San Francisco Examiner, Cincinnati Enquirer, Atlanta Journal/Constitution, Toledo Blade, Chicago Tribune, New York Daily News, New York Post, Milwaukee Journal,* AP Radio, ABC Radio News Network, NBC Radio Network, Cable News Network, and the *CBS Morning News.* To list every one of the 191 newspapers, magazines, radio stations, and television outlets that carried the Dramamine Screamers story would take up an entire page in this book. And that does not count 1,236 radio stations that were interested enough in the story to receive PR-produced audio feeds of it. What a waste of journalistic manpower.

Dramamine Screamers shows how PR can exercise a strong degree of control over not only press coverage but the content of the press coverage as well. Four important aspects of the PR campaign were carefully designed by Burson-Marsteller to glean the maximum benefit from news reports:

☐ Putting Dramamine into the very name of the contest itself was a bold, aggressive stroke that ensured all news coverage would spotlight the Dramamine name.

☐ The timing of the stories' appearance—May through July—was set to coincide with the "season" during which most people would most likely look for an antinauseant—June through September.

☐ The "fun" aspect of the story helped keep Dramamine from appearing too medicinal. "One of the objectives of this program was to make Dramamine seem less serious," says Morrison.

☐ Choosing seven amusement parks scattered throughout the country allowed for voluminous local press coverage—often as important as coverage in the big national media outlets.

All of this adds up to an estimated 60 million people exposed to these messages, according to statistics in a Burson-Marsteller stewardship report. And Dramamine continued its firm hold on the market despite a $1 million ad campaign by its competitor.

The Dramamine Screamers campaign worked because of a key element in all good PR, the independent third-party endorsement, which gives the message credibility.

Here's how it works.

If GM were to tell you in an ad that its new Corvette is "the most advanced production car on the planet," you would be skeptical, to say the least, because GM has a clear financial interest in telling you that.

But if GM could get someone else—an independent party not connected with the company—to tell you the new Corvette is "the most advanced production car on the planet," you would probably trust that third party. That third party is often the press, which has a well-cultivated image of being a seeker of truth, an independent thinker, an adversary of interest groups operating outside the best interests of the public.

"The news has infinitely more credibility than advertising, and we think we do more with our publicity than all the ad guys in terms of drumming up interest," says Jack McNulty, head of General Motors' PR department. "People don't trust ads because they know where they come from."

The press helps PR people sell their wares by acting as trusted authority. "If *Car and Driver* magazine says this is a good car, there's nothing better that we can do with advertising to generate sales," says McNulty. In the public's mind, the logic is based on the old cliché: "If it's in the newspaper, it's gotta be true." Theoretically, anything appearing in the press has been carefully scrutinized by an already skeptical eye. And anything judged positive by the adversarial—and sometimes savage—press, has passed a special endurance test, a gauntlet of sorts. It *must* be superior. Most of the time, however, reporters are not really out turning over every stone. Coverage in the press also verifies the importance of the product, as attested by the lofty motto "All the news that's fit to print."

The GM case is more than a hypothetical example. When the 1984 Corvette was introduced, GM made sure *Car and Driver* had a sample Corvette to run through the paces. In March 1983 the magazine concluded that the Corvette was "the most advanced production car on the planet."[4] Sounds pretty good, doesn't it? Well, GM's PR wizards apparently fooled the experts at *Car and Driver*; GM had lent the magazine a prototype Corvette, not one from the less perfect assembly line.

Later on, *Car and Driver* did obtain and test a production model. "It rides like a buckboard," concluded technical editor Csaba Csere. The production Corvette's dashboard rattled and its roof liner sagged. Unfortunately, the enthusiastic fifteen-page spread about the car was already history.

The press, of course, does not always write "puff pieces," a fact you might think would cause considerable frustration among PR people. And this indeed is the wild card PR people point to when they claim they can't control how the media will "play" a story. But smart PR people know that in reality they can do much to control the tone and impact of a story not only by "talking it through" with the reporter but also by introducing their own "impartial" authorities. These PR-sponsored authorities use the press as a mere conduit to the public. But the effect is to obtain an implicit endorsement within an endorsement from the press, since the public often responds to the words of an expert (third-party endorser) quoted by an expert press (third-party endorser). *New York* magazine writer Michael Kramer recognized and even condoned this sort of manipulation in a 1984 article intended to give Democratic presidential candidate Walter Mondale advice on how to debate Ronald Reagan. One of his last tips: "You can and should try to influence press coverage of the debate. Have your surrogates ready to praise your performance. . . ."[5]

The best PR, however, carefully conceals the partiality of the source of praise. Instead of having Walter Mondale's campaign manager and running mate pat their own man on the back—as turned out to be the case—Mondale's PR people would have been better advised to dig up for the press a (seemingly) less biased source of praise: a media expert, a Republican-just-turned-Democrat, a formerly critical Independent.

Such "experts" are superb "independent" third-party endorsers who have the ability to appear distanced from what they're promoting, even if their affiliation is clear upon close examination. PR firms for corporations like Dow Chemical—a maker of dioxin—sent scientists, toxicologists, and environmental specialists around the country on media tours to advance and support Dow's side of the story.

"The best way to get credibility is to get credible people out there speaking for you," says Jim Callaghan, a Hill & Knowlton PR man who worked on the Dow account. Each expert gave some ninety interviews a year to newspapers, magazines, television talk shows, and radio phone-in programs. These third-party endorsers have an impact, despite the fact that they are on Dow's payroll. The public perceives scientists as being above bias.

Authoritative front men, however, are only the most obvious part of the "unbiased" third-party-endorsement ruse. Because PR people know how reporters work, they have infiltrated the very newsgathering process. Often, journalists will depend on PR people to provide them with the names of experts in a field—invariably favorable to the PR person's point of view.

PR people have also identified the key authorities whom journalists rely on for tips, ideas, and "expert" opinions in a given field. Then PR sets out to influence these primary authorities with presentations and material before the journalist gets to them. Thus the journalist is not always aware of how PR has played a part in his story.

A good example is image PR—whose purpose is to sell not only stock, but more importantly the company management. Wall Street stock brokerage houses like Merrill Lynch and Paine Webber have their own research people who study stocks and suggest which ones are the best to buy. These in-house analysts will recommend potentially good stocks to the brokers. The brokers, in turn, tell their customers—you, the public—which stocks to buy.

"There is an old myth that you've got to deal in numbers with stock analysts," says Peter Osgood, president of Carl Byoir & Associates PR firm. "That's not true. Analysts are subject to impressions—and they're impressionable—just like anyone else."

And if the PR firm can influence the most important, most listened-to of the thousands of stock analysts in the U.S., it can give its message more credibility and get a bigger audience.

Says Tom Daly, a partner of the New York PR firm of Kekst & Co.: "Some analysts are more important than others. An analyst for Merrill Lynch can influence a lot of people—directly [because of Merrill's large broker network]. There are also analysts who sell their research to others—investment houses, portfolio managers. The art of it [for PR people] is in trying to figure out what interests these people. Who out there is watching the company? Who'd sit down and listen to this company's story? And who, if we could interest them, would take the ball and run with it?"

Comments one incredulous Fortune 500 executive from a company in the metals industry, "I'm surprised how much some of the analysts covering our company—and well-respected analysts at that—have taken the company's word at face value. If they had actually checked these things out, they'd have found some of our claims were totally false."

Reporters at all the major business publications also seek out these stock analysts for tips and information, which find their way into the business press. Editors and business writers at your local newspaper read the *Wall Street Journal, BusinessWeek,* and *Forbes,* and, in turn, plan their stories and make their recommendations based on what they've read. In the end, a huge pyramid of potential investors eventually hears what has started with just one analyst's research.

One consequence of this piggybacking is that a basic opinion, tone, or story line about a stock or company can be transmitted virtually intact in a huge game of "telephone." Each writer may add new angles or interview additional sources or even write somewhat different-sounding stories, but the basic direction— (i.e., "No one can beat I.B.M."; "A&P is ready to turn profitable") can remain amazingly similar. Journalist Timothy Crouse, author of *The Boys on the Bus,* found the same phenomenon in political reporting and dubbed it Pack Journalism.

By far the most prized behind-the-scenes expert, especially in political reporting, is the "inside source." Journalists just can't resist them because these experts also make reporters look smart, sophisticated, savvy, inside. In an October 14, 1984, *New York Times Magazine* cover story, "The President and the Press, the Art of Controlled Access," *Times* chief White House correspondent Steven R. Weisman gave yet another inside look at how the White House controls the press.

After going on at length about how the White House keeps reporters from getting the news, Weisman tells us how cunning, omniscient journalists still outsmart these press manipulators. "The principal way that reporters gather information at the White House is to seek out presidential and administration aides for discussions about decisions, strategies, and policies. Generally the aides are forthcoming," says Weisman.

You know how this appears in the story. The official line of the White House is quoted first. But "inside sources" leak the "real story."

To those familiar with the sophistication of PR, especially as practiced at the Reagan White House, statements like Weisman's are a bombshell of naiveté. If Reagan's press wizards are so good at staging the news, wouldn't even the most basic "inside" treatment of the *Times* story question whether these "forthcoming" aides are part of the White House PR plan? Why are they so forthcoming?

According to David Gergen, director of communications at the Reagan White House through early 1984: "There are many different kinds of leaks. One of them is the purposeful, planned leak . . . for what can be a variety of reasons."

Former secretary of state Alexander Haig goes much further in his book, *Caveat*:

> In the Reagan Administration, [leaks] were not merely a problem, they were a way of life, and in the end I concluded that they were a way of governing. Leaks constituted policy; they were the authentic voice of the government. It is not surprising that this should have been so. The President's closest aides were essentially public relations men. They were consummate professionals—wizards is not too strong a word. In my view they were the most skilled handlers of the press since the New Deal. . . .
>
> The White House wizards understood the great intangible power that government holds over the press. . . . Information is power; manifestly, the press cannot live without information. It has no information of its own; it follows, then, that it must rely on others to manufacture the stuff.[6]

"White House advisors anonymously brief network correspondents, promoting Reagan's policies and taking potshots at his critics," says *Time* magazine's Thomas Griffith. "Network correspondents then troop triumphantly out on the White House lawn to mouth these comments as if they were repeating inside information instead of the daily administration line."[7]

Once the PR people have their "experts," they must then focus their messages on a "target public": the group of people they ultimately want to influence. It is here that we really begin to see how sophisticated PR people are.

Let's go back to General Motors in Detroit. You might think GM's target public is primarily made up of people who buy cars. But things are more involved than that. According to an internal GM document obtained by the authors, "GM Public Relations helps to make GM so well accepted by its various publics that it may pursue its corporate mission unencumbered by public-imposed limitations or regulations."

Among GM's various publics listed in the document:

- Employees: A "well-conceived communications program" will "tell GM's employees of the corporation's interest in their individual well-being and that their financial future depends on a strong, internationally competitive corporation."
- Stockholders: They "must be shown that General Motors is a growing, aggressive organization with an excellent financial future in both dividends and capital appreciation."
- Government: GM "works to form political constituencies . . . which will support General Motors' programs and policies in the political area."
- Business partners: GM must be able to influence companies it does business with, such as parts and raw materials suppliers, transportation companies, and some 11,000 U.S. auto dealers.
- Plant cities: People and government in cities where GM plants are located must be shown that GM is "a desirable and integral part of the community."
- Academe: "We have singled out other groups which have no direct relationship with GM, but which have a great deal of influence on public opinion or in Washington—in particular, academics and other thought leaders."
- International: GM's PR attempts to influence opinion, policies, and government regulations to its benefit in thirty-five countries outside of the U.S. and Canada
- News media: "All available communications tools are used by the PR staff to influence public opinion in favor of the business objectives of management. These include discussions and presentations to the media—print and electronic."
- The buying public: Curiously, this group gets least mention in the document. PR's job here, though, is to "foster a greater appreciation of the excellence, quality, and value of GM's products and services."

With so many different publics, there is a multitude of different communications needs. Thus smart PR—that which benefits GM in all these arenas combined—requires much more complex strategy and processing than simply placing puff pieces about fancy cars.

GM must play up the story about tough competition from the Japanese that might threaten the very survival of the company— hardly a positive story. Why does GM even mention this? Possibly to obtain foreign-car import quotas or a better agreement from workers at contract negotiation time.

But GM must also get a story to ballyhoo its sterling financial and competitive position, to make stockholders and other investors happy and confident. At the same time, GM must make much of its ever-rising costs—wages, materials, research, technology—to justify the ever-rising sticker prices that make consumers wince.

If some of these messages seem to conflict with one another, that's because they do. And that brings us back to an earlier point that PR is primarily guilty of lying about the importance or place of emphasis in a story rather than about the facts.

Smart PR plays up the importance of each set of facts according to its needs at the moment. Today, with one target public, the Japanese threat is the big issue. Tomorrow, with a different public and a different publication targeted to reach that public, the strong competitive edge of the company and its ability to take on all comers is what counts.

In such a delicate situation, the only way for a company to avoid the appearance of talking out of both sides of its mouth is for PR to aggressively tap its intimate knowledge of how the various media work. This brings us to the fourth key element in public relations: finding the most appropriate medium to carry the message.

As every advertiser, market researcher, and publisher knows, each media outlet has its own specific audience. People do not spend two or three dollars for a magazine or sit down for a half-hour to an hour with a news broadcast or newspaper if they do not like what they're buying. The tone; depth and content of the coverage; the pictures and presentation; the style of writing, reporting, thinking, or analysis; the readability; and the political leaning combine to make the news outlet attractive or unattractive to each person.

For example, *Cosmopolitan* attracts a segment of the women's audience different from that attracted by *Woman's Day; Boston Herald, New York Post,* and *Washington Times* readers are likely to be of a somewhat different political leaning than those who enjoy the *Boston Globe, New York Times,* and *Washington Post;* and the stratospherically wealthy readers of *Forbes* are worlds apart from those subscribing to *Money.*

Audiences also split decisively along content lines. Business magazines, news magazines, sports publications, literary journals, women's magazines, and trade publications all have different readers interested in specific topics. Employee newsletters, pamphlets, and annual reports have perhaps the most specific audiences.

What this segmentation boils down to is this: as with advertising, PR people can accurately choose the best media outlets for reaching their desired target publics. Want to place a PR story intended to sell "upscale" TV dinners by talking about how they taste better these days? Your buying audience is probably not reading *Fortune* or *Car and Driver*. Some magazines they might be reading, though, are *Working Woman* or *Esquire*.

Want to reach Congress? According to a study by Michael J. Robinson of Catholic University and Maura E. Clancey of George Washington University, the *Washington Post* is the paper in which to place your news. Robinson and Clancey's study shows that Washington opinion-leaders and policy makers spend an average thirty-one minutes per day reading the *Washington Post*. After that, they spend twelve minutes a day getting news from the *CBS Evening News*, eleven minutes with the *New York Times*, and just over ten minutes with the *Wall Street Journal*. Also figuring prominently on a weekly basis are CBS's *60 Minutes, Newsweek, Time,* and PBS's *Agronsky & Co.*[8]

Says New York PR man Gershon Kekst, "A story in the *Washington Post* influences Congress," and in such a simple way. "It makes them aware of an issue. It sensitizes them to the importance of an issue, so when a PR person or lobbyist calls upon them, the Congressman knows he's being called upon for something important enough to be in the newspaper. If they read a story in the paper, they know people are concerned."

This audience information tells the PR person how to package his story to make it appealing to the editors. Reading the publication or watching the broadcast also helps PR people find out what kind of content and subjects the editors are "looking for."

When you take everything we've discussed thus far as a whole, it is shocking to realize that PR people are often more in touch with this business of communications than are the communications carriers themselves. Good editors are often described as having an instinct for what makes a good story, for what is news, for what readers want. By contrast, the smartest PR people do not operate on instinct; they deliberately research the situation and *know* what will sell as news, what will "package" like news. PR people *know* the vulnerable spots in the system. With that in mind, PR people then uninnocently and nonaltruistically try to mold news into such a shape that, when the journalist is finished with his or her own hammering, it will still resemble the message the PR people want communicated.

This much is frightening for the media to accept—which is why their natural protective instinct is to deny it exists. But the only way journalists will be able to repel PR is to study what makes PR work as carefully as PR has studied what makes journalism work. That will start only when journalists stop and take a second look at all those PR "flacks" they so underestimate.

five

Who Are These Guys?

THE PEOPLE AND THEIR TOOLS

> PR MAN: Mr. McCormack, I can't take respon-
> sibility for this.
>
> MCCORMACK: What's your alternative? Let this ma-
> niac wash out a billion-dollar invest-
> ment? At least this buys time. It'll
> take the press at least an hour to get
> here.
>
> PR MAN: I wouldn't count on it.
>
> MCCORMACK: I'm counting on you to take care of
> the goddamn press. Now you do your
> job and I'll do mine!
>
> PR MAN: Yes, sir.
>
> —THE CHINA SYNDROME[1]

Just as there is much misunderstanding about what PR is and how it works, there are plenty of misconceptions about the people who practice it themselves. Perhaps because of journalists' us-and-them bias which places journalists on one of the highest moral planes and relegates public relations people to the bottom rungs of the ladder—next to the used-car salesmen, advertising people, and purveyors of snake oil—the public may get a distorted view of the profession.

PR people are portrayed as constantly suffering from ethical indigestion, as in this *Wall Street Journal* front-page headline:

The Image Makers.
In Public Relations, Ethical Conflicts
Pose Continuing Problems.
Lies, Stonewalling, Cover-up To Protect
The Company Often Are a Way of Life.
Indecent Burial of Bad News.

That covers just about everything—except for wife beating.

From our interviews with hundreds of PR people of every stripe and in every setting, we've concluded that "ballyhoo boys" are the exception, not the rule, and such Barnum & Bailey types are usually among the least effective pitchmen.

At the highest level of the profession, PR people are low-key, candid, creative, knowledgeable, warm, witty, charming, friendly, personable, self-confident. The best ones communicate as well as or better than some of the best journalists today; they are true communications technicians. We found few hollow shells of human beings, bereft of moral conviction and marching in step with whatever "orders" their clients or employers bark out. Many were genuinely excited about their profession; some were swell-headed; only a few harkened back to their journalism days to assure us they were really "okay."

Then, too, we saw no cabals or international PR conspiracies to control the public's mind—though quietly controlling minds is, in fact, what PR people attempt to do on a case-by-case basis. PR people have chosen their profession, and most seem reasonably satisfied with being effective advocates for their clients. They prefer to describe their job as the business of persuasion, even though that persuasion goes on covertly, employing third-party endorsers and taking full advantage of every flaw in press operating procedures, the public thinking, and the very processes of communications itself. Some will even admit that what they do is manipulation, but manipulation with a noble, higher goal in mind: defending or advancing the cause of their client. There are two sides to *every* story, goes the argument. They are in a sense, the equivalent of attorneys in the court of public opinion.

"Sure, PR is manipulation," says Kent McKamy of McKamy & Partners. "I used to view manipulation as negative, but it is also a positive word. If I can manipulate my children not to play in traffic, that's a positive effect."

Whatever it is they say they do, the important thing is that PR people do it extremely well. If journalists look down at PR people's abilities to truly manipulate public opinion in a way that will benefit a special interest, they are greatly underestimating the opposition.

"Look around our organization at the top five percent or ten percent," says Harold Burson, of B-M. "In our perception, they've achieved four things: these are bright people—intelligent, well read—they have good minds.

"They are aggressive, highly motivated. When a project ends, you don't have to tell them to get started on something else.

"They have an ability to get along with people; they are people who really adapt to just about anybody they come in contact with.

"And above all they have a great ability to communicate exactly what they want to say. The most successful people are not necessarily good writers, they're good communicators."

We do not disagree.

Doug Herle, director of human resources for Hill & Knowlton, adds a fifth key element for the making of a successful PR person: "We look for a sense of creativity in the way they approach things. We want them to transcend the ordinary."

We would break out a sixth important ability: understanding how the media really works and thinks; knowing what is news and what is not news; and knowing what sparks a journalist's interest, curiosity, and investment of time in a story.

That is perhaps why so many PR people are drawn from newsrooms. They bring with them an important understanding of what makes news news. PR people with journalistic experience know how to "package" a story to "sell" it to their editors. They know what editors are looking for. And they know how to cleverly "write around" weak spots in a story, having undoubtedly camouflaged weak reporting at times themselves. If that can be done for legitimate news, it can be done in the service of PR.

But PR people are also being increasingly drawn from the

ranks of other professions that border public relations: advertising, marketing, sociology, psychology, finance, and law. "We've even had a couple of philosophers in our training program," boasts Hill & Knowlton's Loet Velmans.

One need not even be officially in the public relations profession to be successful at PR. We know one retired fisherman who successfully battled the Army corps of engineers and a professional New York PR firm in his fight to stop pollution in New York Bay. He had credibility and right on his side, but more importantly, he understood politics and public relations. He knew how to get local press coverage.

To be sure, there are plenty of potential ethical conflicts in PR to keep the bad image alive.

For example, in 1975, Ruder & Finn took on some PR work for the (pre-Ayatollah) Iranian government airline. The PR firm put Marion Javits, wife of then-Senator Jacob Javits of New York, on the account. The problem was that this meant the wife of a U.S. senator was, in effect, representing a foreign government.[2] Finn maintains that the Iran account involved no political activity and adds that Ruder & Finn—now Ruder, Finn & Rotman—has a twenty-five-year-old ethics committee, which reviews accounts. As a result of the Javits controversy, Ruder & Finn returned its advance fee to Iran.

Similarly, ethical questions have been raised about U.S. PR firms that have done work for foreign dictators: Norman, Lawrence, Patterson & Farrell's PR for General Anastasio Somoza, when he was Nicaragua's dictator; Burson-Marsteller's work for Argentina's military junta; and Carl Byoir & Associates' PR work for the German tourist information board in the 1930s.[3] Byoir later quit the contract and was cleared of wrongdoing by congressional investigators.

And, of course, "There's plenty of misleading PR going on out there," says Hill & Knowlton's Jim Callaghan. But, he says, PR people who have to pitch another story to the same journalists tomorrow must deal in truth to maintain their credibility.

"I know the popular view of PR is the poor PR guy in *China Syndrome*, but that's bullshit," says Kent McKamy. "Once a PR person starts lying, he's instantly destroyed his credibility."

Besides, McKamy and others point to a number of ways out of ethical binds. "A friend said to me just the other day, 'Why is it that the things that put me to sleep in the day keep me awake at night?'" recalls McKamy. "I don't have trouble sleeping at night. If a client tells me to do something I don't think is right, I tell him what I think. Life's too short to be troubling yourself like that."

In fact, PR people say an important aspect of their job is to be frank with the client. After all, as communications experts, they know what will and what won't wash with the press or public. "Why waste your money on PR if you're not going to do something that will really make you look good?" is one argument PR people will confront an obstinate client with. There are other ways of manipulating public opinion without overtly lying, as we have shown.

There are, of course, other less forthcoming ways to avoid lies. "If your client is doing something illegal or immoral, you either don't talk about it in your PR or simply don't do the PR," says Judith Bogart, a past president of the Public Relations Society of America. Answers like, "I don't know," "No comment," "I don't have anything for you on that," "We are examining all the facts before we comment," "There's nothing I can say about that right now," or "I won't dignify that with comment," keep the PR person from lying.

Sometimes an issue is so sensitive, the PR people take off altogether. Pentagon spokesman Michael Burch admits he "made myself unavailable" to the press the night before the Grenada invasion.

For every negative anecdote about PR, however, there is a positive one.

In 1933, just after Adolph Hitler took power in Germany, one of his representatives approached Edward L. Bernays about doing PR for the Third Reich. "He wanted me to do some work for the German railroad or one of the concerns he was in charge of. I turned him down," says Bernays. "I also turned down Somoza—and Franco, too, even though the U.S. accepted Franco.

"In public relations, the public interest—rather than pecuniary reward—is the primary concern."

And, while Bernays did help get women to smoke cigarettes in 1934, he regrets having been so successful. "That was before anybody knew cigarettes were carcinogenic. I later worked to get tobacco advertisers off radio and television to ease my guilt complex," he says.[4]

After White House spokesman Larry Speakes was not told about the impending invasion of Grenada—causing him to deny to the press the night before that there was an invasion in the works for the next day—he was reportedly so furious about being used to mislead the press that he discussed resigning. "The credibility of the Reagan administration is at stake," he is said to have complained in a memo to then-chief of staff James Baker and counselor Edwin Meese III.

Reagan's deputy press secretary, Les Janka, who also served in the Nixon and Ford administrations, did resign, to protest the administration's so-called press blackout. "I worked through Watergate," Janka told the *Village Voice,* "and this time when the finger pointed to me to lie, I said, 'No way.'"[5]

There is also plenty of PR work done for charity. Hill & Knowlton does *pro bono* PR work for some 185 civic, charitable, educational, and cultural organizations from the Boy Scouts of America to the National Committee for Prevention of Child Abuse to the Chicago Symphony Orchestra.

Ray Hiebert, professor of communications at the University of Maryland and president of Communication Research Associates PR in College Park, Maryland, did PR for the International Year of Disabled Persons.

More than twenty years ago, David Apter & Associates Public Relations in Washington did PR for the 1963 civil rights march on Washington. The firm also did PR for the tenth- and twentieth-anniversary marches. "Coretta Scott King came to us three weeks before the [twentieth anniversary] march because it was more than they could handle by themselves," says Mark Apter. "What was getting into the press was that the Jews weren't backing the march, some blacks and Arabs were dissenting. Because it was such a broad-based coalition, it was not able to speak with one voice, and the media were looking at the small unhappy incidents. About two weeks before the march, we were able to focus the coverage on the agenda of the march."

Nor should other public interest PR go unmentioned: campaigns to prevent forest fires, to stop smoking and drug use, and to combat drunk driving.

If PR people are little understood and greatly underestimated, so too are their tools. The kit bag of the modern public relations person is a wonder of communications, marketing, and opinion research technology. Time was, many PR people like to say, the only tools needed to get a story in the newspaper were a press release and a bottle of liquor to wrap it around. Today, the business of manipulating public opinion has gone high-tech.

Video press releases are now commonplace to attract television coverage, and TV news uses them liberally. Hill & Knowlton, Burson-Marsteller, and Carl Byoir & Associates, the three largest PR firms, each has its own fully manned television production studio, as well as video crews for location shooting.

So when the Food Marketing Institute held its 1983 convention and for the first time in three years the number one issue was not food prices but rather better-quality service, Hill & Knowlton, FMI's PR representative, jumped in and did three video "news stories" that looked like the genuine article about the convention. "We got enormous pickup on that," says H & K's George Glazer.

Sometimes the videos are simply taped statements—"actualities," they are called—by a PR firm's client in response to a charge. The idea is that a TV news broadcast reporting the accusation will give better play to a corporate defense if pictures are already taped and delivered to the TV station.

Often the best way to get these videos out to TV stations around the country is via satellite. In August 1982, Carl Byoir launched regular satellite video transmission service for its high-tech press releases. The By/Media Satellite Network serves more than 400 commercial television stations and some 1,000 cable news systems via the Westar V Satellite.

The satellite connection also allows live transmission of PR material like that surrounding the opening of Epcot Center in Florida (see Chapter 6). And during the 1984 Democratic presidential primaries, candidates Mondale and Hart held live satellite interviews with TV journalists in several cities to expand and "personalize" coverage.

Not only is this whiz-bang PR aimed at the news media, it is also targeted at some very specific publics. For example, By/Media broadcast a live satellite teleconference about a new mutual fund to forty-six U.S. cities for Prudential-Bache.

A two-hour video/satellite hookup by Hill & Knowlton, promoting business in Egypt, was a PR extravaganza. H&K hooked up an investment company in Cairo with seven hundred interested businessmen in five different U.S. cities. The program included videotaped addresses by President Reagan and Egyptian President Mubarak.

Hill & Knowlton also provides broadcast and video facilities to television stations in return for publicity. At the 1984 GOP convention in Dallas, the PR firm set up an anchor booth on top of the Marriott Hotel for TV anchors from small local markets sending stories back home.

"They come out, shoot their stand-up, go downstairs to the editing facilities, then put it on the satellite uplink," says Glazer. "All we want is an identification like, 'I'm speaking to you from the roof of the Marriott Hotel in Dallas.'"

Radio is not forgotten either. Audio actualities are prepared in the same fashion as are videos and are often sent via the Associated Press and United Press International audio circuits. "We're getting ready to do an extensive actuality feed tomorrow," says Glazer. "There's a congressional hearing for over-the-counter prescriptions involving one of our clients. We're going to Washington to tape excerpts of their testimony; we'll edit it, then call five hundred radio stations and pitch our tape to them.

"Whether you like it or not, radio is still the first medium," he says.

Even the old-fashioned press release has been high-teched. Instead of mailing press releases or messengering them to a couple of key news outlets, more PR people are zapping them via their own news wire services. The largest of these is PR Newswire, which transmits about 150 stories a day and has direct lines right into some 600 newsrooms, including those of the *New York Times, Wall Street Journal,* NBC Radio Network, *Newsweek, Daily Variety,* the *Hollywood Reporter, San Francisco Examiner* and *Chronicle, Washington Post,* ABC Radio Network News, *Boston Globe,* WABC-TV, WNBC-TV, WCBS-TV, and *USA Today.* Some 10,000 companies send press releases and feature PR stories via the wire. A corporate PR department can write its release on its own word processor and shoot it quickly to PRN via telephone. Press release by wire adds speed, wide or selective distribution and impact. "Your news appears immediately on high-speed teleprinters or right in newsroom computer files editors watch closely," says promotional material for the service.

Perhaps the most important news organizations to have the installation are the wire services—AP, UPI, Dow Jones, Reuters, and Knight-Ridder Financial News. If these services "pick up" a PR Newswire story, either by doing their own story on the same subject, adding their own reporting to the PR material, or simply rewriting the press release, the PR Newswire byline usually falls off. "I don't know that it's a more credible story coming from AP as such," says Roland Eckman, PR Newswire's executive editor. "The main advantage is that AP has rewritten our story into good newspaper style, and editors hope AP has picked out the important elements. Newspapers will run an AP story without question."

The news wire also has lines into computer databases like Nexis, Newsearch, NewsNet, and Standard & Poor's News Online. Financial analysts use these databases as information sources.

AP also allows PR people to buy time on its satellite network to send press releases.

Perhaps the most important tool PR people now have at their disposal, however, is an outgrowth of the spate of PR firm acquisitions by advertising firms in the early seventies. Over the last ten years, PR people have begun applying market research techniques to discern and monitor existing public opinion on an issue, to find which target publics need to be influenced, to single out the most appropriate media vehicles to carry the PR message, to keep track of what and how many PR messages the target public has been exposed to, and to learn what effect the PR has had on altering opinion and whether additional PR is needed.

"The use of polling data in PR for issues management has been a major development in recent years," says Mike Dowling, president of Ogilvy & Mather Public Relations' Washington office. "Anytime we talk to a client, we ask, what is the latest polling data? Demographics? Who's against you? Where are your enemies located?

"Polling is getting very sophisticated too. They'll ask people,

'If you knew this, what would your opinion be?' Let's say the answer is "Against.' Then they say, 'If you knew this and this about the issue, how would you feel?' Suppose the person moves a little closer to your side. Then they ask, 'How about if you knew these two more facts?' Then you home in on those facts that'll help you, and that's what you print out in news releases and everything else."

One of the most spectacular examples of both the power of PR and the importance of research was the litigation brought by Vietnam veterans against the chemical companies that manufactured Agent Orange for use as a defoliant during the war. The chemical companies decided to settle the suit and pay the veterans $180 million largely because opinion research showed that public opinion would accept nothing less. That proved the vets' own PR campaign had succeeded, thus eliminating the need for a judge and jury's final verdict.

Campaign Strategies, a New York opinion research outfit working for the Vietnam vets, began with a telephone survey of public attitudes toward the case in the eastern federal court district of New York, where the giant class-action suit was being tried and where the jurors would come from. The polling covered attitudes about chemical companies, the Vietnam War, environmental issues, and attitudes toward chemical company executives and scientists who would be testifying. "It was a very good way of measuring the effectiveness of the PR campaign," says Hank Morris, vice president of Campaign Strategies. "Eighty percent of the people had heard about the case. That's phenomenal."

Next, the survey participants were read a "fact pattern" that closely followed what would be presented in court and were asked whether they would find for the vets or the chemical companies. "Three-quarters were against the chemical companies," says Morris. "The PR and attention given this issue four years before the trial played an enormous part in that decision."

The survey also asked how much should be awarded to the veterans. Answers ranged all over the place and up into the billions.

More specific opinion research was conducted when the judge presiding over the case allowed both sides to survey the pool of 500 potential jurors with detailed questionnaires. Some of the information sought included occupation (chemical industry employees, lawyers, and journalists were bounced); whether the person was pro-or antibusiness; whether the potential jurors had negative or positive attitudes toward chemical companies, Vietnam war protesters, Vietnam vets, World War II vets (to see if there was a bias for or against veterans in general, rather than just Vietnam vets), environmentalists, insurance companies, pharmaceutical companies, government; a series of agree/disagree questions to statements like "My country right or wrong," "I am embarrassed by the U.S. role in Vietnam," "I worry about cancer," and "A soldier is supposed to follow orders"; and whether the person had been personally affected by the war by having had a friend or relative who fought or was killed there.

The questionnaires were analyzed by computer by both sides, and the 500 potential jurors were ranked in order of each side's preference. The survey showed that the chemical companies didn't have a chance. So before a jury was even empaneled, before the opening statements were made, the suit was over, won by PR in the court of public opinion.

The effect of this on the public relations business and litigation in the years to come may be staggering. "This is the cutting edge of a major legal trend," says Morris. "Three years from now there won't be a major litigation without both sides having public opinion experts. And it will have an enormous impact on the PR before the trial. They'll start to track changes in public opinion, and, for example, if there is a major unrelated disaster that could affect opinion, like the Union Carbide gas leak in India, the lawyers will say let's delay or speed up the case, depending on which side they're on."

Group Attitudes Corporation, a subsidiary of Hill & Knowlton, conducts thirty different kinds of opinion research surveys, including public policy research that tracked public opinion toward the Food and Drug Administration's proposed ban on saccharin; a seventy-two hour quick-tab poll to find what the public thought about a client strongly criticized on *60 Minutes*; a Washington thought-leader survey of prominent senators, congressmen, and executive-branch officials and their view toward both a corporation and a scandal in its industry; and secondary analysis and monitoring of polls taken by thirteen other research organizations.

This research capability is being honed to a formidable edge by combining the best qualitative techniques taken from investigative reporting with the best quantitative methods of social science research. Walt Lindenmann, the ebullient president of GAC, created something he calls the "community case study." A researcher is sent to infiltrate a community and live there undercover for a week or so. The purpose is to collect intelligence data that will identify leaders, assess the scope of a particular problem and find out who is creating the problem. Lindenmann himself did this for a southwestern utility he would not name and discovered that the company's PR problem was that it was addressing only the more traditional members of the community while ignoring the increasingly influential minorities and others—who should have been the company's real target public.

Lindenmann has also done such work for companies wanting to locate manufacturing facilities in specific locations—often a source of community resentment. "By going right in, you can tell what the people will settle for in a compromise," says Lindenmann, giving the company a decided edge over the unsuspecting community.

Sometimes the benefit of the research is to learn that no PR can help. Lindenmann studied one company's product-liability problem, tracking every bit of media coverage with the help of a service called MediaScan, and the resultant public reaction through public opinion polls. "It was a frightening finding," he says. Every time the media was negative, soon afterward the public was negative, as expected. But even when the stories were positive, the public's hostility increased. Lindenmann concluded that the client had lost too much credibility. "I suggested: for the time being, shut up! You're in a no-win situation," says Lindenmann.

Other research tools, which categorize the characteristics of the readers of the nation's newspapers and magazines, are well established and have been serving advertisers for years. The Stanford Research Institute has pigeonholed readers into numerous Values and Lifestyle (VALS) types, including Survivors (living in extreme poverty, little education), Belongers (conservative, puritanical, conformist), Emulators (trying to make it big), Achievers (leaders in business and professions), and I-Am-Me (individualistic, narcissistic, exhibitionist).

Claritas Corporation, another research firm, has its own more detailed sketches of readership based on what zip codes they live in—the Zip-Market Clusters. Group S1,* for example, is made up of "educated, affluent, elite white families in owner-occupied, green-belt suburbs," and includes the Blue Blood Estates, Furs & Station Wagons, Two More Rungs, and Pools & Patios groups. Naturally, PR can benefit from this information by directing its publicity at only those publications read by the desired target public.

But perhaps the most crucial question research is only now beginning to answer is: does PR actually work?

"Ten years ago, you'd just write a bunch of press releases and send them out," says John Morrison, vice president of sales and marketing for G. D. Searle. "You wouldn't test market with the media. Now we are trying to get a scientific measure of how effective the PR is."

So when the new product—Searle's tabletop aspartame sweetener, Equal—was test-marketed in Pittsfield, Massachusetts, and Marion, Indiana, the effectiveness of the advertising and PR campaigns was tested too. The PR was scrutinized because research showed that "advertising had limited ability to deliver credibility to the claim" that Equal really did taste like sugar.

Why? Manufacturers of saccharin had been making the same claim about their product for years, but consumers had found saccharin to have a bitter aftertaste. Once burned, consumers were twice shy.

Pittsfield, Massachusetts, a small, industrial community in the northwestern part of the state, is a frequent product test market. When BehaviorScan, a market research firm, set up shop there, it covered all points of sale. All the grocery and drug stores in town are equipped with scanner-type cash registers, which allowed researchers to measure on a daily basis exactly how much Equal was being sold. By comparing advertising and PR inputs

*Other Zip-Market readership groups that should delight you next time you read your favorite magazine: Levittown, U.S.A., Sun-Belt Singles, Bunker's Neighbors, Big Fish/Small Pond, Norma Rae-ville, Coalburg & Corntown, Shotguns & Pickups, Money & Brains, Marlboro Country, Hispanic Mix, Back-Country Folks, Tobacco Roads, and Hard Scrabble.

with daily sales, the researchers could get a deadly accurate reading of what ads or PR plays moved product off the shelves.

The PR gimmick was the Equal Slimathon, a five-week weight-loss contest between two teams of local celebrities, headed by Mayor Charles L. Smith and Louis J. Perachi, Jr., administrator of the Berkshire Regional Transit Authority, and sponsored by Equal. Searle would donate $100 to the local United Way for every pound lost on the winning team. "It's for a good cause," attested the *Berkshire Eagle,* whose managing editor, Thomas O. Martin, was totally unaware of the PR campaign.

Publicity also came from news articles and recipe stories about Equal. Television and print advertising and store promotions were also thrown into the marketing mix. Similar testing also took place in Marion, Indiana, another good test market.

Through the six months of testing in 1981 and 1982, the publicity (not including advertising) had generated 1.5 million impressions—exposures to mention of the product—in the two markets, or an amazing 31 impressions per household. "There was a tremendous amount of newspaper and radio coverage," says Burson-Mursteller's Jan Norton. That was then compared to sales.

Explains Norton: "The first two weeks, we just had publicity, and we saw sales start to take off. Can publicity generate sales? We know, within an isolated situation like this, yes, it can."

Then the advertising started as the Slimathon began, and sales rose more. Finally, as the PR and ads continued to run, store display promotions were added. The combination of the three worked the best to generate sales.

Meanwhile Equal was being publicized in *Newsweek,* the *Washington Post, Chicago Sun-Times, Fortune,* and *Mademoiselle.* In separate tests, Searle found that PR by itself was more effective in delivering customers than the TV commercials were. The commercials, once again, lacked credibility when they made the claim that Equal tasted like sugar.

So Searle went back to the drawing board for its commercial, inserting quotes from the PR-generated news into the ads. The idea was to use press comments within the commercial—the media's third-party endorsement embedded in advertising—to generate the credibility that Searle's own claims lacked. A new fifteen-second "Sweet Life" commercial was born:

> Now, the revolutionary new sweetener discovery you've heard about is here! Introducing Equal. A news story in the *Washington Post* reports, "Good-bye sugar, saccharin, and calories." A story in the *Chicago Sun-Times* reports, "A taste virtually indistinguishable from sugar." New low-calorie Equal tastes like sugar, and it's made without saccharin and no bitter aftertaste. Mmm-mmm. Welcome to the sweet life of Equal.

The original "Sweet Life" commercial had a persuasion score of 11.6 percent. When the two editorial endorsements were added, the persuasion score almost *doubled*. "That made it more than twice as persuasive as the normal commercial for that category," says Norton.

As the product was being rolled out nationally, Searle PR tested a larger market in Atlanta with radio, TV, and print publicity—but no ads or store promos. The Slimathon name was changed to the Equal Challenge to facilitate brand-name identification and more local celebrities, including TV anchorpeople, were used. To get onto the air at radio stations during the important morning drive time, the PR people got attractive women wearing Equal T-shirts to bring morning disc jockeys their coffee with Equal. Once past the receptionists with the ploy and into the studio, they chatted on air with the DJ about Equal and how much it tasted like sugar. Often the DJ cooperated by tasting the product and giving it a personal endorsement on the spot. "This really does taste like sugar," said one between gulps of coffee.

The ultimate conclusion of this research, including additional PR test marketing in several other cities, was that PR worked best when used in concert with advertising and in-store promotion. The Atlanta PR, for example, did not generate as much awareness as that in Pittsfield and Marion because there was no ad support.

All of PR's tools taken together—the sophisticated research, the high-tech tools, the talent and abilities of the people themselves—demonstrate that today's PR people are a force with which to reckon.

*　　*　　*

In a conference room at the offices of Jeffcoat, Schoen & Morrell on Manhattan's Upper East Side, partners Sydney Morrell and Nathan Turkheimer trade war stories from their days as young, gung-ho journalists. Morrell recalls leaping out of a bush in London to catch a reluctant interview subject on his way to church.

Talk turns to the important career change years ago. Families were young and struggling, the money in PR tempting to men constrained by a reporter's salary. Then there were the PR triumphs, spectacular by most any standards—first some years with Henry Ford, then acting as management consultants to business leaders throughout the globe. Turkheimer mentions a campaign on behalf of the International Ladies Garment Workers Union to draw attention to the recent re-emergence of illegal sweat shops in New York. He had chartered a bus to take reporters on a surprise behind-the-scenes tour. Results were spectacular: armed guards, guard dogs leaping at the television cameras.

Does he ever have regrets about leaving the lofty pursuit of journalism? he's asked. He pauses, smiles. "Of course you have regrets. But I think there are always regrets about things you might have done, no matter what you do."

But hasn't he accomplished a great deal where he is? Bringing the sweat shops to the attention of the media and the public, the armed guards, the snarling dogs?

Here the smile becomes almost bittersweet. "Yes. But in the final analysis they weren't snarling at me."

six

Lights, Camera, Hype!

ENTERTAINMENT PR

We are in a television studio for the local news. The red light on the camera winks on live. Our appropriately coiffed anchorman leans one shoulder into the camera and reads two or three "talking head" stories—brief, almost headline-style stories delivered by the anchor and without any accompanying film.

That done, the anchor switches positions to a second camera. Inserted over his shoulder on the screen is a graphic showing a home-computer keyboard. Anchor puts on his pleasant-but-serious face and begins:

"Millions of people swear by personal computers. But some of us remain a little leery of the devices. In this report, the second in our series, we'll see that there are some solid reasons for those feelings of suspicion."

Videotape rolls, the director flicks a switch, and the story goes out on the air.

The news story, prepared by World Information News Service, begins with a montage of shots showing mainframe computers in action.

REPORTER: Computer crime has become one of the major growth industries of the eighties. And it's understandable, when you consider that computers transfer over 400 billion dollars every day.

The scene cuts to another montage, showing military personnel monitoring the sophisticated computers at the North American Air Defense Command (NORAD) headquarters buried deep in the Rocky Mountains.

REPORTER: It is even a threat to our national security. As depicted in the new motion picture *WarGames,* the U.S. has been brought to a full military alert, all because a typical computer whiz kid has inadvertently gained access to our military computer system and ends up playing a deadly game of Pac Man with the Pentagon.

We see the whiz kid, played by Matthew Broderick, sitting before his home computer in a clip from the movie. He starts typing in commands on the keyboard in response to the screen, which asks what game he would like to play.

"How about: Global Thermonuclear War?" he asks, typing same on the screen in blue phosphorescent letters. After a brief pause, the computer responds in a metallic voice:

"Fine!"

CUT TO: another montage of *WarGames* scenes showing NORAD on missile alert.

REPORTER: This may seem outrageous, but according to a computer security specialist for a major defense contractor, Don Williams, it could happen.

CUT TO: medium shot of Williams.

WILLIAMS: The rules say that this should never occur, and they have procedures set up to say that it won't occur, but in reality, 'cause people are real, they do things for convenience. Because it's a way to get a job done, these holes develop.

We cut again back to NORAD on alert.

REPORTER: There have been, in fact, numerous instances when

America has been brought to military alert due to human or computer error. *WarGames* director John Badham:

CUT TO: medium shot of Badham.

> BADHAM: In 1980, there were a number of false alerts that got NORAD all cranked up and had them tracking a flock of geese over Alaska because all the machinery is so sensitive, it starts picking up peculiar things that have nothing to do with supposed missiles coming in, or airplanes flying over, and they're constantly checking and cross-checking with one another trying to avoid these mistakes, but they do seem to happen.

Over still more exciting scenes of NORAD, the reporter brings the story to a close.

> REPORTER: While the probability of triggering a nuclear incident by accident is remote, the technology to do it exists in millions of American homes right now.

CUT TO: medium shot of Badham.

> BADHAM: The possibility that a youngster could do this on a fluke is a very real, real possibility.

The picture of Badham's serious face freezes.*

It looks like news. It sounds like news. It even has the feel of a genuine news story, right down to the imperfect oratory as the interview subjects gather their thoughts on camera.

But it is not news. Nor is World Information News Service a real news organization. Both are only the latest in Hollywood PR, 1980s-style.

The above news story is part of an impressive "video press release" from MGM/UA. It is also a marvel of imitation news.

Inside a neat, dark-blue loose-leaf binder from MGM/UA is a three-quarter-inch, broadcast-quality videotape. On the thirty-

*Copyright 1983, World Information News Service.

five minute tape are three news features ready to roll: 1) "From Pac Man Junkies to Computer Wizards"; 2) "The Potential Threat of Home Computers"; and 3) "Re-Creating NORAD for Hollywood." Each "news" feature—which looks surprisingly like a real news story—eventually gets around to plugging *WarGames*.

The tape also contains a personality profile on stars Matthew Broderick and Ally Sheedy, and a featurette about *WarGames* itself.

All of these stories contain "A" and "B" sound tracks. The "A" track holds the background sounds and voices of the on-camera interview subjects. The "B" track has narration by a World Information News Service announcer. If the local TV station wants to make it look as if the story was done by one of its own reporters, the flip of a switch turns off the "B" track and the reporter can dub in his or her own voice.

And there's more in this PR package: "teaser" commercials for the news program to alert prime-time viewers to what's coming on the eleven o'clock news; film clips; unedited interview segments for especially creative TV journalists who want to do their own cutting; and artwork for those screen inserts that appear over the anchorperson's shoulder to help introduce the story.

There are even "happy talk" scripts for anchors to use to lead into the story:

> Success doesn't come easy, right? It takes years in a profession as chancy as show business to become a star overnight. But as our profile on the two stars of *WarGames* shows, this old maxim isn't always right.

And there are happy-talk scripts to tag on after the story:

> A little frightening, isn't it? Maybe we should all take courses in computer programming just to make sure what the kids are up to.

If this ability of PR people to mimic real TV journalists is worrisome enough, how about this: sent to some 230 TV news directors around the country, the *WarGames* video press release was

used in some form by roughly 170 stations, according to Al Newman, vice president of publicity for MGM/UA.

"I'd say forty percent of the stations used it as-is, and the
remaining sixty percent played with it: either eliminating our
narration track—we provide a script for them to read themselves—or re-editing it," says Newman. "But even if they re-
edit it, we are still able to maintain pretty good control. They
only have so much material to work with."

Entertainment PR is probably the most widely recognized form
of the business. Who doesn't know what a Hollywood publicity
stunt is? Indeed, it is part of our pop culture. Remember the
1955 *I Love Lucy* program in which Ricky Ricardo's new press
agent suggests he jump into a swimming pool to save a "drown-
ing" woman at the Beverly Palms Hotel just to get mentioned in
Hedda Hopper's gossip column? It's a classic that has undoubtedly fostered the image of the Hollywood press agent as someone unabashedly full of wacky, fun, and harmless schemes to get
attention in the press. It runs all the way back to the 1830s and
P. T. Barnum.

Edward Bernays, in his authoritative history of the field,
Public Relations, recounts a famous publicity stunt for *The
Greatest Show on Earth.* Barnum used the press to publicize the
addition of Joice Heth, an ancient negro slave who—so Barnum
said—had nursed George Washington a hundred years before.

Barnum's assertion had raised a furor of scientific and editorial debate, and was covered far and wide in the press. Barnum's
PR work kept the debate boiling with fake letters to the editors,
both pro-Barnum and anti-Barnum, written by himself.
"Barnum did not care whether the newspapers praised or attacked him, as long as they spelled his name right," says Bernays.[1]

Continues Bernays: "When Joice died, an autopsy revealed
she might have been eighty. She could not possibly, the doctors
said, have been one hundred sixty years old, as Barnum had
claimed. Barnum was deeply shocked. He publicly admitted that
he had been deceived!"

The ghost of Barnum still walks our sophisticated world today, revealing itself in what is by now a cliché of television jour-

nalism: the arrival of the circus in town. Local TV reporters, without fail, will be seen riding one of a string of elephants walking to the Big Top.

But while these charming shenanigans still thrive and help keep the age-old image of the press agent alive, a whole new, more sophisticated, more manipulative, and more powerful form of entertainment PR has sprung up. And the *WarGames* video press release is only the tip of the iceberg.

Universal Studios claims it pioneered the video press release when it used the device for *Psycho II*. "They become editorial pieces, not just an overt plug for the picture—though subliminally they are," says Charles Glenn, Universal's executive vice president for advertising, publicity, and promotion.

Universal also sends out video interviews with film stars and directors so that local TV people can insert themselves into the interviews and appear to be rubbing elbows with the Hollywood elite. The reporter tapes himself asking the question; then the camera cuts away (or so it appears) to the star answering the reporter's question.

While some people might wonder how the entertainment critic from a small TV station in, say, Binghamton, New York, ever had the budget to go to Hollywood, let alone the contacts to set up an interview with Burt Reynolds, Glenn, who is paid to know how these things are received, doesn't see a problem. "Anything you see on TV, you believe might have happened," he says. "Besides, it's not something the general public looks at and says, 'How could this local TV guy be there?' If it's on TV, it's within the realm of possibility."

MGM/UA and Universal are not alone in this business. All three television networks produce similar PR "news programming" on upcoming miniseries for their affiliate stations. The networks also stage "star weekends" to allow affiliate station news reporters the opportunity to promote upcoming series.[2]

Even the local stations do PR themselves for network programs. (Don't forget, the stations stand to gain, too, from running the programs and boosting ratings.) One of the best of these sophisticated PR puff pieces was a twelve-part news series by WABC-TV New York anchor Bill Beutel called *The Path to War,* which aired in February 1983. The "news" series ran the same week as ABC's miniseries *The Winds of War,* and was an excellent vehicle for priming viewers to watch the program later the same evening.[3]

Modern entertainment PR, though, is more than just electronic press releases. PR for a movie—even a movie with a guaranteed audience—is a well-planned, long-term project. "Publicity doesn't just happen by accident," says Susan Trombly matter-of-factly. Trombly does PR for Lucasfilm Ltd.

As soon as a studio decides to go into preproduction, a unit publicity person is hired to "live with the movie," explains MGM/UA's Newman. "A film becomes extremely visible when it goes into production, either because of the subject or the stars in it.

"We go to *Time* or *Newsweek* or the women's books and talk about possible story ideas. For example, we'll start filming a picture in the next few months starring Jack Nicholson and Timothy Hutton. It's a comedy that takes place in Kansas. A modern-day cattle drive that ends up in Kansas City. Either *Time* or *Newsweek* could respond to our ideas by deciding, 'It's time we do something on Tim Hutton. Let's cover this.'"

There isn't much arm-twisting, since the media need entertainment stories to help boost readership or ratings. That's especially true for a guaranteed blockbuster like *Return of the Jedi.* Every news organization was greedy for a piece of that action, and the movie got coverage in every major magazine, with probably twenty covers, including *Rolling Stone, Life, People, Us,* and *Time.* Every major TV market had film clips. WABC-TV's Joel Siegel did a four-part series. *Entertainment Tonight* and *PM Magazine* did segments too. Even *Today* did a "Jedi Week," as did *Good Morning America.*

Presented with an opportunity like that, PR people don't just sit back and enjoy an easy paycheck. They take full advantage of it to try to do more than just get the movie's name in the paper; they try to mold coverage exactly to their own specifications. Don't forget, *Return of the Jedi* was the third film of what is supposed to be a nine-part series. Trombly, who did PR for *Jedi,* didn't want to run the risk of any trouble from that—however remote the possibility. After all, even the big guys have flops; remember Steven Spielberg's *1941?*

"Our job was to stress that this movie was different and that it not be seen as just another film in the series," says Trombly. "The public relations strategy was also to make it absolutely clear the film would answer all the questions." To that end, the future six parts were downplayed and the first three in the series were dubbed a "trilogy."

It should then come as no surprise that the May 23, 1983, cover story in *Time* boldly proclaimed: "*Return of the Jedi* triumphantly completes Lucas' *Star Wars* trilogy."

"We got an early commitment for the *Time* cover of George Lucas and the characters," says Trombly.

While good story ideas and hot tickets are keys to the newsroom, media friends and press contacts do help. Says Glenn, "Obviously there are a lot of other people also trying to promote their projects to national magazines. But if you've got a personal and professional relationship with someone in the magazine, you've got a better chance of receiving the favor from that magazine than the other six guys. Well, it's not a favor, but they're quicker to respond. Obviously, the merits of the individual story determine whether the piece appears or if you get a cover; however, your relationship on a PR level ensures that you get a fair hearing."

Of course a *Time* or *Newsweek* cover is great publicity in the sense that it puts the motion picture before millions of readers. Equally important, though, it influences the opinion makers. "The rest of the media all of a sudden become more interested and watch the movie more carefully," says Glenn. Once again, pack journalism.

But a simple proliferation of publicity is not enough. Another major aim of PR is to "position" the movie, a process that prepares the public not only to want to see the movie in the first place but also to like it when they finally do sit down in the theater, which then helps with word-of-mouth recommendations, which then draw more viewers in to see the movie.

"If we have preconditioned you for a movie incorrectly, you'll hate the movie," says Charles Powell, a former MGM/UA publicist and now partner in the Los Angeles PR firm of Powell & Young. "That's why *Heaven's Gate* was a flop. The publicity preconditioned the audience for something the movie couldn't deliver. On the other hand, *Arthur* was positioned as a sly drawing-room comedy. Had it been sold as a laff riot, you'd have hated it."

Proper PR positioning can really pay off on Oscar night, some PR people insist. A concentration of some 90 percent of the 3,000–4,000-member Academy of Motion Picture Arts and Sciences lives in southern California, and they are not immune from the PR that collects there nor from the national PR. "The members of the Academy are as much affected by the media and what they read as is anybody," says Newman.

"When you get right down to it, the Academy is not much different than the guy on Third Avenue trying to figure out what movie to see," adds Powell. Both Powell and Newman attribute *The Deer Hunter*'s 1978 Oscar for best picture to good PR positioning. "Here was a picture that was basically violent and negative, yet they were able to build an aura that made it appear to be an important film," explains Newman.

Says Powell, who did *The Deer Hunter* PR, "This was still a time when Vietnam was anathema. How do we sell it? As a Vietnam film? No. There had never been a successful Vietnam film. We couldn't sell it on stars—Meryl Streep wasn't a big star yet. We didn't have a Spielberg or a Lucas directing it. It was Michael Cimino's first mega-film. So we sold it in a way that would position it to the public as an important, controversial event."

Gandhi and *Chariots of Fire*, two more recent best-picture Oscar winners, were similarly positioned as, respectively, a sociopolitical imperative and a classic.

Universal hardly did any prescreening of *Deer Hunter* to the media. That created mystery and "gave the impression before anyone saw it that they should get ready for a major event," says Powell. Nor did the stars do the standard talk-show appearances—which communicated by implication that they, as artists, and the movie, as art, were too important for such commercialism. The advertising contributed to the aura with a set of lonely white deer antlers on a dead black background and only the name of the movie.

"That picture could have died, but it was watered like a

flower. The whole thing was a marketing gem," says Powell.

The positioning of the sixties classic *Easy Rider* is another example of PR's ability to home in on its target publics like an Exocet missile.

So as not to turn off target counterculture publications like the *Village Voice, East Village Other, Boston Phoenix* and *Real Paper,* and the *Berkeley Barb,* Easy Rider's PR people wanted to avoid any big-studio taint on the low-budget film, which in reality was a big-studio release from Columbia Pictures. So PR man Lee Beaupre set up shop away from the studio in his own home. He never used Columbia Pictures letterheads for the press releases and never held a screening on Columbia property. "It seemed like another American International Pictures movie, like *Wild Angels,*" recalls Beaupre, a former reporter for *Variety.*

Getting endorsements from the Establishment press was important too, and Beaupre knew exactly how to do that discreetly within the context of the aura he was trying to create. Instead of going to a magazine's entertainment editor, Beaupre invited the art director to a screening. A staffer like that would likely be more counterculture and would talk about the film among his or her colleagues. Eventually the entertainment editor would be contacted, if the powerful word of mouth within the magazine hadn't caused him to contact Beaupre first.

Brilliant positioning was part of *WarGames'* successful PR too. Publicist Pat Kingsley lured some seventy-five members of the House of Representatives, the Senate, and the Reagan Cabinet to a preopening screening in Washington.

"A lot of them did not know what they were going to see," says an amused Kingsley. "They thought they were going to the MPAA [Motion Picture Association of America] to have dinner and a nice screening. That was fine. Whatever it took to get them there." MPAA president Jack Valenti was instrumental in marshaling guests, and General Alexander Haig's presence on the MGM board of directors also helped. "He didn't really get involved in this, but it didn't hurt to say he was on the board," says Kingsley.

After the screening was over, CIA Director William Casey stalked out—telling Kingsley, who was soliciting comments to give the *Washington Post,* "I have nothing to say about this movie." (Then) White House budget director David Stockman, Kingsley claims, was not far behind Casey.

Congressman Ed Markey (D-Mass.), however, was quoted as saying, "Every senator should be strapped into a chair and made to watch this!"

The ploy "got editorial space," recalls Kingsley happily.

Soon after the Washington premiere, Kingsley's Los Angeles-based PR firm, PMK, got intermediaries to convince President Reagan to screen the film at Camp David. He liked it. "He obviously didn't know what the movie was about," Kingsley says, "but there was an article in the *Washington Post* shortly after he saw it." The President was in a meeting with some congressmen concerning the MX missile and he was telling them about *WarGames*. One of the congressmen protested, "'Don't tell us the ending,'" as Kingsley tells it. "And then Reagan looks over at the chairman of the Joint Chiefs of Staff and says, 'You wouldn't like the general; he's the heavy.' So we got another boost. Just when we thought our campaign was about over, we get this bonus which we hadn't expected."

As so often happens in PR, publicity leads to more publicity. *WarGames* and Kingsley got ABC's *Nightline*, which explored the issue of whether it was possible for a civilian to tap into NORAD's computer. Taking point/counterpoint were one of the movie's technical experts and an expert from the aerospace industry. The half-hour program was an excellent vehicle for the film, validating the slightly outlandish plot and providing free advertising; the first several minutes of the show were basically film clips from the movie. "To buy that air time would have cost a fortune," crows Kingsley.

Third-party endorsement was sought—and received—from yet another source: kids. Three weeks before the film premiered, "sneaks"—sneak previews—were shown in about 300 theaters nationwide on a Friday night—Friday to ensure that a young audience that didn't have school the next day would be in attendance. "These kids have a network that's like their own little newspaper or something, and they suddenly all know about the movie," says Kingsley.

WarGames is an example of the increasing number of "message" movies coming from Hollywood. As the Office of War

Information found during World War II, motion pictures are a powerful force for building political support and effecting social change. Hitler knew this, too, and his propaganda machine successfully used the movie *The Eternal Jew* to incite hatred against the Jews and to build acceptance for the Third Reich policies.

WarGames' message, of course, was an antinuclear one. So another goal of the PR, in addition to selling the movie, was to sell parts of the antinuclear theology: nuclear weapons are dangerous; ergo, we should not be putting more in Europe and should be figuring ways to get rid of the ones we do have.

Indeed, Kingsley admits to being a strongly committed antinuclear activist for whom *WarGames* was "like a baby." The end result was that the *WarGames* PR created a credible mixture of political, public, and media endorsement for the movie and the antinuclear philosophy. What advances the cause of the freeze movement advances the cause of the movie, and vice versa. The result is an interlocking network of government, media, business, and political interests joined together—wittingly or unwittingly—by PR. Meanwhile, the public is duped into believing they are simply watching an entertaining movie, or an interesting "news" story [actually generated by the PR] about the entertaining movie.

If PR seems to be around every corner in Hollywood, that's because entertainment is a business almost totally dependent on the creation and influence of opinion. Take motion pictures. Aside from a handful of classics about which almost everyone agrees, the real quality of what Hollywood turns out each year as entertainment and as an art form is a matter of highly subjective opinion. There is no objective scale against which one can measure the true quality of *WarGames* or *Heaven's Gate*—no "facts," if you will. Even box office receipts often enough bear little relationship to quality. This helps to explain why the industry whose success or failure rides so much on the creation of favorable public opinion or interest should be so saturated with PR people.

The movie studios, of course, are not the only ones dependent on good PR. Every facet of the entertainment business must manipulate perceptions to survive.

Seven years ago, Kathryn Schenker, vice president of publicity for A&M Records, had a no-name rock group on her hands. She used her media connections to get them listened to. When we interviewed her in late 1983, Schenker had to worry about overexposure in the media. Naturally she thought that her group—the Police—was "the biggest band in the world." Perhaps, but there is more involved here than just taking anything said about someone in entertainment at face value, or even at half the face value. On one level, everyone knows it's a Barnum & Bailey world.

Still, for a time frame measured in the weeks or months that some entertainment commodity is "the hottest in the world," before the next "hottest in the world" comes along—the public suspends disbelief. For one split second, the fairy tale is true because PR has made it true.

How?

As with any PR, it involves getting the third-party endorsement. When the Police went through New York City on a 1983 concert tour, most television stations in the city covered the band on the five o'clock, six o'clock, and eleven o'clock news. The media were leveraging the excitement on behalf of the PR people; only a few years ago that excitement could be felt only by fans actually going to the concerts.

"TV news looks very 'hip' to have the Police on," observes Schenker. However, getting to that point on the ladder to musical stardom—where the media clamor for the client—requires a great deal of climbing. Central to the ascent is getting radio airplay for the songs.

Getting airplay for a record on the radio and getting press coverage are two interrelated areas that often feed on each other like elements in an M. C. Escher sketch. Says Schenker, "If *Rolling Stone*, the *New York Times*, and *USA Today* are all writing about Oingo Boingo [a lesser known client of Schenker's], and radio stations are not playing the record, I can go to the radio station people and say, 'Everybody in the world is writing about this band. Why aren't you playing their songs?' If the radio's playing the hell out of Oingo Boingo, I can call *Rolling Stone* and say, 'Why aren't you writing about them? You have a responsibility to your readers.' If a publicist says, 'You have a responsibility . . .' nine times out of ten they'll write something."

Sometimes the media will get so caught up in the PR, they'll go way out on a limb in their coverage. Such seems to have been the case with the Puerto Rico-based band Menudo. NBC *Nightly News,* ABC *World News Tonight, The CBS Evening News, Entertainment Tonight, Good Morning America,* and local TV news reported Menudo's June 1983 arrival in New York as causing an outpouring of fans not seen since the Beatles. ABC's *20/20* also did a segment on the band, and *Time, Newsweek, People,* and teen magazines covered the group.

The claim that Menudo and the Beatles are in the same league—repeated time and time again by serious newspeople—is a heady one indeed. Where did this idea come from?

The original source of the Beatles/Menudo Connection seems to have been New York's hyperbolic mayor Edward Koch. As politicians are wont to do, he made the comment when he met the group in February 1983. According to Eric Parham, publicist for ABC's children's programming, it was the group's promoters and chief financial beneficiaries, Paquito Cordero and Edgardo Diaz, who "came up with the idea of comparing Menudo to the Beatles." Whichever publicity hound devised the idea, once it was uttered, numerous interested PR parties spread the word far and wide. It appears in press releases from New York Spanish television station WNJU, Channel 47: "Menudo, the Puerto Rican group that has been described as greater than the Beatles . . ." Menudo has a regularly scheduled series on Channel 47, and, according to Barbara Shales, assistant to the station president, Channel 47 notified the press, alerted viewers, and promoted Menudo's June visit to New York.

Why didn't the press pooh-pooh such an outrageous claim? We cannot say for sure, but we must point out an interesting coincidence for one major media force. Four programs owned by the ABC network played a large part in publicizing the band—WABC-TV's *Eyewitness News, World News Tonight, 20/20,* and *Good Morning America;* ABC Entertainment, meanwhile, had just signed the group to do regular four-minute appearances on Saturday mornings in a show called *Menudo on ABC.*

Menudo was also signed up by Embassy Communications to do up to five motion pictures. Embassy, co-owned by Norman Lear, owns Channel 47 and produces the television sitcom *Silver*

Spoons, which runs on NBC. Menudo also made an appearance on that program.

To *Time*'s credit, its Kurt Andersen and Janice Simpson were about the only two journalists to have seen at least part-way through the hype, without delving into the PR connection. Explaining the outpouring of excitement that surrounded the group's New York appearance, *Time* said Menudo "arrived within 24 hours of the huge Puerto Rican Day parade down Fifth Avenue and so rode the crest of local ethnic pride." Concluded the level-headed Andersen and Simpson: "Beatles redux? Hardly."[4]

Stars themselves are promoted by PR too, of course, but usually only in conjunction with something they are selling, like a movie or an album. Ever notice how often comedienne Joan Rivers appears on the cover of *People* just when she happens to be standing in for Johnny Carson on *The Tonight Show*? Likewise, Barbra Streisand was making herself available exclusively to ABC's *20/20* when *Yentl* was being released.

And who can forget the lavish promotion and coverage Canadian talk-show host Alan Thicke received when his new syndicated late-night talk show *Thicke of the Night* was revving up to "challenge" Johnny Carson? The idea of an unknown Neighbor from the North being a serious threat to Carson is almost as extravagant as Menudo challenging the Beatles, yet the press gave the thought as much credence as any other feature story. Thicke's backing by Carson's ex-boss Fred Silverman undoubtedly helped sell the story.

But, as history shows, Thicke never really was a contender for Carson's audience. "I'm not nearly as good as Silverman keeps saying I am in the papers," said Thicke on one of his first programs. "If I'd been that good, you would have heard of me before." Commented Thicke later, in a *TV Guide* post mortem on the show, "Our advance publicity was so good, I couldn't wait to see myself."[5]

Even TV news programs have PR people to generate favorable publicity. Some in that business describe entertainment journalism as an area ripe for manipulation, because most entertainment editors, writers, and columnists don't have editors second-guessing or watching closely over their shoulders. They have a lot of free reign. And they are often more interested in filling up space than in the content of what they write.

A PR person for a major-market local news station tells one such tale. The station was considering several candidates to fill the news director position for the evening news broadcast. The PR person at a rival station tried to plant a story in the press that one individual, who had a questionable background, was to be picked for the job. The story was actually untrue. But a local newspaper columnist called the station to ask about the rumor.

"I know for a fact it's absolutely not true," said the PR person. There was a pause, then the columnist replied.

"Well, I don't care. I need copy, and I'll run with the story anyway, saying it's a rumor."

Rather than plead with the columnist not to do that, the quick-thinking PR person said, "Wait. I've got something else you can substitute." The substitution was a quote by a local politico heard in the news program's "green room," which snippet later ran verbatim in place of the objectionable "rumor." The PR person kept a potentially volatile piece of gossip out of the paper, and the entertainment editor got the "copy" he needed. One hand washed the other.

Book publishing is another area of entertainment that is increasingly learning to use PR to help leverage tight budgets and get around high advertising costs. Everyone knows about "plugging" a book on the talk-show circuit. But book PR is going beyond that most basic of promotions.

One gimmick that works very well is to get the press to do a story not about the new book, but about the subject the new book deals with. There are several reasons this is so successful. For one thing, the journalist writing the story has much of his work already done for him—by the author of the book.

For the author there are benefits too. His book gets publicity, of course, as well as explicit mention, but it doesn't look like publicity. This is not a "boring" story about a book. Instead, the author and the book are treated as expert, authoritative sources necessary to telling this other interesting feature news story. That moves the product off the book pages of the magazine or newspaper and onto the more widely read news and style pages. *Time* admits to frequently using PR-promoted books as the basis of feature stories; *Newsweek* says it does so only sometimes. For example:

- An October 1, 1984, *Time* story in the "Behavior" section dealt with mother-son relationships. Buried more than halfway down the first column was the plug for *Mothers and Sons,* a just published book by Carole Klein.
- *Newsweek*'s "Life/Style" section ran a November 14, 1983, piece on the symbolic underpinnings of home decorating. Underpinning the article was the book *Home-Psych: The Social Psychology of Home and Decoration,* by Joan Kron.
- Another *Time* "Behavior" section story reported about a psychologist who questioned the value of all therapy. It seems to have been based on a newly released book by psychologist Bernie Zilbergeld, *The Shrinking of America.*

Broadcasters do it too. Explained ABC news president Av Westin, "We are preparing a report right now based on a new book about couples that was probably called to the producer's attention by the publisher's PR department, and yes, we are running it tentatively around publication time.

"I see no conflict in that. They don't tell us what to do. In fact it works the other way: because of our clout, the publisher and author will accommodate us to help us do the story."

Publishers' PR people frequently try to position their books by giving exclusive first access to *20/20* or *60 Minutes,* says Westin. The reason is simple. Exposure on *20/20* or *60 Minutes* calls the book to the attention of 14–16 million potential buyers. "Our viewership includes a lot of upscale, educated book buyers," says Westin proudly.

PR people for books also depend on getting newsworthy material that is buried in the book out into the headlines. For example, when Seymour M. Hersh's book about Henry Kissinger, *The Price of Power,* was released, publisher Summit Books' PR people helped make it easier for the press to make news about it. "The news release was in two parts," explained Summit Books president James Silberman to *Publishers Weekly.* "One [part] was to tell one or two news stories and the other was an elaborate guide to what was new in the book. Those media that wanted an easy story—simple to explain—had the first release, and those who wanted to go behind that and do more were provided with a way to go about it."[6]

Commented writer Joseph Deitch, who covered the Hersh book in the *PW* article on "Books as News," "The news revelations [about *The Price of Power*] excited people to the point where they wanted to read for themselves and bought well over 200,000 copies. (There was no advertising until . . . eight weeks after publication.)"[7]

Of course, a book about a prominent subject helps "justify" the news. But it is the PR people who make sure the news breaks at the most profitable time. That's why when May Pang's book, *Loving John*, about her eighteen-month love affair with John Lennon, hit the stands, it had wide coverage. Warner Books director of publicity Ling Lucas had arranged a *Newsweek* "Newsmakers" piece on Pang; two appearances on *Good Morning America*; a *20/20* segment featuring the author; a *Donahue* appearance; a *Merv Griffin Show* appearance; a story on *Entertainment Tonight*; a national press conference about the book; an MTV video press release about *Loving John* as well as an MTV interview with Pang; and an eighteen-city publicity tour.

No detail was overlooked. Lucas also prepared an open-ended "interview" tape for use on local rock radio stations throughout the country which allowed disc jockeys to ask questions from a prepared script and press a button for Pang's taped response. The listening audience, of course, would think they were hearing Pang live.

Warner's PR also saw to it that a very important target public—booksellers—was taken care of too. They were invited to a publishing party at Studio 54 in New York to help make them feel part of the jet-set excitement with plenty of loud disco music, dancing, and free drinks, though there was a noticeable absence of real "jet-setters." A *PM Magazine* video crew covered the event.

And to kick this whole campaign off, "somehow," says Lucas, galleys of the book were "leaked" to syndicated gossip columnist Liz Smith. "Want to read about a weird love triangle for our times?" asked Smith. "Just wait until the May Pang book, *Loving John: The Untold Story*, hits the bookstores. . . ."

As we have said, entertainment PR can seem to be relatively innocuous. But it is not. It is a beachhead for other, more damaging forms of PR. Entertainment PR is the first little white lie the press allows itself to tell.

Acceptance of PR as necessary for access to Hollywood stars, or because "everyone knows about hype," making it theoretically harmless, creates an opening for more important types of PR that have a more significant effect on everyday life.

PR people have learned to move the news, events, and issues of the day out of the arena of quantifiable facts and into the realm of more subjective public opinion. Why? Simply, this is the battlefield where PR has the advantage and can take the lead. It is in the area of subjective opinion, rather than of fact or knowledge, that PR can most influence our perceptions.

What is true of *WarGames* is true for the rest of the news. The critics love Cabbage Patch dolls, the critics hate Cabbage Patch dolls; the critics love nuclear energy, the critics hate nuclear energy; the critics love the Soviet Union, the critics hate the Soviet Union. The difference between the highly subjective entertainment field and the rest of the news is that the rest of the news' critics can point to facts to support their opinions; entertainment critics depend on a lot of "magic," and "I don't know why, but I just like it, and you will too!"

Ultimately, of course, the facts upon which all news is based are filtered through journalist and viewer subjectivity to translate into opinion, which is why PR has been able to move outward from its entertainment beginnings to conquer all areas of the news. More and more, PR is muddling the news with plenty of facts that support plenty of opinions. They may or may not be important or relevant facts—but PR knows how to make them appear thus. The final opinions these facts support may or may not be the best choices, but PR makes them legitimate, believable, salable.

The news business is becoming show business. And PR people know how to generate plenty of drama. In the end, as the definition of news is altered and as the limits of credibility are stretched, the public can no longer be sure what is genuine news.

This is why our last example of entertainment PR is seen as "news" by some very reputable arbiters in the media.

If you picked up a newspaper or magazine or listened to radio or TV in October 1982, chances are you heard about the opening of a new amusement park in Florida. Of course, the news didn't describe it as just any amusement park. This was EPCOT Center, usually described as "Walt Disney's greatest dream."

Ecstatic coverage appeared on the three network evening news programs, cable television, foreign TV from six countries, major magazines, U.S. daily newspapers large and small, and local TV and radio. *Fortune* and the *Wall Street Journal* had cover stories about the event that hit the newsstands the same day. *Good Morning America, Today,* and *The CBS Morning News* all originated live from Orlando on opening day.

To really appreciate the proportions of this coverage, one must visit a small room at Walt Disney Productions' Buena Vista Studios in Burbank, California. There rests a priceless treasure trove of more than 100 thick loose-leaf books, each heavy with some 200 news clippings on EPCOT—20,000 stories in all, or almost one-fourth the coverage accorded the Tylenol poisoning story. On another set of shelves are scores of black-cased videotape cassettes containing 40 hours of TV news stories on EPCOT. Some members of the press have stated that the coverage of EPCOT was second only to that given the space shuttle. Suddenly, this neatly stored publicity largesse looks like something more than just happenstance.

Indeed the PR surrounding EPCOT was a highly orchestrated use of the media, engineered by Disney PR men Erwin Okun and Jack Lindquist. "Our objective was that every man, woman, and child in the country know that by midnight on October 1, 1982, something called EPCOT had opened in Orlando and that it was exciting and important," says Lindquist. "We didn't achieve that, but we came damn close."

The PR, culminating in the abundant opening-day coverage, began taking shape about two years prior to the ribbon cutting. As EPCOT was being built, Disney PR people began collecting information, picture possibilities, and story ideas. A quarterly newsletter, *EPCOT Center Today,* was born and sent to some 20,000 print reporters, radio and TV broadcasters, disc jockeys, talk-show hosts, travel writers, and government tourism and travel agencies around the world. The purpose was to sustain awareness of the project.

One of the biggest PR problems to deal with had to do with the entire premise of EPCOT. EPCOT Center, as built, is not the EPCOT the late Walt Disney had originally envisioned. Disney actually wanted what the acronym described: an Experimental Prototype Community of Tomorrow. He wanted a place "where people actually live a life they can't find anywhere else in the world," he explained in his last movie—about EPCOT—made in 1965.[8]

The real EPCOT is not unlike an updated, permanent 1964–65 New York World's Fair. It is an exposition, an amusement park, whose only permanent residents are hundreds of audio-animatronic robots.

Disney PR explained that away in the opening-day press kit: EPCOT is "our interpretation of Walt's greatest dream . . . [and we think] he would have heartily approved of the evolution of his idea."

That dispensed with—and the press apparently made little of the matter—the opening-day PR was carried out with frightening control. "Our problem has never been quantity of exposure," says Okun, "Reporters, editors, and news directors were children too, and now they are parents. Our concern for publicizing the opening of EPCOT would rather fall in the broad areas of control, organization, and timing."

How do you do that?

□ Half the hundreds of journalists who came to Disney had their bills paid by Disney Productions.
□ To accommodate the 2,000 members of the press who were brought to EPCOT on a personal basis, the press was brought in in groups of 150–200 for three-day visits extending over the first three weeks after opening day. Sound like a press pool to Grenada? It should, because that's basically what it was.
□ Opening-day ceremonies, as well as individual pavilion dedications over the three weeks, included stage shows, dances and songs by entertainment groups, thousands of balloons and fireworks. These were "visual press events that were carried by the TV media over an extended period," says Okun.
□ Disney provided and paid for satellite uplink facilities and time on the Westar V satellite so reporters from some thirty local TV stations across the U.S. could have the rare opportunity to rouse viewer interest back home with lines like "Welcome to *Houston Afternoon* live via satellite from Orlando, Florida!" Among stations and programs using this toy were KSLA-TV, Shreveport;

WDTN-TV, Dayton; the *At Twelve* program in Milwaukee; KXAS-TV of Dallas-Ft. Worth; WISH-TV, Indianapolis; the *California Afternoon* program; *AM Pittsburgh*; and WRGB, Schenectady. "In many cases, it was the first time they had ever done anything like that," says Okun. "It, in effect, localized the story for them."

□ Similar accommodations were made for radio stations.

□ A press kit containing twenty separate stories for print reporters—including pictures and slides—was provided.

□ Videotapes, radio news material, and aerial photography were provided free to the media.

□ In the month before the opening, Disney Productions "staged" a photo with 5,000 construction workers at EPCOT which appeared as a two-page photograph in *Life*. *Fortune*, the *Wall Street Journal*, the *New York Times*, the *Los Angeles Times*, and the *Washington Post* all did business stories on EPCOT and Disney during that period.

□ Countless radio and TV stations and publications were running PR/marketing sweepstakes offering free trips to EPCOT.

Said Okun, the Disney vice president of public relations who has jokingly referred to himself as "Mickey's personal PR man," in a speech to shareholders: "In my recollection, no venture in free enterprise has ever been treated so well and with such acclaim by the media of the world. The time, space, and attention they devoted to EPCOT Center immediately established it as an international landmark. . . . No other entertainment event in history ever received such saturation media coverage. . . . [The media] came, they saw, and EPCOT conquered."

Correction: entertainment PR conquered.

seven

PR in the Cabbage Patch

PRODUCT PR

The use of modern public relations techniques to sell products and services began in the 1920s and 1930s. But at that time, only the most sophisticated in corporate America—industrial leaders like Ford, General Motors, Sears Roebuck, Procter and Gamble, Bethlehem Steel, the American Tobacco Company, and AT&T—recognized PR's value.

Product PR was an outgrowth of World War I and the "world-wide program of public relations," by the U.S. Committee on Public Information, explains Edward L. Bernays, whose own PR business blossomed then. "The purpose of public relations during the War was to build our morale here, win over the neutral to back U.S. goals, and deflate the enemy. After the War, we took that broad idea and realized we could work in the same fashion with profit-making and nonprofit firms," says Bernays.

Consequently, Bernays' public relations helped create many consumer beliefs and actions which we take for granted today. For example, working with Procter and Gamble, Bernays helped spread the acceptance of soap by children in the early twenties. Kids hated soap, he learned, because it hurt when it got in their eyes. So he launched a national campaign to change the image of soap in kids' minds. Working with schools across the nation, P&G sponsored soap-sculpting contests. "That made it possible for the soap that children hated to become something they loved, something that would gratify their creative instincts.

Within a year, 22 million kids were involved in soap sculpture."
Naturally, P&G soap sales boomed.

Bernays was also responsible for instilling in Americans the belief that there are health benefits attached to a heavy, high-calorie, high-cholesterol breakfast. Beech-Nut Packing, a producer of bacon, had told Bernays its sales were suffering because people were eating light breakfasts. Exploring the question, Bernays asked his own doctor whether a light or heavy breakfast was better for people. "Heavy," replied the doctor.

"I asked him if he could confirm that with five thousand physicians, which he did," says Bernays. The survey, which urged Americans to eat heavy breakfasts to stay healthy—and heavy breakfasts contained eggs and bacon, of course—fast became news. "Overnight, bacon sales went up," says Bernays.

Women can also thank public relations for their achieving the "right" to smoke cigarettes. On behalf of the American Tobacco Company, Bernays in 1934 contacted debutantes across the nation to make a stand for women's right to smoke just like men. As a result, hundreds of women marched on Boston Common, Union Square in San Francisco, and Central Park in New York to light up "torches of freedom."

PR has come a long way since then, baby. Today, business is using PR heavily to help boost product sales in conjunction with advertising—or by completely replacing advertising. Which brings us to the unassuming West Side Manhattan offices of Robert S. Wiener, at the time, executive vice president of Richard Weiner, Inc., PR.

Wiener is responsible for perhaps one of the greatest product PR campaigns to come along yet; he launched Coleco's Cabbage Patch Kids.

If you were among the millions of Americans crowding into your local Toys 'R' Us store around Christmas 1983 to seize a Cabbage Patch Kid, you probably concluded that the insanity was just another permutation of this country's materialist, faddist mentality. After all, Americans did buy a million Pet Rocks in 1975. And there was a flood of news stories attesting to the Cabbage Patch madness on all the evening network news shows, the morning shows, local TV news, and major newspapers. *Newsweek* devoted a cover to the story. Even pop psychologist Dr. Joyce Brothers and Johnny Carson were talking about it.

If, however, in the wake of the oil crisis, Ralph Nader, *Indecent Exposure,* and Three Mile Island, you are cynical about American businessmen, their motives and their ethics, you probably concluded that this was the work of a scheming Coleco which deliberately held back shipments of the dolls to create artificial shortages. There is reason to believe that Coleco should have known roughly how many dolls to manufacture as early as February 1983, when the company received orders at the New York Toy Fair indicating demand for 1 million Cabbage Patch Kids. Coleco president Arnold Greenberg's eight-and ten-year-old daughters took two of the dolls home from the toy fair and wouldn't let go of them. "That's when I knew we had a winner of unusual proportion," he says.

By June 1983 a market test at Macy's in New York sold out instantly.

But there is no solid proof Coleco held product off the market. Indeed, the Nassau County (New York) Consumer Affairs Office charged Coleco with conspiring to "offer goods and services without intent to supply reasonably expected public demand." But after hearings in 1984, the watchdog agency concluded there was no conspiracy and dismissed the complaint.

Finally, if you're the least bit savvy about the manipulative power of modern advertising, the Cabbage Patch craze might have looked like an excellent example of Madison Avenue at its slickest. "Enflamed by advertising," explained *Adweek,* an advertising-industry trade publication, "demand for [Cabbage Patch Kids] has exceeded the supply. . . ." But there is a glaring flaw in that theory. Coleco did not run the kind of multimillion-dollar ad campaign used to launch Diet Coke or a new cigarette; only several hundred thousand dollars were spent on ads, which were discontinued on November 28, 1983. So logically it *must* have been a spontaneous consumer madness.

Don't bet on it.

Wiener's PR campaign for the Cabbage Patch Kids began back in late 1982. In keeping with the concept of the original Cabbage Patch Kids, designed by Georgia sculptor Xavier Roberts, Coleco's Kids would be "adopted" by consumers—not bought. Wiener saw potential trouble here, especially after test marketing of the dolls in Canada prompted complaints from real-life adoptive parents.

(That's the kind of foresight top PR people must have. PR people have to know how to create news, but they also have to anticipate—and avoid—news that could hurt sales of the product. Imagine if Coleco produced two million Cabbage Patch Kids only to have people boycott them because the concept of adopting an inanimate object is offensive when so many real children go unadopted.)

So Wiener got Brandeis University psychologist Malcolm Watson to study what made the Kids so attractive to children. One of the strong positive characteristics Watson came up with was that the physical appearance of the dolls inspired a nurturing instinct in children. The "adoption" idea contributed to that instinct and was therefore good. "We developed a position paper on that, including it in the press packages, and the adoption question never exploded," says Wiener. Ravelle Brickman, another PR person working with Wiener, wrote the "Parenting Guide" that came with every doll.

In June, a New York press conference was held to launch the doll. Some 200 reporters attended. At the same time, Wiener and his assistants were luring the major women's magazines to write stories about the doll as a Christmas gift idea. Those stories would appear in the fall—and just in time to spur Christmas sales.

By early October, Wiener's publicity machine was running full speed ahead. Coleco spokeswomen Kathy McGowan and Karen Gershman were creating demand for the dolls on a fifteen-city tour of the television and radio news/talk-show circuit in major markets like Boston, Chicago, Los Angeles, Dallas, and Atlanta.

Other news "events" were invented. One involved a mass adoption of the dolls by a group of Boston schoolchildren—enticed to the affair by the promise of a free doll. Corny, yes, but the press ate it up.

At the same time, fourteen PR staffers were busy mailing press kits to major daily newspapers. The adoption and nurturing concepts and the dolls' individual names were played up to help sell the story idea and spark the "news" interest of editors. And, capitalizing on the media's interest in anything "high-tech," the PR material pointed out that the computer-run manufacturing equipment minutely altered the facial features of each doll so that no two Cabbage Patch Kids were alike. Hair and clothing differences aside, the computer-borne facial differences, of course, were so minute as to be more in the mind's eye than in the eye's eye, but that's just the sort of perceptual manipulation at which PR is adept.

The "message" hammered home again and again and again in this whole concert? With only preliminary indications to go on and—let's face it—before the fact, the PR simply and confidently stated that the Cabbage Patch Kids were "the hottest item for Christmas," says Wiener. "It was a self-fulfilling prophecy. There is no question PR helped fuel the demand that created shortages."

By fall, however, the Cabbage Patch Kid "phenomenon" was still limited to fifteen local markets—not a national phenomenon. But smart PR would change that.

Wiener's people had been unceasing in their efforts to sell the story to the networks. The networks were not buying—yet. But with the groundswell of publicity and the consequent demand in local markets, Wiener now had the "proof" he needed to convince the national media that the Cabbage Patch Kids indeed had the potential to be the hottest item for Christmas nationally.

The PR agency became a quasi-news organization. If Wiener's clipping services—which scan newspapers coast to coast, looking for mention of the Cabbage Patch Kids—found a local story about shortages of the dolls, Wiener would pass the article on to AP and UPI. The wire services were one route to national coverage. Wiener's office also subscribed to TV news monitoring services—similar to clipping services—and when they turned up a local story, Wiener's people would alert the appropriate network news organization to tell it what its local affiliate was reporting. That way, the network wouldn't have to take Wiener's word for it; it could check with its own newspeople.

The Cabbage Kids' big break came from the *Today* show. Wiener's people had sent the show's pregnant hostess Jane Pauley her own doll. But more important, it was publicity that begat publicity. "The *Today* show doesn't put us on just because a PR man says this is the hottest toy of the season. There was a reason they did it; we showed them all the articles and videotapes about the dolls," says Wiener. "Good PR people perform a service for the media. You propose programming based on a knowledge of their needs."

Wiener got five and a half minutes on *Today*. That made the story real. "After *Today,* we found the media started coming to us," says Wiener. "*Today* gave our story credibility through the third-party endorsement. When Bryant Gumbel or Jane Pauley or Connie Chung says, 'Here's this season's hottest item,' it means more to consumers than if Coleco says the same thing. The credibility that achieves far outweighs an advertisement."

Similar spots on the *CBS Morning News* and *Good Morning America* followed, as did segments on the three network news programs. In late November, an NBC *Nightly News* crew traveled to Hartford to interview Greenberg. Wiener advised Coleco to tell NBC it was pulling its Cabbage Patch advertisements. Why? The idea was to show that Coleco's interest in public safety was stronger than its pursuit of sales and profits; some of the toy-store riots were beginning to get violent. Besides, Coleco was getting nervous about legal liability.

Of course, pulling the ads was superb PR sleight of hand, because it wasn't the ads that were generating the insatiable demand, it was the PR. And even after the ads were discontinued, the public relations efforts did not let up.

That is an excellent example of how PR can lie without lying: Coleco pulled the ads to stop generating demand that could be detrimental to the public safety. So far, so good. But what they didn't tell anyone was that the PR, which was even more instrumental in creating demand that could jeopardize the public safety, did not stop. Did Coleco lie? Well, no; the press simply never asked about the PR efforts.

If the PR continued to generate demand that Coleco knew it could not fulfill, could that not be construed, as the Nassau County Consumer Affairs Office originally charged, as "offering goods and services without intent to supply reasonably expected public demand?" Therein perhaps lay the misleading business practices that many suspected but could not quite put a finger on. The PR shadow is often too intangible for ready identification, too ethereal to actually grab.

While Coleco could not get enough dolls into the stores, somehow it found all it needed for PR promotional purposes in ten major markets. The company started lining up radio and TV stations and newspapers that would offer the dolls free as circulation and ratings boosters—the most basic of PR attention getters. In New York, for example, WYNY radio, the *New York Post,* and WNBC radio's *Imus in the Morning* program all had Cabbage Patch giveaways.

Dolls were also given away by Coleco to kids in hospital wards too—"not to be exploitive," says Wiener, recognizing that some people might jump to that conclusion, "but the gesture did bring back benefits to Coleco." In other words, it provided more publicity.

Wiener even arranged to have First Lady Nancy Reagan give Cabbage Patch dolls to two Korean children who were in the U.S. for heart operations.

In the end, on a PR budget of "way under" the reported $500,000, says Wiener, "the Cabbage Patch Kids were on every major TV station in every major newspaper and magazine and general-interest magazine in the U.S.—and not just once. Everybody in the U.S., whether or not they were parents, knew about the Cabbage Patch Kids."

[Incidentally, for Christmas 1984, Wiener was busy making two more toys popular, Mattel's Rainbow Brite doll and Hasbro Industries' Transformers robot toys. And if you didn't believe transformable robot toys were expected to be "the most successful first year for a new toy, eclipsing the record $60 million of Cabbage Patch dolls sold in 1983,"[1] Wiener need only to have shown you the front page of a July 1984 *Wall Street Journal* which said exactly that.*]

Wiener and the Cabbage Patch Kids are, of course, only one super-successful example of product PR. Today, you cannot avoid such "advertisements" in the "news" media. Everything, from toys to flowers to vacation resorts to cruise packages to food and computers, is now marketed through PR. "When I look at TV or read an article, I look for the product plug," says Wiener.

---

*Later that year, the *New York Post,* after getting involved with another PR-hatched giveaway, claimed the board game Trivial Pursuit was "even hotter than Cabbage Patch dolls were last year."

Unless you have a trained eye, though, it is often difficult to separate product PR from "news." You can begin shining a light on PR by looking a little more closely. Take this *New York Times* example:

> An era in communications begins today with the inauguration of pay telephones on airborne commercial jets.
>
> Passengers on 20 wide-body jets owned by six airlines will be able to call anywhere in the United States while flying across the continent.
>
> The service, which is expected to be greatly expanded in the coming months, uses cordless phones. . . .[2]

The October 15, 1984, *Times* article was "advertising" airplane-to-ground telephone service for Airfone, Inc., which had blitzed the United States media with the story that day. Awareness of a new product's existence is the main purpose of this first-stage PR sell. Similar coverage of this momentous event, in different forms and with differing story lines, appeared in press outlets throughout the nation.

Then there is this piece from the food pages of the *Orlando Sentinel*:

> The season's bounty of fresh fruits can be especially delicious when featured in spicy desserts, such as Fresh Fruit with Anise Custard. . . .[3]

What looked simply like another helpful recipe story was actually a pitch by the United Fresh Fruit and Vegetable Association, designed to boost demand for fresh fruit.

And, again to the uninitiated, what else could these good stories be but good stories in the high-tech eighties:

- ☐ An interesting *Forbes* magazine story about the use of computers in developing professional football strategy.
- ☐ A *CBS Morning News* story about the same thing.
- ☐ A segment on the WEWS-TV program *The Morning Exchange* in Cleveland showing how computers helped the Tampa Bay Bucs defeat the Atlanta Falcons.

- A WABC-TV *Eyewitness News* story by sports anchor Spencer Christian about computers in football, run during the football strike of 1982.
- Another story about the use of computers in football distributed by NBC Sports to 200 of the network's affiliates during the Super Bowl 1983.
- A *BusinessWeek* story about the San Diego Chargers and the computer-designed 372 F Shoot Pump play.
- A WNBC-TV news story in New York by *Live at Five*'s Jim Ryan showing how computers will enable runners in the New York City Marathon to compare their results.
- WCBS-TV and WNEW-TV, New York, segments on 2,500 runners testing the computer system to be used in the New York City Marathon.

All of the stories eventually got around to mentioning or showing a Quantel computer. That, of course, was no mere coincidence, because all of the stories were generated in the media by Quantel Business Computer's New York PR firm, Makovsky & Co.

Sometimes PR does not even necessarily involve the press. PR people seek out other authority figures. When your doctor recommends a certain hospital for an operation, an endorsement increasingly coveted these days as hospitals compete with one another to survive, a natural assumption is that the recommendation is based on such factors as quality of patient care.

But according to Judith Bogart, former president of the Public Relations Society of America and head of public relations for Jewish Hospital in Cincinnati, hospital PR people are seeing to it that doctors' endorsements are courted with nursing staffs more attuned to their needs, fancy equipment, and comfortable doctors' lounges—complete with doughnuts and coffee. "Patients will usually go where their doctor tells them to go," explains Bogart.

Meanwhile, Manufacturers Hanover Trust, the nation's fourth largest bank, sponsors corporate challenge running races in twelve major U.S. cities. The 3.5-mile races tend to draw a lot of young up-and-coming executive types whose businesses

Manny Hanny would love to have as customers. Each race costs the bank between $30,000 and $60,000, but it's money well spent, says Charles McCabe, Jr., senior vice president and director of marketing. The events give the bank "ins" to hundreds of businesses. A 1983 race in Houston turned up twelve prospective corporate clients; shortly after running in another MHT race in New York, the treasurer of one company switched banks and brought the bank a $250,000 account.

Fleischmann's Yeast uses home economics teachers and 4-H clubs to implicitly endorse its product to children. "We've got eight hundred thousand kids working with Fleischmann's Yeast and learning about bread," says Hill & Knowlton's B. J. McCabe.

The purpose of Fleischmann's program with children is to get tomorrow's consumers loyal to the product at an impressionable age. "We did a survey of children involved in this program and found that ninety-two percent of those kids were still working with Fleischmann's ten years later," says McCabe.

Of course, media endorsements are still the main target. Food publicity is one of the biggest areas of product PR. Why? The press is always hungry for stories about food, and food-company PR people always have plenty of story ideas. It's a match made in heaven.

One way PR people and journalists rationalize these free ads is if the product can somehow be connected to the news. So when Welch's bought the "Official Juice of the Olympics" title in 1979, McCabe helped produce three one-to three-minute "news" films about the Lake Placid Olympics. "We were able to work in the product message tactfully," says McCabe. A couple of hundred local television stations used the material.

Likewise, when Jimmy Carter became President, Hill & Knowlton had someone for its client, Planters Peanuts, on the talk-show circuit showing how to make Georgia peanut soup.

When news hooks are not immediately available, smart PR people like McCabe have no problem; they create their own excitement. McCabe sent Fleischmann's home economist Melissa Moore out on the talk show/lecture circuit to hype a new "trend"—home bread baking—for which yeast is a key ingredient.*

Moore talked about baking bread and pizza on television programs like *AM Buffalo, PM Magazine* in Cleveland, and the *What's New* morning show in Minneapolis. She did the same thing at department stores like Gimbels and Lord & Taylor, which also gained media attention. McCabe says some 70,000 people "attended" Moore's pizza-making demonstration (in person and via KFAB and KGOR radio) at an Omaha, Nebraska, shopping mall.

Even Wisconsin dairy farmers have PR people out plugging for them—and it ain't no corn-pone campaign either. Each year, four or five target markets are identified for special attention. PR people enter the markets about ten months in advance of the media campaign and alert food brokers, cheese distributors, and supermarket representatives about the coming program. That way, these people can prepare well ahead of time to order Wisconsin cheese so it's on the store shelves when consumers are looking to buy it.

About six to four months before the event, the dairy PR people will hold a breakfast with these same people to explain the details of the campaign.

About six weeks before the main event, the dairymen line up their TV, radio, and print advertisements. The PR people also start making contact with the local media, offering for interviews experts on cheese, as well as Wisconsin's "Alice in Dairyland," a beauty who talks about cheese.

Just before the ad campaign and store promos break, the dairy farmers' spokespeople meet with the media at a cheese and wine party. The upshot of all this is that advertisements, store promos, and PR-placed news stories create an atmosphere in which one cannot avoid hearing about Wisconsin cheese.

Can "Alice in Dairyland" really pull one over on the public and the press? "After the promo is over," says Al Breseman, an agricultural economist at the University of Wisconsin, "they get

---

*A note of accuracy. Moore is actually a PR person employed by H&K. Explains McCabe: "When she goes out for Fleischmann's, she's from Fleischmann's; when she goes out for Planters, she's from Planters." Her audiences don't know this, though. To them she is a professional—a home economist—who represents a third-party endorsement of the product.

a report on sales. It is not unusual to see the cheese distributors and supermarkets involved in the campaign show a three hundred percent to four hundred percent increase in cheese sales."

The microcomputer industry—both the hardware and software side of it—almost owes its life to public relations. Small start-up companies with tiny advertising budgets had to get attention at a low cost somehow. Then, too, while anyone and everyone with a garage, soldering iron, and some semiconductor chips from Radio Shack was getting into this easy-entry business—all of them vying for attention at the same time—each had to figure out a way to be heard above the racket. "Our new company had to differentiate itself from this throng of little known, small-time players," says Adam Osborne. "We could make it only if consumers perceived our new company as among the industry leaders."

PR filled the bill perfectly. With the birth of the new industry, the hype and the growing interest, computer magazines began springing up overnight. "News" had to be found to fill those publications, and PR was there with more than a few suggestions. The general press saw a need to have stories too, because of all the excitement. Computer manufacturers "flooded us with so many announcements about this new development or that new development," says ABC News's Av Westin, "that *20/20* finally did a piece about computers."

There were other advantages to PR. With all the confusion and clutter about computers in the public mind—in part created by all the PR hype, as each company claimed yet another important difference customers should look for in a computer—positive reviews in computer magazines became increasingly important. "I've come to think the articles are better than our advertising," says James Johnson, president of Human Edge Software in Palo Alto, California. Christopher Morgan, the PR man at Lotus Development, which produced the best-selling Lotus 1-2-3 program, was the fourth highest paid officer in 1983.

"Public relations has been very important in taking computers up from being just for hackers to a mass market item," says Donovan Neale-May, director of Dudley-Anderson-Yutzy PR's West Coast office. "The more media attention—articles continuously talking about the impact of computers—the more attention by the public. It's like a bandwagon. PR fueled the whole message about computers and created demand in much the same way as happened with the Cabbage Patch Kids. We're generating millions of media exposures for our [ten computer] clients."

One of Neale-May's more prominent clients was Eagle Computer. His job for that company was to make Eagle known as the leading clone of the extremely popular IBM Personal Computer. "The idea was to position it so that, in an industry roundup story, when they talked about IBM clones, Eagle would be the first one they'd mention," along with Compaq, Columbia, and a host of others. Eagle succeeded in that task by calling its PC an IBM copycat right from the start, a concept whose brashness apparently caught the imagination of the press.

Osborne, another PR wizard, understands well the value of knowing what turns on the press: "My public statements were always deliberately phrased provocatively enough to attract media attention. Thus *BusinessWeek* wrote about the company's early success under the [headline] 'From Brags to Riches,' while the *New York Times* coined the heading: 'Brat Makes Good.' It was all superb media coverage. The public loved it, and they remembered our name when they entered the computer store."

So the press loved a story about the audacity of Eagle and other companies mimicking the IBM PC. In the public's eye, meanwhile, the Eagle name did not suffer for its infringement on IBM's copyright.* Rather, the public remembered the name of the bargain-priced computer that did almost everything the overpriced IBM PC did. The PR message got across.

Not talking to the press—or at least giving the appearance of not talking—is sometimes even better PR for the big computer makers. IBM claims it never talks about its new products before they are introduced, yet somehow—we do not know exactly how, but somehow—detailed information and even engineering specifications slip past the heavy security at IBM's Armonk, New York, headquarters, and magically fall into the hands of stock analysts and the press, which is just aching to break the story.

Hewlett-Packard admits it considered "controlled leakage" to

---

*Eagle was eventually sued by IBM for copyright infringement. Of course, that only further added to the Eagle image. The suit was later settled.

generate "preannouncement hype" in the words of Roy Verley, manager of corporate relations. An exclusive story given to one major newspaper can ignite the interest of other editors, adds David Simon of Simon Public Relations.

Regis McKenna, a Silicon Valley PR man who hypes Apple Computer, among others, uses what he calls the "multiple exclusive." Instead of giving just one news organization exclusive access to a story, McKenna allows several news organizations exclusive access to only one part of the story.

Thus when the Apple Macintosh computer was introduced in 1984, *Newsweek* and *Rolling Stone* were given entrée to the group of computer design "wizards" who developed the Macintosh; *Byte,* the computer magazine, was allowed to do the technical story; *Fortune* reporters were allowed to interview key management people at Apple; and *Forbes* had a marketing piece about the television commercial introducing the Macintosh. No longer were the PR people merely trying to control the news; McKenna was now in effect telling the "independent" journalists exactly what they would be allowed to write about.

In addition to this, some sixty news organizations had one-on-one meetings with Apple and Macintosh people about the new computer during the six-week period before formal introduction, with the proviso that the information be embargoed until January 24, 1984. That way everyone would be primed to write about Apple for the January 25 editions and have all the information hit the public at once, creating a kind of fever. The press allowed itself to be told not only what it could write but also when it could write in order to purchase the favor of an exclusive interview on one facet of the product introduction.

McKenna also uses the techniques discussed in Chapter 3—influencing the industry analysts and experts that journalists depend on for information. "If you bring those people into your fold," he says, "and educate them about your product, your technology, and the future of your business, and then you go to the press, the press is just going to reflect what you've already told the infrastructure." Apple co-founder Steve Jobs adds that such PR is "essential" to a computer company's bottom line.

The diverse list of products and services being pushed by PR goes on—literally everywhere one turns:

□ Humana Corporation's $20–$30 million sponsorship of one hundred artificial heart transplants was in part designed to boost the image—and income—of the $2.6 billion-a-year (revenues) for-profit hospital chain. Continuous repetition of "Humana Hospital-Audubon" in the news, as the press followed the progress of William J. Schroeder, spread the Humana "brand name" far and wide. At the same time, Humana's move dispels criticism that for-profit hospitals do little to advance the cause of science. "We're making a major contribution to the advance of science," says Humana Chairman David Jones. "The gain can only come to our reputation."

□ Oberlin College, famous for its conservatory of music and for being a quality liberal arts college, was suffering a 10 percent drop in applications in 1982. The culprit, PR consultant Hill & Knowlton concluded, was lack of national exposure; prospective students just didn't think of Oberlin because they didn't know what the college had to offer.

H&K was paid $55,000 to generate publicity, and it did: a *Washington Post* story about the president-elect of the college on a jazz-playing tour of Russia; an Associated Press story in which Oberlin's expert on library theft was interviewed; interviews with an expert on the Falkland Islands when war broke out there; coverage of computer-related projects at the college on the *David Susskind* show and in the Associated Press; and numerous other stories.

When H&K got advance word that Roger Sperry would be awarded a Nobel Prize for his work on the brain, "we wanted every reporter to know he was an alumnus of and former professor at Oberlin," explains PR man Christopher Tennyson. So yearbook photos of Sperry as captain of the Oberlin basketball team were sent out; *Good Morning America* mentioned that Sperry had wanted to be a basketball star at Oberlin before he settled on a career in science.

And when the Royal Shakespeare Company had a six-week residency at the college, there were stories about it on CBS's *Sunday Morning* and in the *Christian Science Monitor*.

The result? "Applications . . . are up fifteen percent in the College and forty percent in the Conservatory so far this year," beamed an editorial in the *Oberlin Review* student newspaper. There are other less tangible but equally important benefits too. "There's pressure on Oberlin to be known," explains Tennyson. "If the parents of a student headed for Oberlin are at a cocktail party, they won't be too happy if they have to explain to their friends what Oberlin is. But if Oberlin was mentioned in conjunction with Trevor Nunn and Ben Kingsley on CBS that morning, the reaction is. 'Oh yeah, I saw that the Royal Shakespeare Company was there,' which makes it more prestigious."

□ Vacation spots are regularly promoted by PR people who will usually pay all expenses of the travel writers, a practice frowned upon by journalists—in theory. Forty-six of fifty state travel and tourism departments bring travel writers in on such junkets, according to the U.S. Travel Data Center. Boasts the Ohio Office of Travel & Tourism: "In August 1983, a free media blitz was implemented which resulted in over 140 electronic [broadcast] and print interviews . . . a videotape produced by this office aired on *Good Morning America*."

And remember how all those stories about Cancún, the Mexican resort, surfaced at about the same time? Hill & Knowlton helped get wide coverage for that destination between 1974 and 1979; later, the Mexican government arranged to hold a summit conference of world leaders in Cancún to further promote the resort and enhance its prestige and status as an international destination.

Hill & Knowlton also did PR for the Knoxville World's Fair after the *Wall Street Journal* ran an article that asked the stinging question, "What if you gave a World's Fair and nobody came?" The *Journal* article was written because the fair was not getting much support from corporations. H&K's first advice was to stop the fair's PR efforts aimed at the national media, because "you have no story to tell and you'll only get negative coverage that way," said H&K's Fred Berger. Instead, PR efforts were focused on creating a videotape that would help get corporate and governmental sponsors. President Reagan even appeared on the tape to endorse the Knoxville fair. That did the trick. "Then we went back to the media with a satellite press conference announcing China's participation in a world's fair for the first time since 1943," says Berger. "After that, the *Wall Street Journal* had a story saying Knoxville will make it."

reopened by Sea Containers Ltd., was successfully promoted by Carl Byoir PR, with stories in *Time, Newsweek, People,* CBS News, NBC News, and numerous other media outlets.

□ Even the news media do PR for themselves. *Time* and *Newsweek* send advance copies of their magazines, complete with press release and synopses of the most potentially newsworthy stories, to AP and UPI the day before they hit the stands; that is where stories like, "*Newsweek* magazine will report . . ." come from.

BusinessWeek does the same thing, with distribution to appropriate media. *New York* magazine has WMCA radio personality Barry Gray host an hour-long weekly program whose purpose is to discuss what's in the latest issue of the magazine. *Money* magazine's Editorial Public Relations Department has its Ken Prewitt do a regular business report on the CBS news radio network. "Promotion wins new subscribers, flatters existing ones—besides alerting them to stories they shouldn't miss—and boosts newsstand sales," says a senior editor at one major magazine.

TV news does it too. Often news stories on ABC *World News Tonight* conveniently lead into mention of Barbara Walters' latest "newsworthy" interview to be broadcast later that evening on ABC News's *20/20* or into a promo for the news division's *Nightline* program.

Is this hype of virtually everything necessarily bad? That depends on whether you believe journalists should be doing news or product promotions. One could argue that, if the product plug and PR source of the story are made perfectly clear, and if product promotion stories are kept to a minimum in the press, there is probably little harm.

Unfortunately, the media do not seem to be moving in that direction on either count. News stories advertising products and services are becoming more—not less—prevalent in the news. The sources of such stories and the promotions being practiced are likewise becoming more buried, rather than more clear.

For example, back in 1976, comedian George Gobel traveled the talk-show circuit promoting a new holiday, Mother-in-Law Day. Gobel—a television personality with enough credentials to appear as a talk-show guest in his own right—was actually a paid spokesman for Florists Transworld Delivery. Indeed, the holiday was created by FTD lobbyists in Washington. "FTD asked us to look at whether it was possible to have another floral holiday like Valentine's Day," to stimulate sales, explains Berger. "Our research showed that if it were treated lightly and tongue-in-cheek, we could do Mother-in-Law Day." The PR was supported by advertising and in-store promos.

The result was anything but tongue-in-cheek. The first year, some 75,000 extra wire orders for flowers were placed for the holiday, which falls on the fourth Sunday in October. Typically, for every wire order, FTD florists fill 3 more local orders, which means that some 225,000 people responded to the pitch. The demand for flowers by wire for that occasion peaked at 125,000 to 140,000 (i.e., 375,000 to 420,000 total) in the third year.

"Generic" news stories are another way of burying a plug. Carl Byoir & Associates produced a videotape news story about how cognac is made in France. Innocent enough, it seems. Newsworthy, maybe. But the real purpose of the video, part of Byoir's public relations for the Cognac Institute, was to get people "drinking more cognac," says Peter Osgood, Byoir's president. "The video didn't mention any brand name, so it was more appealing to TV producers who needed a feature or filler."

Similarly, when New England ski resorts were suffering a year with no snow in the late seventies, the National Ski Areas Association wanted the press to sing about the virtues of machine-made snow, which some enthusiasts believe is inferior to the kind that falls out of the sky naturally. Berger of H&K got his coverage. "We got reporters to go out to some local resorts to talk about the problem and the machine solution," he says. "We had one reporter from Channel 7 [New York] making snow with a machine in a garage. We even got the weathermen to talk about where skiers could find machine-made snow."

At a level even further below the surface are PR product plugs that appear to have nothing to do with plugging a product at all. Take this one.

A beautiful blonde is in her bedroom in the nude. We see her from the back slipping into a pair of purple silk panties. "I love silk," says the woman. "It makes me feeeeelllll, mmmmmmmm-mmm, with soft Italian silk from Berlei. Berlie knows how to bring out the best in . . . me. Mmmmmmmmmm," she moans.

That steamy, attention-getting scene was not shown in some Times Square porno theater, it was broadcast on WNBC-TV's eleven o'clock news in New York in May 1984. The "news"? The woman with the silk panties was part of a "controversial" cable TV commercial-in-the-making for Berlei USA. "I'm shocked and saddened," commented the anchorwoman after that story ran. (WNBC-TV, however, was not too shocked to run the sexy bedroom scene a half-dozen times between 9 and 11 P.M. as a teaser for the late news program.)

The controversy was created by Berlei's PR man, Wil Gagen, who tipped off the media—including *Women's Wear Daily, Advertising Age,* and *USA Today*—to the story. In exchange for sexy pictures, controversy, and shock value, the media gave Berlei a free plug. Gagen, by the way, helped create another controversy several years earlier over Jordache's sexy, tight-jeans commercials.

Another PR product plug that doesn't look like one comes again from Apple Computer. Co-founder Steve Wozniak's US Music Festivals have to rank among the best publicity stunts because they manage to unite youth and its antihero, Corporate America. Officially, there is no connection between the Cupertino, California, computer firm and the two US Festivals, which received lavish media coverage. But Wozniak owns a half-million shares of Apple. "At the first US Festival, we gave away forty thousand pieces of literature about the company along with a helluva lot of Apple decals," says Stan Devon, Apple's head of investor and press relations. What's good for US is good for Wozniak is good for Apple is good for Wozniak.*

PR has also positioned the computer as what most people mystically refer to as "High Technology." People are intimidated by these amazing machines, which is why retailers are able to charge thousands and thousands of dollars for them. PR has also bestowed mystical powers on some computer makers—most notably Apple, IBM, and at one time, before their fall, Atari, Texas Instruments, and Osborne Computer—which

*The computer company also sows its own PR seeds without the media—and with taxpayer assistance. In California, Apple's "Kids Can't Wait Program" has donated 9,000 of its machines to public and private schools. Apple gets a tax deduction for its "philanthropy" and builds brand recognition among the young, who, it is hoped, will think Apple when they buy their own models in the years to come. A similar giveaway promotion is available for colleges and universities throughout the U.S.

helped color investors' decisions. There may be many computers more powerful or faster than the IBM PC; but IBM has a certain aura. Adam Osborne is more down to earth about computers. "There is nothing high-tech about computers anymore," he says. "They are mass market items, like washing machines, televisions, and dishwashers."

Good PR also has the effect of altering the journalist's perception of reality. When the Macintosh was introduced, *Fortune* writer Ann M. Morrison was apparently so taken in by her exclusive entrée to Apple that she was literally enthralled by the factory that produced Macintoshes. She quoted Steve Jobs describing the Fremont, California, plant as "one of the most automated computer factories ever." It was "full of factory-of-the-future technology," Morrison swooned.

Morrison's story gave credibility to Macintosh advertisements—running at the same time—which drew a strong futuristic image of computers—not people—and machines building the Macintoshes at Fremont. In reality, however, computers are not building Macintoshes, admits one Apple executive, because, simply, the manufacture of a personal computer does not lend itself to automation. In reality, *Fortune*'s and Apple's "factory of the future" was little different from many other computer-making facilities.

And to this day, business journalists are still under the impression that Federal Express is far and away the biggest carrier of overnight packages. "After years of assaults by competitors, Federal Express remains at the top of the heap," wrote Ruth Hamel in a 1984 *USA Today* story.

Federal is bigger—in revenues, because it charges more—but in terms of numbers of packages delivered, Purolator Courier has Federal beaten hands down: 52 million overnight packages a year delivered by Purolator in 1982 versus only 38 million by Federal. That story—which indicates Purolator is a more efficient company, if it can charge sometimes drastically lower rates for the same service—has gone almost totally unreported. Why does this inaccurate perception linger? Federal has a good, persistent PR department that constantly reinforces and encourages the "biggest" myth; Purolator, on the other hand, has done almost nothing to get press attention.

Having accepted entertainment PR as "normal," having wel-comed and validated product PR people as legitimate "news sources," the press has lulled itself into a false sense of security about PR.

With its foot in the newsroom door, PR is now ready to flex its muscles and start tinkering with perceptions, news coverage, and opinions on more important levels. PR is ready to exert more significant influence and control.

eight

Raising the Stakes

BUSINESS PR

The week of December 10, 1984, was a busy one for the PR profession. That week, public relations itself was in the media spotlight—albeit fleetingly—on three major business stories.

☐ The *New York Times* had a December 14 story about crisis management and public relations at Union Carbide, as the company came to grips with the gas-leak disaster at its Bhopal, India, subsidiary, where more than 2,000 people had died.[1]

☐ Two days before, the *Times* had reported about ITT Corporation's suspension of its chief PR person, Edward J. Gerrity, Jr., and two other ITT PR people. That article, and a longer follow-up on December 13, strongly linked the three PR people to leaking unfavorable stories—primarily to syndicated financial columnist Robert Metz—about a move by some shareholders to liquidate ITT. "They [ITT management] believe that [Gerrity] is behind it, and they are investigating to see if it's so," said Patrick Wall, Gerrity's attorney. The suspension was "completely unrelated to the Metz article or any question of the stock price of ITT," Wall asserted.[2]

[Coincidentally, perhaps, the negative articles appeared shortly after takeover specialist Irwin Jacobs had acquired substantial holdings of ITT stock. Gerrity, through his attorney, denies the charges of wrongdoing and has since left ITT.]

□ Finally, on the fourteenth, UPI reported the charge from a lawsuit that Mesa Petroleum used public relations in its efforts to take over Phillips Petroleum—a potential violation of Securities and Exchange Commission law, said Phillips. "[Mesa Chairman T. Boone] Pickens has undertaken a systematic public relations program of press conferences, public meetings with securities analysts, and extensive newspaper and television interviews to condition the market in advance of filing of proxy consent solicitation papers," said Phillips in its lawsuit.[3] A Mesa Petroleum spokesman denies Phillips' charges and says the suit has since been dropped. Phillips' Director of Media Relations Jerry Smith explains that Phillips agreed to drop all litigation against Mesa when Pickens signed a settlement (on December 23, 1984), and agreed to cease and desist takeover attempts for fifteen years.

What this trio of stories points up is the increasing use of public relations to help grease the gears of business. Using PR to sell Cabbage Patch dolls or aspartame is one thing, but achieving efficiencies of operation, getting special treatment from government, and launching a corporate takeover—or protecting management from a takeover attempt or other crises—are just as important to the bottom line. PR is gaining greater clout in the business of selling corporate goals, projects, programs, and philosophies.

No longer are PR people relegated to the role of press liaison somewhere way down the corporate ladder; they are now being given entrée to the executive suite. They are becoming an integral part of management and planning. And they like this new power, thank you; for a profession that has long been the little respected, scarcely valued poor relation of business, this is indeed a rags-to-riches story.

Business PR falls into three distinct categories:

1. Image PR, which tries to put a company in a good light so that it can go about its business with as little interference from the public and government as possible;
2. *Ad hoc* PR, which attempts to achieve a specific goal beneficial to the company by actively and sometimes aggressively influencing certain target publics; and
3. Crisis PR, which hopes to protect the company and/or manage-

ment from problems that shake the very foundations of its survival, and which we will cover in the next chapter.

The first of these is the most basic and is summed up in an inside document describing the goals of Caterpillar Corporation's public relations department: "The continuing objective of public affairs is to help Caterpillar achieve the understanding and support it needs to operate a worldwide enterprise successfully." Caterpillar PR aims to "develop a better, truer public 'impression' of Caterpillar" as a service-minded organization, a "quality house," a well-managed enterprise, a good company to do business with, a responsible corporate citizen, and a multinational company whose products are doing important, constructive work around the world.

This good image or reputation pays real dividends. If bankers believe these things about Caterpillar, that opinion can translate into lower rates on huge corporate loans; if employees, suppliers, and business partners believe it, they might be willing to "give" Caterpillar more in bargaining for the pleasure of doing business with such a trustworthy, reputable firm; if governments and the general public believe it, they might give the company more regulatory leeway. All of that often translates into increased sales and, of course, higher profits.

Caterpillar PR's image building apparently works. For two of the last three years *Fortune*'s annual survey of thousands of business executives have placed Caterpillar in the top spots of its industry's "most admired corporations."

Similarly, DuPont's PR people continuously push the image defined by its corporate motto, "Combining Technology and Imagination." To that end it sponsored the *Gossamer Condor*, the man-powered aircraft made of tough but lightweight DuPont Kevlar and Mylar. After the historic achievement of man-powered flight, DuPont PR put the *Gossamer Condor* on a one-year national tour of museums, which gave DuPont's technology-and-imagination image voluminous media coverage. The Wilmington, Delaware-based chemical company did the same thing with the *Solar Challenger* solar-powered aircraft that flew from Paris to New York. DuPont ranked first of 10 in *Fortune*'s 1984 corporate reputation rankings for the chemicals industry, with a 7.41 score out of a possible 10.

A good corporate image has great value for the implementation of a company's business plan. Because of good image PR, a new DuPont chemical plant would probably be welcomed into a community more warmly than, say, a new plant for Hooker Chemical, whose dark Love Canal reputation precedes it.

Conversely, negative images can prompt increased government regulation, hurt employee morale, and make it harder for individual companies to recruit workers.

While image PR, like all PR, involves some degree of manipulation in pointing to the good rather than the bad, it also requires deeds, not just words. To create a believable image, the company has to be committed to a long-term, continuous program of actually practicing what its PR preaches. Thus, there is a strong element of truth to this type of PR. That is less so the case with *ad hoc* PR.

As mentioned, the purpose of *ad hoc* PR is to get a specific job done. One such job is getting investors interested in a company. PR helps bring that company—especially a small one—to the attention of investors. But public relations people are reluctant to boast about exactly what they can do. "If we told you what benefits we provide, the SEC would close our doors," explains the chairman of one New York PR firm.

Good PR can manipulate stock prices—which is, of course, illegal. Small companies tend to have a small number of shares—perhaps several hundred thousand as opposed to, say, Exxon's 900 million shares. If *Forbes*'s 700,000 readers run out and start buying shares of a tiny company favorably described in the magazine's pages, the stock price could shoot up overnight. Some public relations people talk anonymously about real-life cases in which they helped push a small company's stock price up to $10 from $1; up to $22 from $2 in one and a half to two and a half years' time; from $6 in August to $45 in November.

Another New York PR firm, specializing in getting media attention for small companies, uses its New York media contacts so that a typical PR implementation report to a client might read like this one: "An ongoing [two-year] publicity program in the financial press resulted in features and stories in . . . *Business-Week, Investment Dealers Digest,* the *Market Chronicle,* Associated Press, United Press International."

National press coverage is important, but it is not the only third-party-endorser PR looks to influence. This firm also takes the company chairman or president and his story to the grass roots to meet local stock analysts, local business people, and local media in Boston, Springfield, Hartford, Nashville, Dallas, Minneapolis, Columbus, Cleveland, Scottsdale, Arizona, Grand Rapids, Spokane, San Francisco, and a dozen more cities. "We believe Wall Street begins in New York and meanders all across the country," we were told.

Nor are these trips scattershot. There are specific target publics: "Minneapolis is an Over-the-Counter city, where the brokers are oriented toward low-priced stocks." "Boston is conservative. Florida and Scottsdale are looking for income-oriented stocks and care a lot about dividends. San Francisco is a mixture that looks for all kinds of stocks."

The firm also pitches the companies to New York stock analysts and stock advisory services like Value Line, Standard & Poor's, Moody's, and Argus Research. "Argus provides an important and highly influential telephone reporting service for forty brokerage houses around the country," they explain. "Nothing might appear in writing, but a good part of those forty houses will move on an Argus phone recommendation."

Ad hoc PR is involved in all kinds of business matters. Not long ago Carl Byoir & Associates helped a Connecticut-based developer locate a $24 million high-rise apartment complex for upper-middle-income tenants in the Boston bedroom community of Newton, Massachusetts. Why PR? Well, there was a small hurdle to overcome: Newton's zoning regulations required multifamily housing units to set aside 10 percent of their space for low-income housing—which would have been off-putting to the well-heeled tenants, says Byoir president Peter Osgood. Talk about a PR problem: how do you keep low-income people out of a housing project and avoid that ugly word discrimination?

Leave it to PR.

The Byoir people studied the city's demographics and discovered a need for housing for the elderly. The elderly can qualify as low-income—but they're not just any low-income riffraff. Without mentioning that detail publicly, Byoir's people influenced the press to accept the developer's idea and also pressured a key alderman on the housing committee. Osgood's people were able to win a zoning variance that would set aside just 5 percent of the project to low-income elderly housing.

More builders and developers are recognizing the value of good PR. "The building industry, for the most part, lacks any significant public constituency," says Roy L. Diez, editor-in-chief of *Professional Builder* magazine. "Builders are regarded by many as profiteers. And new housing developments are usually associated by the public with community change and environmental disruption."

That's why large corporations, like McDonald's and Burger King, use PR people to anticipate and help soothe public opposition to its restaurants as standard procedure. To get more of what they want with less trouble, the small, independent companies that make up the bulk of the building industry must similarly "win public opinion and they must do it early in the game," says Bernard Ury, a Chicago PR man. "It's not enough to work with a select group of municipal officials and homeowner groups; you have to work with the public at large and be open with them early in the game. This business of playing your cards close to the vest for fear of irritating the public only accomplishes what it seeks to prevent."

PR will be especially important as smaller, cheaper housing mandated by changes in the economy rises to challenge traditional building standards, requirements, and zoning laws. To this end, *Professional Builder* got into the PR business itself by printing a twenty-page "educational handbook" called "Smaller Housing, Higher Density Housing Can Be Beautiful" in its September 1983 issue. "Essentially, the report was a builder 'image piece' designed and written for builders to pass along to their local government officials and concerned citizens to help win approval for more affordable, down-sized, and higher-density housing," admits editor Diez.

Builders apparently are winning public opinion. Remember when more affordable, down-sized, and higher-density housing meant cheap, cramped developments packed together like matchboxes with no yards and no place to park a car?

That perceptual alteration is a small accomplishment compared to what some PR people have done in the way of changing public opinion—or, more correctly, public opposition.

Shortly after France's Concorde supersonic jet was christened, strong opposition to its landing at JFK airport in New York welled up. Richard Aurelio of New York's Daniel J. Edelman PR stepped in. "There were stories going around Ozone Park [the Queens community near JFK], for instance, that the Concorde made your ears bleed, that it was bigger than a 747, that it gave you skin cancer, and that it broke your teacups," says Aurelio.[4]

Aurelio's people set out to measure the levels of noise in a New York subway, at Studio 54, and at Notre Dame with the organ playing. All were louder than the Concorde. Mock-ups showed that the Concorde was not bigger than a 747.

Meanwhile, Edelman's Washington office lobbied Congress to defeat two environmental bills that would have hindered the plane, and got the U.S. Department of Transportation to allow the Concorde landing rights at Dulles Airport so the effects of the plane could be tested.

Finally the PR people persuaded the New York business community that New York would lose its stature if the Concorde landed in Houston instead of New York. To drive the point home, Aurelio got France's then-president Valéry Giscard d'Estaing to fly from Paris to Houston on the Concorde. The flight got wide coverage in the press, including a front-page story in the *New York Times*. The message: with the Concorde's supersonic speed and no landing rights in New York, Houston was closer to Europe (in flight time) than was the Big Apple. That was the beginning of the end of opposition to Concorde.

What *ad hoc* PR can do for business, it can also do for labor unions. In September 1983, $1.4 billion (revenues) Continental Airlines, in financial straits thanks to increased competition from nonunion airlines sparked by deregulation, filed for bankruptcy. Its argument was that it could not survive without huge wage concessions from labor. Continental eventually got reduced wages.

Shortly thereafter, claiming it had heard unsolicited reports of safety problems at Continental, the Air Line Pilots Association launched a PR campaign which Continental describes as a "smear campaign" designed to ruin the airline's reputation. By having ALPA's 30,000 members looking eagle-eyed for the slightest infraction of safety regulations by Continental's scab pilots, then cataloging and reporting those infractions to the Federal Aviation Administration (FAA), ALPA created the impression that Continental was an unsafe airline.

Coincidentally, *60 Minutes* did a segment on just the question of how safe it was to fly Continental. Continental says ALPA instigated the *60 Minutes* story. ALPA's Director of Accident Investigation Harold Marthinsen agrees. "We did initiate the story," says Marthinsen. "We sat down with the producers from *Sixty Minutes* and laid out our story. They decided to do their own investigation." Harry Moses, *60 Minutes* producer of the segment on Continental, however, denies through his secretary that the story originated with ALPA.

Little matter that the *60 Minutes* piece didn't really answer the question it raised. The doubt served the PR needs of the pilots' union and the programming needs of CBS. Once again, a perfect marriage of the press and PR. [In an April 1984 industrywide inspection, the FAA found Continental to be one of the five safest airlines in the United States.]

Airline pilots are apparently big customers for PR. Back in 1971, the International Airline Pilots Association was trying to get international cooperation in the handling of airplane hijackings. Unfortunately, the United Nations ambassadors who might have acted on the agreement were not doing much to bring it about. So Kent McKamy, a New York PR man, lent a hand.

The IAPA chartered an airliner and invited the appropriate UN members for a special air excursion to view the fall foliage in the Northeast. Special clearance had been given for the plane to fly lower than normal, the foreign representatives were told. Sixty UN ambassadors accepted the junket.

Once aloft, the PR plan went into action. Four hijackers—ski masks, guns, explosives, and all—barged into the cabin and seized the plane. No one was told this was just a PR stage play, and for five minutes, McKamy kept his target public in terrorized suspense.

Finally, the hoax was revealed and the message delivered: This was only a five-minute demonstration of the kind of terror hijackers perpetrate. Now imagine how much worse a real hijacking is. At that, the in-flight movie screen descended and the sixty UN representatives were shown a one-hour film about hijacking as their plane circled the New York area. Talk about a captive audience. Within two months, a multinational agreement had been reached.

Ad hoc PR does not always act so aggressively, but it can be just as manipulative with the soft sell. For instance, some 46 million Americans in movie theaters across the country in the late seventies viewed an interesting short subject called *Ridin' the Edge.* The flick ran with such features as *Hooper, Smokey and the Bandit,* and *A Matter of Time.*

The film showed the making of a movie stunt in which a man crashes a car into a brick wall with only the protection of an air bag restraint—the first time the controversial airbag was ever used with a live human. But the film was more than that. Produced by Allstate Insurance Company's PR people, the short was an exciting vehicle with which to stump for requiring air bags in automobiles. The air bag in the film worked, of course, saving the stuntman's life. It was a hit in molding opinion too. Allstate surveyed viewers before and after the film was shown, and audience opinion clearly moved in favor of air bags after the film was seen.

Air bag foes—automakers, who don't want yet another expensive government-mandated safety device adding to already heavy sticker prices—have their own PR campaigns, which brings us to sunny Orlando, Florida, and Walt Disney World.

True to its billing, EPCOT Center is a stimulating, interesting tourist attraction. It is also a vehicle for injecting corporate philosophies and ideas into carefree, happy vacationers. In EPCOT's Future World area of the park, General Motors presents The World of Motion, which is sold as "an amusing look at man's age-old quest for freedom of movement."

Indeed, the ride is an amusing demonstration of Walt Disney's audio-animatronic robots. But the pavilion is also part of the field operations section of GM's huge public relations department whose goal, according to company documents, is "to take the General Motors story of our products and plants, our people, our policies and our programs to . . . key publics on a personalized and tailored-to-fit basis."

Once the World of Motion ride is finished, visitors are directed to the TransCenter, where several PR pitches bombard the senses on a level that is not always completely conscious:

- A dramatic video of the effectiveness of automobile seat belts builds support for that much less expensive restraint device.
- Demonstrations of endurance tests of doors, locks, hoods, etc. prove how much GM cares about making sure that unsafe and substandard automobiles do not leave the factory.
- A mini-showroom allows visitors already primed for the future to see "the most technologically advanced line of General Motors cars and trucks."
- And a lighthearted demonstration, "The Bird and the Robot," shows the "possibilities" of robotics. The soft-sell PR message is that robots do a better, more exacting, more dependable job in manufacturing than do human beings. This helps create acceptance and demand by the public for machine-manufactured autos. It also prepares human employees for the competition with machines in the work force.

GM is not the only one to have discovered the value of this somewhat subliminal PR at EPCOT. A short walk away from the GM pavilion is Exxon's Universe of Energy, a dramatic multimedia presentation and ride that shows the "nobility" of the quest for energy. The real pitch here is for "uranium energy" (which everywhere else is known as nuclear power), a business Exxon is already in. "As we leave [The Universe of Energy], although we know the challenges are great, our spirits are lifted at the potentials and options that have been set before us," is how an EPCOT guidebook sees visitors receiving the experience.

On the other side of CommuniCore, The Land, presented by Kraft, takes millions of visitors on a ride through the history of agriculture. Just before visitors are exposed to the hydroponic agricultural technology of tomorrow, they see a turn-of-the-century family farm. The subliminal message: the small farm is a thing of the past—outdated. Until the wonders of hydroponics become feasible, the next best thing to replace this agricultural antique today, logically, is the giant corporate farm.

Over in the World Showcase section of the park is more obvious PR: France is showing a tourism film; Mexico is also selling tourism in its borders, under the thin guise of *El Rio del*

Tiempo: The River of Time ride; and Coca-Cola and American Express associate themselves with freedom in The American Adventure.

A brasher PR vehicle is issues advertising, full-page advertisements that express a company's PR message. Issues advertising doesn't pitch a product, but rather philosophies and corporate images. The goal here is not so much credibility as getting people to hear and think about the company's position on issues affecting the company's business. Such advertisements are akin to "the ancient and honorable art of pamphleteering," says Mobil Oil PR man Herbert Schmertz, the person generally credited with inventing issues advertising. "It's important that a pluralistic society's participants speak their mind because a better informed public will make more rational decisions. We don't think we should leave all the informing of the public up to the media, because they don't do an adequate job."

One of the best examples of the power of issues advertising is R. J. Reynolds' campaign to present "both sides" of the smoking issue. While it is unlikely that many people believe much of what Reynolds ads have to say ("We don't want young people to smoke," and, "You may assume the case against smoking is closed . . . but this is far from the truth"), what they do is stir up controversy and publicity. The ads were widely covered in the press when they were first introduced in January 1984.

The idea is to have the controversy raise doubts about the real health hazards of smoking in general and secondhand smoke in particular, increasing recognition of which has hurt cigarette sales. "Antismoking groups have had a four-lane highway to attack the industry, with no one to rebut," says E. A. Horrigan, Jr., chairman of RJR Tobacco.

The issues advertisements were introduced at a time when many municipalities across the country were considering stiffer no-smoking laws governing public areas. There is little way to measure success this early, except, perhaps, for this, an editorial in the *New York Times* that concluded:

Where smokers are prohibited or segregated, rules are successful substitutes for courtesy. . . . Still, how many of us would really welcome more rules and more laws to govern behavior? Where smoking sections are practical—as in planes and trains—they're a happy solution. Failing them, have we so far transcended tolerance that a simple 'Do you mind if I smoke?' is a thoroughly improbable question? And the occasional 'Not at all' an inconceivable answer?"[5]

Con Edison, the New York electric utility, also employs issues advertising to keep its nuclear reactors at Indian Point, New York, safe from shutdown by antinuclear forces influencing the public and legislators about the very real potential for another Three Mile Island accident—or worse.

So Con Ed's "Neighbors for Safety" campaign draws on the third-party endorsement of Indian Point workers who live near the plant—guys like Bob Tandy, a maintenance mechanic who says, "More than twenty members of my family and most of my friends live within a few miles of Indian Point. When they ask me about the plant, I tell them the truth: I believe this is the safest power plant in the country." Note an important distinction that passes for truth in Tandy's answer: Tandy's truth is that "I believe" Indian Point is safe, not that "it is safe" and not that "a deadly nuclear accident could never happen here."

But while much of public relations efforts are aimed at the public itself, one way or another, most *ad hoc* PR is really intent on influencing that small "public" that ultimately has final say on almost every issue that can affect a company, industry, trade association, or union: government.

For example, back in Florida, Walt Disney World maintains an ongoing public relations program with state and local government leaders to make sure it gets what it needs from them. According to WDW corporate papers:

> In the area of government relations, the [public relations] department and company believe in fostering relations on an informal basis through a number of special events. Each February, the department hosts the 160 state legislators and their families for a weekend of tours and informative sessions on the Walt Disney World Resort Complex future plans.
>
> Periodically, the department monitors legislation which affects our industry at the state and federal level. Special care and attention is also taken to ensure the company is properly represented in regulatory and advisory boards and commissions pertaining to tourism.

Plans are underway to host an annual event for our City/County officials.[6]

But for much of business PR, Washington is the big prize, and PR manipulation of government bodies there, through the manipulation—and creation—of entire issues, has become the way of doing business today. The recently popular buzzwords for this kind of *ad hoc* PR are "issues management."

The issues of the day have always been managed to some extent. In fact, some would argue that they were "managed" to a much greater degree twenty or thirty years ago, when both the administration in Washington and the heads of committees in Congress wielded more control over the dispersal of information. The legislative process was much simpler, and third-party points of view were not needed to support the position of a corporation or industry.

"To present your side of an issue, you only needed to get up to the Hill and to the administration and talk to five or six critical people," says Jim Jennings, executive vice president of Gray & Co., Washington's premier PR firm.* "But all that changed with Lyndon Johnson's Great Society and the proliferation of government into the lives of Americans at all levels, both business and personal."

With the rise of myriad public-advocacy groups, all clamoring to be heard at the legislative level, and the increase in dispersal of federal revenues, the influence of committee and subcommittee chairmen began to diminish until today "it exists among many other points of power," says Jennings. "Junior members of Congress have much more influence. There's a proliferation of critical caucuses: industry, Hispanic, women, black."

To complicate matters, the media changed in response to the changed climate of the sixties. Consumerism, environmentalism, civil rights, and other movements focused attention more and

*Robert Gray, the affable, white-haired man-about-Washington for whom Gray & Co. is named, denies he had any PR campaign of his own to help develop that "premier" image. However, numerous glowing profiles of Gray appeared in the *Wall Street Journal*, the *Washington Post*, the *New York Times*, UPI, *Forbes*, the *Business Review of Washington*, and *Venture* magazine—just about the time Gray quit as head of Hill & Knowlton's Washington office to start his own PR firm in 1982. More articles about him appeared in *Fortune*, *Barron's*, and *Time*—just around the time Gray & Co. made a public offering of its own stock in 1984.

more on Washington, which drew more reporters to the scene. Watergate put the cap on the whole thing by encouraging more investigative reporting in Washington.

For business, the turbulence of change was a nightmare of new regulations and increasingly vocal interest groups that needed pandering to. The rules of the game had changed, and new ways had to be found to at once get what one needed from government, shout down the opposition, and harness the power of interest groups for one's own benefit through persuasion.

On top of all that, much of what occurred was done under the watchful eye of the media—or at least ran the risk of being in the spotlight. So business had to look good in the process of getting government to work for it in these new, more public smoke-filled rooms.

PR stepped in to fill this tall order. Influence peddling became more issues-oriented and less personality-bound. Contrary to the popular perception, maintains Jennings, "It's not really a question of who you know. That only gets you an audience, but you'd better be incredibly convincing if you're going to have an impact on the person in a powerful role."

To help convince congressmen on issues on which they have not yet formulated a strong position, Gray sends his minions into the congressman's home districts to whip up grass-roots support that will in turn influence the congressman.

"In many instances, before you can change a congressman's opinion, you've got to change the constituency's opinion first," explains Bob Gray. That means sending a team of three or four PR people right into the legislator's district. "We can land in Topeka, Kansas, and in thirty minutes we'd be able to find and make contact with the key media people there: editors, talk-show producers, TV and radio news directors."

That done, the team attempts to get op-ed pieces published, encourages talk shows to interview the client, stirs editors' interest in doing stories on the subject, or sends audio and video "actualities"—taped statements by the client—to radio and TV stations.

The purpose of this is to stimulate interest. "If you talk to a housewife in Iowa, the first things on her list of priorities are probably family, home, church, community," says Gray. "The MX missile is not very high on that list. You've got to move that issue up the list, and you do that by talking about the side economic benefits to the regions affected; tax revenues, jobs, economic growth. Then you begin to spread your support base."

The problem, though, is that *ad hoc* PR's increasing sophistication and proliferation push the complex, real issues aside in favor of simpler, more manageable ones. It changes the battlefield to one where the PR people can win more easily. So Iowa housewives may support MX because it brings jobs, regardless of whether it's a good defense system or not; they leave their trust in the hands of powerful interest groups—an unwise abdication no matter what the issue. That erodes true public debate and consideration, which is the heart of the democratic process.

Let's look at one such battle in detail to examine how the truth of a particular position winds up becoming a nonissue.

Recently Gray & Company came up against Burson-Marsteller in a complicated wrangle between the television networks and the Hollywood studios/producers. Buried beneath the complexities of the issue was a very basic element for both parties: money—about $800 million a year's worth.

Here's the issue. On behalf of NBC, Gray tackled a 1971 FCC ruling known as the "Financial Interest and Syndication Rule," which barred the networks from owning any syndication rights in programs produced for them by independent production companies. Thus, after the CBS network makes its money from the first run plus one rerun of, say, *Dallas,* the producer of the program, Lorimar, can syndicate the program to Metromedia or a hundred independent television stations for rerun and does not have to give a penny to CBS.

The ruling's original intent, asserts Gray & Company's Jeff Trammel, arguing his side of the story, was to prevent the networks from owning a share of prime-time programming at a time when they dominated the industry. Subsequently, he charges, a handful of Hollywood studios became even more dominant, so it became appropriate for the rules to be repealed or modified. The networks wanted a piece of that $800 million a year in syndication money.

The network PR people brewed up a storm of controversial claims designed to attract support from a variety of public interest groups during the so-called "public comment" period of FCC hearings, when testimony is solicited from all interested parties throughout the country. Gray & Company got such diverse groups as the National Council of Senior Citizens, the Hispanic caucus in Congress, the former president of the United Rubber Workers, and the city commission of Miami to file letters of support during the comment period.

Were all these groups worried about NBC's and the other networks' bank balances? Not really. Low-income and labor groups coalesced around the issue of "access to free, quality programming in TV." Without additional income from owning and syndicating a piece of the programming pie, the argument went, networks would not be able to compete against cable and other pay systems, and presumably free TV would be run out of business.

Oh no, the networks were not interested in lining their own pockets. They just wanted to make sure the Hispanic and elderly communities would not have to go without *Three's Company, Laverne & Shirley,* or *TV's Foulups, Bleeps and Blunders.*

Furthermore, future sports spectaculars may well be inaccessible to noncable viewers, Trammel hinted darkly, because the networks would simply be too poverty-stricken to compete successfully in the bidding. "HBO was the highest bidder for Wimbledon last year," he lamented, "but Wimbledon decided to go with the networks because they have a larger audience. The first time the Olympics are not on free TV—and it may be Seoul in 1988—" Trammel predicted, "you're going to hear a tremendous uproar." [The broadcast rights to Seoul have not yet been granted.]

Meanwhile, Hollywood's own PR people were out drumming up interest for their side of the issue. In April 1982, the Committee for Prudent Deregulation was born. CPD is a coalition of the Hollywood movie studios; major producers like Lorimar Productions; independent television stations and group owners such as Cox Communications and Metromedia; stars like Alan Alda, Larry Hagman, and Jean Stapleton; and others. Burson-Marsteller won the CPD account.

"One of our recommendations was that this probably could not be made into a public issue in the sense of mass public opinion," says Timothy Brosnahan, a senior vice president at B-M's Washington office. "But the issue could be brought out of the

FCC and discussed with congressmen, the media, and interest groups."

Burson-Marsteller got on with the more mundane tasks of reducing huge filing statements and reports from lawyers and economic firms into more simplified, condensed information kits. These were then used to inform, persuade, and enlist additional support groups like Action for Children's Television, the American Civil Liberties Union, and the Council of Churches of the City of New York. The abundance of coalition members and outside supporters totaling well over 200 provided plenty of filings to impress the FCC with the scope of interest.

The PR kits were also used to stimulate interest in four key national newspapers—the *New York Times, Los Angeles Times, Washington Post,* and *Wall Street Journal*—and with *Time* and *Newsweek.* "Those four newspapers have an impact on discussions like this," says Brosnahan. After CPD met the editorial boards of the *Washington Post* and *Los Angeles Times,* both papers ran editorials favorable to Hollywood. There was less contact with the *New York Times,* Brosnahan recalls, since that newspaper took an early position in favor of the New York-based networks. [CPD says it did, however, manage to get an Op-Ed piece by MTM Enterprises executive vice president Mel Blumenthal into the *Times,* and the paper did run a profile of MTM, which quickly got around to mentioning "the prospects of changes in Federal regulations that could make these independent producers . . . totally subservient to the networks. . . ."]

Hollywood's PR sideshow issues chosen to help sway these opinion leaders centered on fairness: if they won, the big networks would virtually control all the programming on free TV, and smaller, more independent producers would be shut out. (That argument brought, for example, the support of an important voice familiar on Capitol Hill for its continual efforts to improve children's programming, Action for Children's Television.)

Then there was the threat that the networks could hurt independent stations by forbidding some very popular syndicated shows from running against, say, the *Tonight* Show, or the *CBS Evening News.*

Perhaps the best appeal-to-fairness argument was that producers, at best, break even or take a loss on their shows' network runs in "the hope that the show will do well in syndication," said some of the press handout material. That press release and an August 15, 1983, *Time* magazine article pointed out that *MTM* Enterprises' *Hill Street Blues* series—despite its great popularity—loses more than $1 million a year for the producers. NBC, meanwhile, the press release continues, makes a $20 million gross profit.

What neither the press release nor the *Time* article mentioned was that, in syndication, one hit show like *Hill Street Blues* could probably make back enough money to finance one hundred years of million-dollar-a-year losers and still have much more than $100 million in profits. MTM Enterprises would not divulge how much *Hill Street Blues* is pulling down in syndication, but MCA's *Magnum, P.I.*, a show of comparable standing, has grossed some $200 million for its first several years of reruns. And with all the production costs of these shows already paid for—except for the minor deficits—most of that $200 million is pure profit.

Agencies like the FCC are most subject to the opinion of Congress, which created it in 1934. Indeed, running parallel to the FCC consideration were bills in Congress that would have imposed a six-month-to-five-year FCC moratorium on changing the rules. Burson-Marstelller's publicity was thus intended for Congress. Admits Brosnahan: "The FCC ultimately makes the decision, but people in Congress do have an influence on the FCC."

The West Coast also had another PR high card: stars like Larry Hagman and Charlton Heston were brought in to testify before the FCC and Congress and to meet personally with key congressmen. While Brosnahan downplays the impact of this on Congress, he admits it certainly impressed them.

"Sure, it dazzled the press and some members of Congress," grouses Jeff Trammel. "The stars made visits to congressmen's offices, hosted parties and screenings, and flew ten senators to Hollywood. Many of the stars didn't know the issues at all. Most couldn't even respond adequately to questions during their congressional testimony."

Another trump card for Hollywood was Ronald Reagan's letter to Congress endorsing a six-month moratorium on FCC action. Six days later, the House voted to prohibit action on the FCC repeal until June 1984. In June, the moratorium was extended further still.

Here we have the essence of *ad hoc* PR communication: no calculable lies, no overt manipulation of the truth: simply opposing sides slanting their interpretations of the information to suit their needs. Why did the whole focus move from the FCC, where Congress had first authorized a $2 million study of the issue as long ago as 1978, to the halls of Congress itself? Because the FCC had already made a tentative decision to partially repeal the rules as the networks requested. "When the studios' recommendations lost on merits in the FCC, the studios ran to Capitol Hill to bail them out," cries Trammel on behalf of NBC.

The other side has a different view. "The networks wanted to keep it behind closed doors in the FCC so no one would hear about it," counters Brosnahan on behalf of the CPD.

What all this hullabaloo managed to accomplish was to obscure the real issues—which might have been just as well for the PR people and their efforts to marshal support. Jacob Clayman, director of the National Council of Senior Citizens, admits he didn't have time to "explore in every corner, seen and unseen" before throwing his organization behind the networks in FCC and congressional testimony. But he did examine the arguments printed up neatly by both sides and decided, along with others in his organization, to indulge a bias he's had for quite a while. "Free TV is so important for the aged, many of them poor and tied to their homes, that our position arises out of the feeling that the elderly shouldn't be required at their stage of the game to spend their last nickel to obtain at least the quality of TV that's available now," says Clayman. "We have no interest in the titanic battle between the giants. But you can't expect an institution like free TV to remain vigorous if its profit structure is impinged upon, as it is with the growth of cable/ pay TV."

It's a mark of PR's effectiveness that so many grass-roots organizations among labor and the poor were mobilized around issues not of financial interest but of free programming and quality productions. Estimated cost to both sides: $20 million.

Commented one Washington PR man cynically, the "financial interest and syndication" issue "is really a case of, are fifty multimillionaires on the West Coast going to become bigger multi-millionaires, or are fifty multimillionaires on the East Coast? When you ran for the subway in the morning, I'm sure your first thought wasn't, 'Those damn networks . . .'"

Credibility is a crucial element to good *ad hoc* PR. PR firms often try to stir up a hornet's nest of controversy and then draw real people into the congressional and agency committee rooms on their behalf. "I used to work on Capitol Hill," says Brosnahan, "and when you start seeing thousands of identical postcards coming in on an issue, you know someone instigated that and you tend to reject it. But when you see a lot of editorials, and a variety of opinion leaders speaking out, that has an impact." Even if the congressman knows PR is behind it, he has to respond if only to avoid appearing unresponsive to the folks back home in the district who have been stirred up.

While Washington is clearly a major focal point for the creation of PR issues that rightfully or wrongfully sweep whole sectors of the nation up into their purposeful, engineered vortex of controversy, it is by no means the only place issues management can affect us. With the immediacy and impact of today's communications, Americans can get caught up in the crossfire of a PR-directed issue affecting a relatively small target public.

Case in point: the threat of Chapter 11 bankruptcy for Eastern Airlines, which made major news in fall 1983, and had even greater impact because it came just two days after Continental Airlines filed for bankruptcy.

For years, Eastern management had suffered stormy relations with labor. By fall of 1983, with more than $140 million in losses piling up for the first nine months, chairman Frank Borman had concluded that a 20 percent wage cost reduction was necessary for the $3.8 billion (sales) airline to survive—15 percent from pay cuts and 5 percent from increased productivity.

The problem was, how to effectively communicate that to the work force? Eastern's management suffered from a huge credibility gap after years of crying pauper to labor. Only six months before, Borman had given in to the demands of the International Association of Machinists after bluffing about an inability to pay; Eastern finally agreed to a 32 percent wage hike over eighteen months.

The answer, says Richard McGraw, Eastern's PR head, was a

videotaped appeal to employees. But it had originally been decided that the threat of bankruptcy would not be broached. For one thing, such announcements tend to scare customers away from booking flights with the airline, compounding the financial woes. A second reason was that Borman personally abhorred the suggestion. "Borman is a former astronaut—he is the Right Stuff—and doesn't like to quit," says one source close to the situation. "Bankruptcy conjures up all kinds of negative feelings that go against the American tradition, like a debtor's refuge, not living up to one's obligations, living on charity."

That videotape was finished and ready for distribution throughout the company for the following Monday. "On Saturday, Continental filed for bankruptcy," remembers McGraw. "We met Saturday and decided to redo the videotape to capitalize on Continental's filing to emphasize the seriousness of the situation." The tape was recut on Sunday to include Borman's threat of bankruptcy if labor didn't accept the 20 percent labor cost cuts. Eastern knew that the media would pick up the story in a big way following so closely on the heels of the Continental filing; Eastern counted on that fact to lend credibility to its claim with employees.

The move was a brilliant one; on Monday, all hell began to break loose.

"Many workers were traumatized," says McGraw, "because they had a mindset that management was lying, yet here was a bunch of new facts—which they didn't believe—being given to them by other people [the media] who were supposed to be trustworthy. They didn't have a place to pigeonhole all that." Clearly, McGraw supposes the thinking went, the media wouldn't have made such a big story of Eastern's threat if it were not true. Eastern managed to procure its wage concessions from labor.

Of course, Eastern was in trouble, but not everyone agrees bankruptcy was imminent on December 31, 1983, as management claimed. "The threat was real," says Louis Marckesano, a senior transportation securities analyst with Janey Montgomery Scott in Philadelphia. "Wage concessions are the only way to immediately resolve the problems. But [Eastern] over-dramatized the situation as far as the timing. Eastern faced technical default by the end of 1983, but I think if there had been progress shown, the lenders would not have blown the whistle."

PR is creeping into another area of business—helping formulate corporate policy.

How did that come about? According to an annual survey of what corporate chieftains do with their time, conducted by Howard Chase Enterprises, executives now spend 50 percent of their time on social responsibility programs, issues management, government relations, regulatory matters, spokesmanship, and media relations—all areas that traditionally fall within the province of PR. Who better to advise management on PR than PR people?

"Our function is to act as management consultants," insists A. E. Jeffcoat, partner in Jeffcoat, Schoen & Morrell, a small but highly regarded New York PR firm. "We help corporations foresee change and take advantage of it in such a way that they get credit for being farsighted instead of being caught short."

Agrees Mike Dowling of Ogilvy & Mather: "In many ways issues management boils down to managing change. If you don't manage it, it damn sure will manage you and you'll always be on the defensive. Issues management is an early-warning system for issues coming up on the horizon. You want to spot them, seize the issue, name the battlefield, and coin the buzzwords. Spotting an issue early is crucial to killing it."

Adds Dustin Lerbinger, dean of Boston University's school of public relations, "PR people today are boundary scanners. They've got to look out there, see what's going on, then tell the people inside the fort. That's why research is so important. With the public learning things as quickly as the leaders, thanks to rapid communications, emphasis is placed on anticipating problems."

Thus it was PR people who first spotted the impact environmentalism would have on business—in some cases a full six years before Earth Day in 1970 officially launched the movement. In 1964, Sydney Morrell, of Jeffcoat, Schoen & Morrell, commissioned what he believes to be the first research project on air and water pollution for a corporation.

Hill & Knowlton was also among the early subscribers to the environmental trend. "Business kept telling us, 'It will go away,'" recalls Loet Velmans, the chairman of H&K. "It took us from 1966, when we established our Environmental Group, to 1971, to convince them that it would not go away."

And it was Henry Ford II's PR advisors who convinced him after the Detroit riots of 1967 not to pull out of the inner city. Instead, they counseled going into the ghetto to aggressively recruit some 3,000 workers, thus easing tensions that could have become expensive for the automaker.

Now H&K is concentrating on problem issues and images in the banking and health-care industries.

Burson-Marsteller, meanwhile, saw a growing threat for business from the religious sector and compiled a sixty-five-page booklet on the subject—almost two years before the U.S. Catholic Conference's pastoral letter on the American economy in November 1984. "Corporations will now find themselves faced with pressures from a variety of religious groups, each with its own agenda carefully wrapped in the robes of a moral vision. . . . Religious representatives believe that religion has a moral obligation to impact corporate behavior," warned B-M.

The range of management activities PR people are getting involved in is far-reaching. Jeffcoat talks about one gung-ho division manager several years ago in a New York Stock Exchange-traded food company who wanted to go out and build new plant capacity to manufacture a new sugar substitute. Jeffcoat advised against it, citing studies that indicated health risks with the sweetener and the fact that FDA approval might tie up production for years. On that advice, the food company gave thumbs down—to aspartame.

"On one hand, you could say it was a bad decision," says Jeffcoat, "but we did save the company money by not having idle factories for the seven years it did take to obtain FDA approval."

Meanwhile, Reece Corporation, a leading maker of industrial sewing machines, was faced with the problem of effecting its first layoffs in the company's 120-year history. Carl Byoir PR people thought of every possible question that could be raised by employees, the local press, stock analysts, and the union, then set out to get answers. They found that a lot of the company's lower-level jobs were subcontracted out and suggested, among other things, that potential layoffs could at least maintain employment by taking some of the subcontracted jobs until the economy improved. Some employees opted for the offer, while others left, but the expected labor unrest never materialized. "We won the plaudits of the local UAW Solidarity House," beams Osgood. In addition, the PR recommendations led to changes in the structure of the sales and marketing force, development of new employee information and compensation policies, and productivity increases.

Finally, H&K's Richard Cheney talks about two PR/management cases he handled involving an extremely narrow public: individual companies' boards of directors.

In the first instance, a company's board had found that its president had embezzled money from the company and demanded he quit. Neither the president nor the company wanted the matter to become public, a fact the president used to try to extort a generous severance package. The company would not have it, though, and after watching the lawyers going back and forth between the board and the president, Cheney stepped in. He had drafted a press release explaining all the dirty details of exactly why the president was being ousted, and had the lawyer take it to the president with the message that the company had decided it would tell all, and here is how it would look. The president's response was quick. He immediately accepted the company's meager severance offer.

In another instance, three of a company's outside directors, who were from an investment institution having financial trouble, were threatening the chairman with a proxy fight. Cheney helped eliminate a management problem and nipped potentially bad press in the bud.

"I suggested the chairman have a clipboard presentation of what he could say about the three board members' institution's problems if they started a fight," says Cheney. "By the time he'd finished with the clipboard and they could see the vividness of their plight and what he was going to do, they had given up.

"Shortly thereafter," smiles Cheney, "they sold their stock and left the board."

nine

The Battle for Corporate Survival

CRISIS PR

With PR finding its way into almost every other aspect of corporate operations—from promoting products to promoting employee and even government relations—it should be no surprise that PR is becoming an influential factor in a much more important area: protecting the company and management from crises.

Corporate crises come in all varieties: industrial accidents; plane crashes; adverse health or environmental effects of a product, and events or mistakes that would tend to bring into question the integrity, quality, or safety of a product. A corporate takeover presents yet another type of crisis. Whatever the actual event, the real business worry for the corporation is usually that any crisis is a potential threat to profitability, could eliminate a product line, or could in some way attract increased government regulation. Crisis PR attempts to minimize these threats.

The job of crisis PR is *not* to make the public believe bad is good. Take the case of dioxin, the deadly toxin used in the defoliant Agent Orange during the Vietnam war. Crisis PR does not attempt to make dioxin look like something you'd want to sprinkle on your corn flakes in the morning. Rather, it attempts to make a solid public perception—"dioxin kills and seriously injures people exposed to it"—into a gray issue—"some people say dioxin is dangerous, but scientists have not really been able to link dioxin exposure to a higher mortality rate."

To the public, this graying of the issue appears to be simply part of the normal, healthy debate in any democracy. After all, public relations' job is simply the noble task of "telling the other side." But the real intent of this "debate" is often to create a smoke screen of "facts" that obscures the truth. Crisis PR people will throw so much information at the press and the public that no one can be quite sure just where the truth lies.

PR people will not come right out and admit that they are generating smoke screens, but listen to Jim Callaghan, head of Hill & Knowlton's environmental and consumer division, which urged Dow Chemical, one of the manufacturers of dioxin, to be more aggressive in using PR to tell its side of the story: "The media don't deal with truth in any pristine sense anyway. What they do is tell you that Joe and Charlie had a fight. And they go to Joe and say, 'Okay, what's your side of the story?' And they print that. Then they go to Charlie and say, 'What's your side of the story?' And they print that. It's the truth in the sense that yes, Joe and Charlie really did say that. But do you really know what happened?"

Callaghan complains about his environmentalist/consumerist opponents' ability to use the media for their own PR purposes. "Environmental organizations are nothing but giant PR organizations themselves," he says. But it is just as true that Dow's PR people can use that same media truth to say, as Callaghan does: "There is simply no evidence that [Vietnam vets] were damaged by Agent Orange." The media have to give weight and coverage to that statement, because it is true; there have been no such scientifically controlled studies. *But,* that true statement does not mean that Viet vets *weren't* damaged by dioxin; it just means no one has conclusively *proven* it.

"It's a battle of opinions," continues Callaghan, "but there is a basic body of science buried under those opinions. There is a body of information that says dioxin is bad; there is another body of information that says it is not so bad." Callaghan's job is to use his media skills to push that second body of "truth" on the public and insist it is the real truth.

That is, of course, how anyone would debate an issue. However, as we have seen, Callaghan and other PR people debate behind the scenes of the news so that their side is often not presented as their own opinion, but as some independent third-party endorser's findings of fact. Crisis PR is not the proper and aboveboard Yale Debate Association; it is guerrilla warfare in the jungle of public opinion.

At the same time, Callaghan must do what he can to erode the public's confidence in the opposing "truth." Says he, "There are one or two things that may indicate there is a problem with dioxin and there is a lot of anecdotal stuff—but anecdotes are not science."

Consequently, Dow PR pushed the "dioxin may not be all it's accused of" story in interviews, press releases, and material provided to the press. Dow scientists also toured the country advancing the company line in newspaper interviews and radio and television talk shows.

By early July 1983, *Newsweek* had recognized the problem, in an article entitled, "Dioxin: How Great a Threat?" which indicates Dow's PR campaign was a success. Said the magazine:

> No wonder people are confused about dioxin. Skeptics downplay its danger, calling it just the latest inductee in the environmentalists' "chemical of the month club." On the other hand, experiments show dioxin to be not only the deadliest substance made by man, but also a possible cause of cancer and birth defects.[1]

Other journalists tilted their conclusions in Dow's favor. Under the title "Dow vs. the Dioxin Monster," a May 1983 *Fortune* article (initiated by the magazine, claims Callaghan) said:

> Where lies the truth in the wide gulf between Dow Chemical Co.'s view of itself as a model environmental citizen and the lurid accusations in the press that it is a reckless polluter of its own nest, Midland, Michigan? Closer to Dow's side of the shore* . . .

*This, despite *Fortune*'s own acknowledgment in the article that Dow helped doctor an Environmental Protection Agency report on Midland, removing a sentence that concluded Dow was the major, if not only, source of dioxin contamination in the Saginaw and Tittabawassee rivers and Saginaw Bay.[2]

Still, this proud old company finds itself sued against and suing, pilloried in Congress, and widely regarded as a threat to public safety.[3]

And:

> . . . Dow needs to adopt a more open, less belligerent stance. Dow scientists can be flinty indeed in dismissing charges based on so-called anecdotal information—that is, not supported by controlled studies. Recent press reports about an increase in soft-tissue sarcoma in Midland created just such an episode. This kind of cancer is so rare that the increase could be a statistical blip. Dow points out that the total cancer and death rates among its Midland employees are below the national averages.[4]

Fortune seemed to conclude that Dow was more the victim of its own poor attitude and wasn't adequately sensitive to the impression environmentalists, regulators, and the concerned public had.

Two months after the *Fortune* article, a New York court released evidence indicating that Dow indeed did know dioxin was potentially dangerous to humans. A 1965 memo by Dow's director of toxicology warned that dioxin could be "exceptionally toxic." Another memo by Dow's medical director said dioxin-related "fatalities have been reported."[5] In 1984 Dow and other dioxin makers agreed to a $180 million settlement of a suit by Vietnam veterans who said they were victims of dioxin in Agent Orange during the war.

As the dioxin case shows, while crisis PR can successfully muddle an issue in the public mind, it does not always win the war. PR people blame that on the fact that crisis PR, by definition, means they are called into a situation only after the corporate house is well aflame. H&K president Loet Velmans and other crisis PR people take great pride, with a smile, in the image of themselves as the "fire brigade."

Crises do not allow for the careful advance planning that PR people know is extremely important for success in molding public opinion. Crisis PR people cannot be the boundary scanners that Professor Lerbinger sees anticipating problems before they happen; they must come in after the fact.

That does not mean crisis PR never works: the chances of a win still make it worthwhile, as in the case of saccharin. Hill & Knowlton also handled that crisis for a coalition of soft-drink bottlers, beginning in 1977, when the Food and Drug Administration started talking about banning saccharin because of a Canadian study on mice, linking the substance to bladder cancer.

Hill & Knowlton immediately set out to discredit the Canadian study. Scientists and doctors on Hill & Knowlton's payroll toured the country talking to local groups, getting media coverage, and appearing on talk shows. A key element of the campaign to erode confidence in the Canadian study was the development of a simple concept, easily grasped by the public.

H&K's people came up with the idea that to equal the intake of saccharin that the Canadian mice were subject to, humans would have to drink 1,250 bottles of diet soda a day. That idea swept the public consciousness in an era when studies were showing that virtually everything causes cancer.

In the end, the PR campaign helped get a moratorium on FDA action until "better material" supporting the cancer link was developed. A warning label which tells of the possible link to cancer—in laboratory animals, not humans—was also part of the deal.

Hill & Knowlton is one of the premier firms in crisis PR—it has handled PR for a wide variety of problems including the Kansas City Hyatt Hotel skywalk disaster, the Three Mile Island nuclear-power-plant accident, the health-risk charges surrounding the morning-sickness drug bendectin, toxic-shock syndrome, and the safety questions surrounding Kero-Sun kerosene heaters. However, Hill & Knowlton is not the only show in town. Burson-Marsteller is big in the crisis PR business too, and has done PR work for Union Carbide and its gas-leak disaster in India; the Girl Scouts after dangerous objects were found in their cookies; and Johnson & Johnson after cyanide-laced Extra Strength Tylenol capsules killed seven people in the Chicago area.

One would think the Tylenol case, which involved both Burson-Marsteller and J&J's internal PR department, should not have required much PR. After all, it soon became clear that J&J

was not at fault; the poisonings were the work of a sick individual.

But the crisis PR's aim was to rebuild public confidence in Tylenol and J&J. Demonstrating the value of research, a key factor of the PR work was a nightly telephone survey which kept tabs, almost from the beginning of the crisis, on what the public was thinking. Early on, the polls showed the public was fearful of the millions of bottles of Tylenol on store shelves, not because they thought J&J was to blame, but because any one of those bottles could be similarly laced with cyanide. Why chance it? No one was going to buy the stuff.

J&J says it was "quite confident" of the safety of the Tylenol on the shelves, but, according to Burson-Marsteller/Johnson & Johnson documents, "The company knew that by removing the product from the shelf, it would be perceived as acting responsibly to the crisis . . . a responsible company would remove it."

So J&J recalled the capsules at a cost of $100 million and, in the process, moved the focus of the news coverage away from negative publicity about Tylenol and onto positive publicity about a corporation acting responsibly.

Now the problem was how to regain the product's 37 percent market share and $500 million annual sales, as competitors began to move in on the market.

Ironically, the tragedy resulted in plenty of goodwill toward J&J, since the company was widely perceived as an innocent victim. Even the press was sympathetic. For example, few journalists ever asked "why tamper-resistant packaging had not preceded the tragedy," says Burson-Marsteller. J&J wanted to capitalize on this goodwill and turn it into a strong marketing force. That is one reason the company stuck with the Tylenol name, rather than abandon the brand altogether as some had advised.

The PR aspects of the launch were two-pronged. First, the 2,500-member sales force fanned out to build confidence in retailers and the medical community that J&J was upbeat about Tylenol's reintroduction.

Second, for consumers, Burson-Marsteller set up a televised, 30-city satellite press conference attended by some 600 journalists. Says the PR firm:

Such a vehicle would allow local media an equal chance at a nationwide story—assuring broad coverage—and would create some level of a "pack psychology" on the meaning of the Tylenol relaunch. A teleconference also offered a characteristic normally associated with advertising—the ability to deliver one message to the world in a relatively controlled format.

A videotape showing the new tamper-resistant packaging was provided the media and got good pickup. Another 7,500 press kits were sent to media outside the 30 cities, and J&J chairman James Burke appeared on *Donahue* and *60 Minutes,* which did a story on the company's response to the crisis.

The result? Extensive coverage of the relaunch on all three television networks, local TV and radio, and in the print media, which devoted an average thirty-two column-inches to the story. This, despite the fact that Soviet president Leonid Brezhnev had died and a space shuttle was launched the same day as the press conference.

But the really important payoff of the crisis PR: Tylenol immediately regained a 24 percent market share after relaunch and, later, climbed back up to the position of top-selling brand.

Big PR firms, of course, do not have an exclusive franchise on crisis PR. Kenneth Makovsky (then of Harshe-Rotman & Druck Public Relations, now head of Makovsky & Company) handled the PR campaign for the $3 billion-a-year aerosol industry when fluorocarbons came under attack in 1974 for damaging the earth's ozone layer.

The crisis started with a September 26, 1974, page-1 article in the *New York Times* headlined: TESTS SHOW AEROSOL GASES MAY POSE THREAT TO EARTH. The article advanced the theory of Harvard's Dr. Michael B. McElroy that substantial ozone depletion, resulting from aerosol use, could cause widespread skin cancer and radical alteration of the climate.

"Within a month, we had a [major] response in the form of a press release," says Makovsky. "The *New York Times* pretty much printed the press release we drafted as a story," in the November 2, 1974, edition.

Makovsky covered all the bases, starting with an analysis of the press coverage to see what needed to be done. The situation did not look good. Press coverage, which mostly centered on the Harvard study, was almost uniformly unfavorable—and at times hostile—to the industry. The press seemed to have adopted the position of those attacking aerosols and tended to bury the industry's position in the middle or toward the end of the news stories. "The headlines were perhaps the most damaging aspect of the press coverage. It is well established that while very few news stories are read thoroughly, the majority of headlines are read or at least scanned," said the press analysis.

The immediate objective of the crisis PR was to inform the public that all the doomsaying was hypothesis, not fact, says Makovsky. "We couldn't deny it, because we had no proof it was untrue."

To get the industry story out, PR people and industry representatives and experts traveled around the country to state and local hearings discussing aerosol bans to make sure the hypothesis story was heard. After hearings, the PR people would make sure the industry's press releases, and excerpts from the hearings, were rapidly made available to the local press.

Since aerosol industry people all over the country were getting questions from the local media and being asked to testify at hearings, Makovsky made sure they were all aware of and espousing the same industry position. He sent them a steady stream of briefing papers, backgrounders, press releases, testimony transcripts, legislative reports, summaries of congressional hearings, and news clippings. This ensured that the industry would "speak with one voice," in much the same fashion the Reagan administration did so by having all official statements about the Grenada invasion come from Washington. That makes it easier for PR to "control" the news.

Makovsky also created a guidebook for witnesses, which gave pointers about testifying ("It is important to remember that elected officials are adept at debate and have the verbal skills required to lead others into making statements that can reflect poorly on the witness himself or the cause he espouses."); dealing with the press (". . . summarize the most important points of your statement in brief, no-more-than-thirty-second statements suitable for television and radio broadcast."); and how to handle possible questions—including hostile ones (QUESTION: If there is the slightest chance that your products are harmful to the atmosphere, shouldn't they be banned? ANSWER: . . . there is a slight risk that thousands of different products could be modifying the atmosphere to one degree or another. I do not think it is reasonable or proper to ban products at random to eliminate a threat that many qualified people doubt even exists.).

Meanwhile, Makovsky worked with the industry's Aerosol Education Bureau to provide information and materials to the public and media. Through the AEB, the PR people developed a "good relationship" with the press which helped generate news stories favorable to the industry. Makovsky points to a stack of articles "generated" by his agency—with headlines much friendlier to the industry—in the *New York Times, Milwaukee Journal,* the *Observer* of London, *Rocky Mountain News, Barron's,* the *Wall Street Journal,* the *National Observer,* the *New York Daily News, BusinessWeek,* the *Los Angeles Herald Examiner,* and *Fortune.* The seven-page 1975 *Fortune* piece was so good, it was included in press kits distributed by Harshe-Rotman & Druck PR for the Council on Atmospheric Sciences, an organization of aerosol and fluorocarbon-related industries.

Was the *Fortune* piece really spawned by PR? "It was one of the first big articles that we generated," says Makovsky, in his office where another article (from the November 31, 1981, issue of *BusinessWeek*) is mounted trophylike on a plaque honoring Makovsky's winning the ICP promotion achievement award for outstanding product promotion. "But be careful in your quote. How would you feel if we said, 'We generated this or that article,' that you wrote?"

The Council on Atmospheric Science figured in the PR campaign too. "We recommended to the industry that they have scientists who are not members of the industry to present our point of view on selected occasions to the public," says Makovsky. Dr. James P. Lodge, chairman of the Colorado Air Pollution Control Commission, was one of the scientists retained by COAS for that purpose, says Makovsky.

"There are vast knowledge gaps that must be filled before we can accurately predict how fluorocarbons or any other man-made chemical will affect atmospheric balance," said Lodge upon his introduction as the COAS scientific advisor.

There was even a catchy concept like the one used for the saccharin campaign. This time the aerosol PR people related the ozone depletion theory to the storybook character Chicken Little's cry, "The sky is falling!" which became part of the increasing press skepticism about the depletion "theory"—"theory," by the way, started appearing in quotes in headlines.

Now here's the surprise ending. In 1977, fluorocarbons finally were banned for use as an aerosol propellant. Ken Makovsky, however, thinks the PR campaign was a smashing success.

Is he blind? No. The view from inside: the real purpose of the PR campaign, explains Makovsky, was to buy time for the industry so it could come up with an alternative aerosol propellant that did not need fluorocarbons. "If we had not taken the offensive in this situation, the ban would have come a lot sooner, and the industry itself would have been unprepared to face the market realities—physically unprepared," says Makovsky. "If they sat back, they might have been wiped out. Instead, while the debate was going on, they were working on alternative methods. By the time the ban came, the industry had pretty much reformulated its products."

While the PR for fluorocarbons largely revolved around theory, sometimes crisis PR must deal with facts. Such was the case with the PR war between CBS and General William Westmoreland. But while many of the facts should have become clearer as the public debate raged—Did CBS treat Westmoreland unfairly? Was Westmoreland guilty of "conspiracy"?—the PR managed to make the formation of a definitive conclusion in the public mind nearly impossible.

For CBS News, the crisis began on January 20, 1982. Westmoreland had just been relaxing with the *CBS Morning News* at his Charleston, South Carolina, home when Diane Sawyer, Mike Wallace, and CBS producer George Crile launched into a publicity segment about an upcoming broadcast on January 23, "The Uncounted Enemy: A Vietnam Deception." As he watched, it quickly became evident that Wallace and Crile were priming the audience for a public lynching—and the subject would be Westmoreland! The general immediately reached for the telephone to call a friend of his in Washington, David Henderson. "Dave, they're trying to make me look like a criminal!" he said.

Henderson, a partner in the Washington public policy PR firm of Alcalde, Henderson & O'Bannon, agreed to represent Westmoreland *pro bono*. The first step was a news conference, three days after the documentary aired, in which Henderson produced military people and a one hundred-page press packet of evidence refuting the CBS charges that Westmoreland had led a conspiracy to underestimate enemy troop strength and keep the "true" numbers from President Johnson.

That was followed by what Henderson describes as an "intensive campaign" to get publicity for the general's side of the story in the media throughout the nation, between January 1982 and September the same year, when Westmoreland filed his $120 million libel suit against CBS. The campaign was a success by any measure, not least of which was an eight-pound stack of press clippings.

Most prized of those clippings, however, was a June 1982 *TV Guide* article, "Anatomy of a Smear," by Don Kowet and Sally Bedell (now Sally Bedell Smith), which charged that CBS News had violated its own policies of fairness and accuracy. Henderson claims he did not personally inspire the *TV Guide* story, but Smith says the January 26 press conference did, along with inside information she and Kowet had obtained from CBS.

"From the start, Westmoreland was clearly winning," says John Scanlon, the CBS crisis PR man. "CBS News had been reluctant to defend itself." CBS News's own internal investigation—first suppressed and only summarized by CBS, until the network was forced to release it by the judge presiding over *Westmoreland* v. *CBS, Inc., et al.*—didn't help its image as "the most trusted news organization" either. It eventually admitted that George Crile, producer of the documentary, had violated the news division's policies by coaching a witness, showing interview subjects tapes of other interviews, and failing to mention that his primary source was a paid consultant.

The internal CBS report, by Bud Benjamin, a CBS veteran with an impeccable reputation for honesty, also cast doubt on the substance of the documentary: "Even today, military historians cannot tell you whether or not MACV [Military Assistance Command—Vietnam] 'cooked the books,' as the broadcast states. The flow of definitive information is painfully slow and may never be conclusive."

And the report agreed that the documentary had treated Westmoreland unfairly.

Westmoreland's PR, of course, had nothing to do with all that, nor did it necessarily prompt CBS news president Van Gordon Sauter to say that "a judgmental conclusion of conspiracy was inappropriate," even though CBS News still stood by the story. Nor did Westmoreland's PR really get Crile suspended with pay in June 1983, though the suspension came just three days after Westmoreland's attorney, Dan Burt, publicized the fact that Crile had surreptitiously tape-recorded a telephone interview with former secretary of defense Robert McNamara.

Westmoreland, unable to obtain an apology from CBS, finally filed suit against the network in September 1982.

After a year and a half taking a drubbing in the press for its mistakes, CBS finally hired PR man Scanlon in the fall of 1983. One of Scanlon's primary missions: to make sure every salvo fired by the opposition PR was offset by PR fire from CBS News. Scanlon was almost a "grounding wire," which eliminated negative electrical charges against CBS in little sparks before they could build up into a single large bolt of lightning that might destroy CBS News's credibility altogether.

"There is a kind of trial in the court of public opinion before the legal trial, and PR can help," explains Scanlon. CBS learned that lesson, sources say, after Dr. Carl Galloway charged in a 1979 lawsuit that CBS's *60 Minutes* had libeled him in a broadcast about insurance fraud. CBS won the case in June 1983. Still "CBS felt it won the case in court, but Galloway won in the press," says one source. There was simply no PR person to push the CBS side in the press. Ironically, a major network seemed helpless when the spotlight of criticism was turned around.

There was another reason for a more aggressive PR stance. As events developed, Judge Pierre N. Leval, who presided over the trial, allowed the jury to follow news accounts of the case during the trial. Thus any PR by either Westmoreland or CBS News that affected the court of public opinion would also have an effect on the tiny target public of jurors in the court of law.

So Scanlon vigorously dogged Westmoreland's PR offensive.

□ Upon getting wind that Westmoreland would be holding a December 27, 1983, press conference at the Hotel Washington, in

Washington, D.C., to present a four-pound stack of evidence that showed how CBS had libeled him, Scanlon scheduled a CBS News conference right after Westmoreland's, just a few doors down the hall in the same hotel, to present the CBS News version of the story. That replaced an all-Westmoreland story in the next day's news with a "Westmoreland, CBS Trade Charges," story.

☐ Scanlon also arranged appearances for Crile on television and radio talk shows that were having Kowet as a guest.[6]

☐ In April 1984, Scanlon launched a preemptive strike against Kowet's book (*A Matter of Honor*) about the CBS News documentary, air-expressing letters attacking the book as "reckless and malicious" to fifty major newspaper and magazine book reviewers a full month before the book's publication date. "It's designed to intimidate the book review editor . . . either to kill the review or alter it," said John Blades, book editor of the *Chicago Tribune*.[7]

☐ And, of course, Scanlon attempted to spark reporters into doing stories that would present a case favoring CBS News. The "hook" was the treasure trove of history being revealed in depositions. "I know a lot of journalists—most of my friends are journalists, and I have a high degree of credibility with them," says Scanlon. "I'd reach out and say, 'You guys ought to look at this.' If anyone wrote an unfair story, I'd try to get another journalist at the same paper to look at the other side."

☐ Scanlon courted the press by serving as a "resource" for documents, summaries, and interpretations of the 400,000 pages of documents in the case. "If you build those relationships, and if over time you've built credibility with reporters, when the time comes that a judgment call has to be made [by the reporter], he'll say, 'This guy hasn't let me down yet,'" explains Scanlon.

☐ And there were the attacks on Westmoreland and his attorney Dan Burt's motives and backing by the conservative Capital Legal Foundation. "Westmoreland is not paying the fees; the case is being subsidized by a lot of conservative right-wing money," says Scanlon. "We did some quick research and found out who's subsidizing Westmoreland. Dan Burt came right out and said this was a shot at bringing down an arrogant news network." A December 1984 *Village Voice* article of Bob Brewin, "Behind the Burt-Bashing," effectively points out all the flaws in

Scanlon's characterization of Burt.

One of Scanlon's last PR moves was to beat Henderson to the press after CBS and Westmoreland reached a settlement in the case. Both sides had agreed to make a joint announcement of the settlement on Monday, February 18, 1985. But the day before, Scanlon, in an "ungentlemanly" fashion, says Henderson, issued his own press release, announcing that Westmoreland had dropped the case. That gave CBS an important first crack at establishing the public perception of the settlement. Thus, the next day's headlines read "Westy Will Drop Suit," not that CBS and Westmoreland settled. Then, in the days that followed, CBS disavowed its intentions in settling. "They made a mockery of it," says a slightly peeved Henderson.

Scanlon's move created the impression that Westmoreland had lost his case. As important, it also set the tone for press coverage of the settlement. The press focused on why Westmoreland settled, and what he had achieved. Scanlon had successfully drawn attention away from the question of why CBS settled. And it's a good question, too. CBS had spent millions to defend its reputation, and the case was only days away from going to the jury for the final verdict. If CBS was indeed confident of victory, what did it gain by settling?

First, it eliminated the possibility that CBS could lose the case by either a guilty verdict or a hung jury—which would reasonably demonstrate that CBS had not proven its case. Even though seven or eight of the twelve jurors were "leaning" toward CBS, the case was far from a shoo-in for the network. "I could have rationalized it either way," said Richard Benveniste, the jury foreman. "I have a hunch he might have come away with more than he settled for," said Myron Gold, another juror. And one juror, Michael Sussman, seemed convinced that CBS had acted with "reckless disregard for the truth."[8]

Too, CBS News was probably losing a lot of sleep over the verdict just weeks before in *Ariel Sharon* v. *Time Inc.* In that libel litigation, the jury found *Time* guilty of falsehood and defamation in its reports about Sharon's role in the 1982 massacre of Palestinian refugees, but not guilty of actual malice, the third necessary ingredient for winning such a suit. In its verdict, the jury also took it upon itself to mention that it thought certain *Time* employees had acted "negligently and carelessly in reporting and verifying,"[9] hardly the kind of criticism that builds public confidence in a magazine—or television news division. CBS News, without a doubt, wanted none of that.

Who won the PR war in the end? Both sides won and lost. Westmoreland and Henderson waged a successful campaign to discredit the fairness and accuracy of the CBS documentary. CBS's own investigation—the only definitive judgment on the matter—seems to support Westmoreland.

CBS never did conclusively prove Westmoreland guilty of a conspiracy, so in a sense, score another one for the general. However, in the public mind—the thing that CBS News was most concerned about for its long-term interests—the perception must be that Westmoreland "dropped the case" because he thought he would lose, even though the public must also have a bad taste in its mouth for all the tricky television documentary production techniques revealed in the press and during the trial.

Suffice it to say, CBS's credibility may have suffered some, but it was not completely blown out of the water.

Credibility and trust were also at issue in another news organization crisis, that of the *Wall Street Journal* and its reporter R. Foster Winans, who allegedly tipped off certain stock traders to stories that were to run in the "Heard on the Street" column, thus allowing those traders to profit from advance information that would affect the price of stocks when it became public.

In this case, the *Wall Street Journal* carried out its own PR. And why not? After all, it has total control over the largest, most respected newspaper in the country, a PR man's dream. Coverage of the story in the *Journal* also provided a direct communications avenue to the target public the paper most wanted to influence—the *Journal*'s 2 million paying readers. So who needed the middle man, and who would suspect the *Journal* of doing PR itself?

The *Journal* had an unusual hammerlock on the information. As a subject of the Securities and Exchange Commission investigation, the *Journal* was privy to information about that investigation that no other news organization was. The *Journal* also had employment records and other inside—usually confidential—information about Winans all to itself. Capping off its control of the news even more effectively than the Pentagon did with the Grenada invasion, the *Journal* urged its reporters not to talk to the press.[10] With so much control of the information, the *Journal*'s own articles about itself became a major source for other news organizations covering the story.

Careful analysis of the *Journal*'s coverage reveals a number of PR techniques aimed at protecting the newspaper's image. First, the *Journal* had the PR sense to "break" its own story about itself on March 29, 1984 (almost a full month after it first learned of the SEC investigation). While the press generally credited the *Journal* with coming clean, the *Journal* really had no choice; the move prevented the creation of a huge, embarrassing negative impression. If another news organization had broken the story first, the *Journal* would have appeared to have been hiding something. The *Journal*'s story appeared on page three, rather than on page one, where the gravity of the story really warranted placement.

On April 2, 1984, the *Journal* did put on page one what many have called a candid, complete presentation of its internal investigation by a dozen *Journal* reporters and editors. But examined with a PR eye, the *Journal*'s coverage, one soon realizes, did not point the finger of guilt at itself. The story put heavy focus of wrongdoing, distrust, betrayal—you name it—on Winans; it did not concentrate on what mistakes the *Journal* may have made to make the scandal possible.

David Shaw, news media critic for the *Los Angeles Times,* agreed that the *Journal* was trying to excuse itself by attaching all the blame to the reporter. Shaw said the editors should have been more watchful of what such a young, relatively low-salary reporter was doing on a column the *Journal* knows is its most sensitive and the most likely to move stock prices.[11] Other business reporters who held the *Journal* in high esteem were likewise buzzing about such a glaring supervisory failure by *Journal* management.

Nevertheless, the *Journal* portrayed its coverage as washing its own dirty linen in public. This linen washing is, however, better described as a journalistic rubout—of Winans. Parts of the story descended to guilt-by-gossip, probing into Winans' personal affairs and casting doubt on his professional integrity both at the *Journal* and before.

The *Journal,* on the other hand, was portrayed as the trusting victim of betrayal. For example, according to the *Journal* story, after the newspaper learned that the SEC had begun an informal investigation of insider trading related to several Winans columns, after the *Journal* "temporarily" stopped assigning Winans to market-sensitive stories, and after the *Journal* launched its own investigation into the allegations, Winans informed managing editor Norman Pearlstine that he was considering a job offer from another publication. "We encouraged him to stay. His performance, from all we could tell at that point, was good and getting better," said Pearlstine (in the *Journal* account), sounding almost as if he were not the aggressive, politically savvy journalist that colleagues know him as, or the cosmopolitan, cerebral, hands-on editor the *New Republic* admired in a profile of the *Journal* just before the scandal broke.

The *Journal* also made sure to point to its "stringent policies designed to protect against ethical abuses," and made it clear that it would get to the bottom of this story no matter what the consequences, no matter how embarrassing. The newspaper also agreed to cooperate fully with the SEC investigation, even going so far as to comply with subpoenas for reporters' notes,[12] an interesting relaxation of the journalist war cry that the secrecy and security of such information is protected by the First Amendment. Such, however, is the price of public relations.

"In an attempt to limit and repair the damage [to the *Journal*'s main asset, its credibility] . . . we can only do what we know how to do best: explore and expose," said a *Journal* editorial. "This is precisely the action we have often recommended to others caught in embarrassing episodes."

However, when journalists dispense this kind of advice for others, they are usually talking about an independent, outside investigation by a special prosecutor, a grand jury, or the press. The *Journal,* however, used its own people, thank you, and some of those people were even reporters and editors connected with the "Heard on the Street" column itself. Pearlstine counters that he also used reporters and editors who had no vested interest in the column. The *Journal* investigation "will not satisfy those who think only an outsider can investigate the *Journal*," admitted Pearlstine, "but I hope we looked professional."[13] A special investigative team of journalists from outside news organizations would have looked just a bit more professional, and a lot less PR-oriented.

As for Winans' possible motives, outsider *Time* magazine suggested it might trace back to—the *Journal*'s policies: "'Heard on the Street' writers are strongly encouraged to dig up scoops, according to one former reporter at the paper. As a result, a column writer could be tempted to swap information with a news source in exchange for fresh tips. 'Out of a galaxy of motives,' said the ex-staffer, 'it is conceivable that there is but one element: simple pressure to get a story.'"

While these crises are serious enough, nothing upsets a corporate-management team more than the ultimate crisis: losing one's job, five-to-seven-figure salary, power and perks to a corporate raider. While the business press concentrates on the personalities, conflicts, and maneuvering of the management and the raiders in a takeover battle, the crisis PR duel usually goes unreported.

But crisis PR is now an integral part of every corporate takeover attempt. PR played such a big part in Mobil Corporation's 1982 attempt to take over Marathon that not even the *Wall Street Journal* could ignore it. That newspaper credited Marathon's win primarily to its extensive public relations. "The takeover struggle was fought principally in the courts, but . . . a careful reading of the judicial opinions in the court cases, combined with discussions with court officials, clearly indicates that Marathon's public relations campaign strongly influenced the court proceedings," wrote the *Journal*. The *Journal*, however, which focused primarily on the financial, personality, and management maneuvering of the battle, had few details about how the PR actually accomplished this feat. Completely missing was any mention of the PR engineer for Marathon behind it all, Hill & Knowlton's Richard Cheney, widely regarded in PR circles as one of the best public relations experts in corporate takeovers.

Cheney, a well-groomed, smooth, immodest man, says he doesn't care that the *Journal* didn't mention him—with his reputation, he doesn't need the publicity. He makes no secret of his feelings about the Mobil/Marathon PR war: "It was the best, most spectacular in recent times."

From the start, Cheney wanted the PR defense to concentrate on how Mobil would be buying existing oil reserves (Marathon's) rather than spending the money to explore for the new oil America so desperately needed. Marathon chief executive officer Harold Hoopman, however, was strongly opposed to raising public issues in the battle, so he needed some PR finessing himself. The public relations people for Ohio senator Howard Metzenbaum and the chamber of commerce of Findley, Ohio—Marathon's hometown—set up a public rally to show that the town and employees were supporting Marathon. Cheney escorted Hoopman to the rally where the Findley High School band began to play, baton twirlers strutted down Main Street, and the crowd began to sing, "I'm in love with Marathon." Cheney watched Hoopman intently until he noticed that the CEO was beginning to get fired up. Then "I asked him to review his decision on a public-issue statement and he warmed up to the idea with surprising alacrity," says Cheney. Hoopman addressed the crowd. Luckily seventeen television crews "just happened to be in town," says Cheney with a smile.

Hoopman lit into Mobil with the attack Cheney supported: "Everybody in the United States who suffered through the energy crisis has got to ask this administration and Congress whether this kind of acquisition is going to increase the nation's oil reserves by a single barrel. How much oil might Mobil find with the five billion dollars they're offering for Marathon? If they'd taken the money they spent for Marcor [another Mobil acquisition] and used it in their oil exploration program, they might have found enough reserves on their own that they wouldn't need ours now."

Cheney's people grabbed a videotape of that angry statement and zapped it to some 200 television stations throughout the country via satellite. A transcript of the same statement was wired to "every editorial writer in the country," says Cheney.

Meanwhile, H&K researchers were reading all of Mobil's issues advertising and pulling out items that would hoist the acquisitor by its own petard. Apparent contradictions between Mobil's stated philosophies and those being implied by the Marathon takeover were pointed out in Marathon's own issues advertising. Marathon's lawyers used the same material in court. "In the end, the Sixth Circuit Court in Cincinnati [upheld] a lower-court injunction against Mobil [acknowledging] that if Mobil acquired Marathon, 'it may reduce Mobil's incentive to explore and find its own new domestic reserves,'" the *Wall Street Journal* reported.

Much of Cheney's takeover work involves digging up dirt on the enemy company, then making sure the dirt finds its way to an eager-to-scandalize press. As Richard Phalon, author of *The Takeover Barons of Wall Street,* puts it, "The search is always on for what Hitchcock called the 'McGuffin'—a pivot on which the plot can turn; a concept simple and easy to dramatize."[14] Thus when General Cable attempted to take over smaller Microdot Corporation in 1975, Cheney's investigators dug up the fact that Irving Trust Company, Microdot's personal banker who presumably had intimate knowledge about the company's affairs, had agreed to be lead bank in financing General Cable's buyout offer, an apparent conflict of interest that Irving denied. "Jack Egan was at the *Washington Post* at the time, and we gave him all the details, and he wrote a very tough story in the *Post*," says Cheney.

To build one PR maneuver on top of another, Cheney sent copies of Egan's article to all the banks in General Cable's financing group and to the Senate Banking Committee, which was conducting oversight hearings and was sparked to grill Irving on the matter. In the end, Microdot went to white knight Northwest Industries. Ironically, just six years earlier, Cheney had attacked that company—and won—when it attempted to take over B. F. Goodrich.

"That was a real knockdown fight," says Cheney of his battle with Carl Byoir & Associates, which was representing Northwest. After analyzing the situation, Cheney found a good angle to pursue. Northwest Industries' chairman Ben W. Heineman, he felt, was taking over Goodrich because his earnings were falling and looked as if they were going even lower. That was good, informed speculation, but what business writer would jump on a story like that? Don't forget, this was the late sixties, before business journalism became exciting, interesting. Cheney knew exactly where to go.

"I called [*Forbes* magazine editor] Jim Michaels and told him what I had," recalls Cheney. "He sent someone out to Akron [Goodrich's hometown], and did a devastating piece on Heineman." The *Forbes* story compared Heineman to Napoleon at Waterloo (complete with a big photo of Napoleon himself to drive home the point) and spent two pages talking about how Northwest botched the takeover, which had been hatched "perhaps out of a desperation born of despair over Northwest's declining earnings."[15]

"We use good tips from any source," says Michaels. "But of course, when the tip is from an interested party, you have to independently verify it."

Cheney then ran the *Forbes* story as an ad, pointing to the credible third-party endorser and saying, "Here's what *Forbes* says about Northwest." Cheney and Goodrich, as we know, prevailed.

As one can see, a crisis PR anti-takeover defense can achieve its goal by questioning the motives of the acquirer or discrediting the management or ethical record of the acquiring company. With intensive investigation, says Cheney, "We've found we can do some devastating leaks if the facts are there." The effect of all this is to cast strong doubt in the minds of several very narrow, very important target publics: a court or judge, bankers financing the deal, legislators who might hurt the acquirer with regulations, and—often the most important of all—the stockholders who will vote for or against a takeover.

Sometimes the PR assault can deal with what might happen if the takeover is successful. Cheney loves the story about the Western Pacific railroad's attempt to take over Houghton Mifflin and savors retelling it over lunch at the Pinnacle Club in New York.

"Hal Miller, the CEO of Houghton Mifflin, said the authors were all upset about the takeover. I asked him if they'd say so, and he said, 'Sure.' So I suggested he tell them to send letters to Mickey Newman, CEO of Western Pacific." Authors like Arthur Schlesinger and John Kenneth Galbraith did just what Cheney suggested; Cheney, in turn, sent carbon copies of the letters to Robert Lenzner of the *Boston Globe,* Houghton's hometown paper. Lenzner did a story. Cheney then sent the *Globe* article to Herb Mitgang of the *New York Times,* who was a leader of the Authors' League battle against conglomerate takeovers of publishers.

Mitgang called Newman, who retorted to the protest letters, "That's got all the spontaneity of a demonstration in Red Square."

Mitgang then took that statement to Miller, who responded, "Does he think I can manipulate J. K. Galbraith and Arthur Schlesinger?"

Consequently, the authors sent another wave of letters to Newman and the Western Pacific board of directors saying that if Houghton were taken over, they'd walk. In the end, it was the board that walked away from Newman and the takeover.

The authors had also said that if Newman thought they could be manipulated by Miller, that showed he didn't understand the first thing about the publishing business. Of course, Newman was on the right track. Cheney and Miller may not have manipulated Schlesinger's and Galbraith's opinions, but they certainly had more than a little to do with subtly pulling the kind of strings that would get the authors to arms and would create news.

Often the outcome of a takeover attempt will be determined by the simple economics of the deal itself, says Cheney, but "there are a lot of instances where the kill can be made only through public relations overkill." One example Cheney admires is McGraw-Hill's successful battle to ward off takeover by American Express in 1978. Kekst & Company, widely regarded as a close number two to H&K in the takeover PR field, handled the McGraw-Hill defense. The PR firm's head, Gershon Kekst, who coyly claims PR has no influence and claims to not even understand what "placing a story" means, worked with lawyers, investment bankers, and the surprisingly feisty Harold McGraw to develop the publisher's PR defense.

"PR's job is to furnish reporters with as much information as possible," says Kekst. So, as part of McGraw-Hill's defense strategy, Kekst "furnished" the Washington press with information that was aimed at bringing an important issue to Congress' attention (Kekst knows that stories in the *Washington Post* get seen by congressmen and spark their interest in a subject): Amex was behaving very much like a bank holding company, yet it was not subject to the same regulations that U.S. banks are. That potential threat of regulation shook up Amex (though one of American Express' PR people, Fred Rosen, claims it didn't have any effect on Amex' backing away from McGraw-Hill).

McGraw-Hill's defense, with McGraw the front man appearing in press conferences and sending letters to shareholders, stock analysts, and the press, also centered on the need for publishers to be independent of control by nonpublishing conglomerates.

Kekst also made much of an alleged "conflict of interest" of Roger Morley, who was president of Amex and a director of McGraw-Hill.

In the end, Amex withdrew. "Very often a company does not want a lot of controversy in a takeover, and I have to believe the senior people at Amex were not looking for it either," says Kekst.

Crisis PR has no influence?

ten

The Ultimate Trip

POLITICAL PR

WASHINGTON NATIONAL AIRPORT, GATE 9, JULY 25, 1983. Peter Dykstra is putting the finishing touches on a planned media "event."

Camera crews from Independent Network News, Metromedia, ABC News affiliate WJLA-TV, WRC-TV and CBS News, and print and radio reporters are ready to record the arrival of Chris Cook, the president of Greenpeace, who had been detained by Soviet authorities for the past five days.

"If you don't mind," says Dykstra quietly to Catherine Ripley, Cook's girl friend, "I'm going to point you out to the press, because you will be a feature."

Ripley explains to an observer, "I've been told I should kiss Chris in front of the cameras."

Over near the maple-paneled wall where the Ikegami 730 and RCA portable TV cameras are pointed, Dykstra regards the American Airlines travel posters for Chicago and London. "Can we get a Moscow poster to tape up here?" he asks an airline supervisor.

As the cameramen check their light meters and test their Omni spotlights, Dykstra checks his blue backpack for The Beatles' white album (containing the song "Back in the U.S.S.R.") and the 750-ml bottle of Stolichnaya vodka. These will be presented to Cook.

Near the arrival area are more props—a half-dozen Green-peace members with WELCOME placards.

At 4:10 P.M., Cook's plane rolls up to the gate and cameras are dismounted from their tripods to capture the plane's arrival. People start streaming out the gate, among them former secretary of state Alexander Haig, but no one has an event planned for his arrival, so the media spotlight does not follow him.

Finally, Cook emerges; Ripley moves in and throws her arms around her beau. One of the cameramen cheers, "That's what we want!"

The Stolichnaya and the *White Album* are presented; the news conference runs maybe fifteen minutes. Dykstra fills reporters in on background. The event makes the evening news.

A similar news event took place at Cook's stopover in Chicago, but neither it nor the Washington one compares to the main PR event which began seven days before: members of the environmentalist-activist organization deliberately violated Soviet borders on the Bering Sea knowing they would likely be arrested—albeit temporarily—creating news. The media had been alerted beforehand, and a telegram had been sent to then-Soviet president Yuri Andropov, telling him Greenpeace was coming. Greenpeace's "story" to the U.S. press was that it was attempting to obtain photographs of illegal Soviet whaling operations. But the real objective was to get caught by the Soviets so as to create a "news event" sufficiently significant that the media would cover it and, in the process, carry Greenpeace's message that the Soviets were killing whales. The event was timed to coincide with an international whaling conference in Japan.

"Risking" capture by the Soviets demonstrated for the media how dedicated the Greenpeacers were, but in fact they knew there was little risk of harm. "We consulted all available experts," says Dykstra. "If there had been any strong indication our people would actually have spent any time in the harsh conditions of the prototypical Siberian labor camp, we'd never have taken that kind of chance." (This, of course, was well before the Soviet Union shot down a Korean Airlines 747 airliner with 269 civilian passengers on board.)

The PR stunt worked, and the media carried the story worldwide. The payoff: "Obviously, if the public supports what we did in the Soviet Union, they will support us [with funding]," says Dykstra.

Welcome to the world of political PR, the most sophisticated form of the business which so smoothly mixes together "real events" and PR special-interest manipulation that the very thin, wavy line separating real news and PR news becomes a gray blur. Political PR has advanced so far that there is often no way the public can distinguish between fact and opinion, news and PR.

"What the hell is public relations?" asks New York political consultant David Garth. "Is it the guy in front of the theater with the tickets in his hat, saying: 'Come in and see the show,' or is it President Kennedy sitting down with Ted Sorenson, saying: 'I'm going to say, "*Ich bin ein Berliner.*" I think that'll work.'?

"Anything done in politics that's worthwhile is done on its merits, but there is also a PR aspect to the way it's done. And the PR game in politics really has a tremendous effect on legislation, getting additional money for, say, New York City, or getting a bond issue passed."

No one knows exactly how many PR people there are working for the federal government, but estimates run to 13,000 people,[1] with an annual bill to the taxpayer as high as $2.5 billion.[2]

The Pentagon alone has more than 1,000 people defined as being in "public affairs" and spends more than $100 million a year in that area. The White House has "well over 100" PR people, says Dave Gergen. The relatively calm Department of Agriculture has more than 650.[3] The U.S. Information Agency alone employs almost 8,000 people on a budget of almost $800 million.

Every congressman has his own PR staff, of course, and every political group—like Greenpeace, the Wilderness Society, Planned Parenthood, or the Environmental Action Foundation—has PR people on staff. Even Pentagon whistleblowers have their own PR people: the Project for Military Procurement. "We act as PR people for alternative points of view on Pentagon spending," says Donna Martin, a project associate. The Project for Military Procurement was behind the 1983 controversy over the Pentagon's paying wildly high prices for spare parts; the project received an anonymous memo on the subject from an inside source in September 1982 and "leaked" it to fifteen or sixteen major news organizations.

Nor is Washington the only center for political PR. State capitals, large cities, anywhere there are politicians or political issues, PR people usually congregate. "There are times in the [New York] City Hall rotunda when there are so many [political] PR men managing so many press conferences that the television news crews resemble passport photographers as the media manipulators elbow their anxious clients in front of the cameras," explained *New York* magazine in a 1979 article on local PR people.[4]

Some 5,000 social welfare organizations, public affairs groups, labor unions and associations, chambers of commerce, and religious organizations throughout the U.S. also carry out PR activities for the groups they represent. This does not include thousands more trade associations that are primarily engaged in business PR, not political PR.

Political PR (often overlapping and blurring the term "politics") is at least as old as the Republic itself and probably older, according to PR historians. For example, Edward L. Bernays points to the Boston Tea Party as the equivalent of today's media event that was "staged to dramatize American resistance to British authority."[5] Scott Cutlip and Allen Center, authors of the textbook *Effective Public Relations,* say President Andrew Jackson's political opponents created myths about "Davy Crockett in an effort to woo the frontier vote away from Old Hickory. Crockett's press agent was Matthew St. Clair Clarke."*[6]

For the public, the problem with political PR is that it is often intertwined with real events or with events that appear to have a significance of their own. Here is a realm of PR in which ideas, programs, policies, laws, and the politicians themselves are the products to be sold. And because of the credibility of threatened congressional or legislative action; of U.S. warships in Central America; of leaks, speeches, and trial balloons; and even of Greenpeacers being detained in the Soviet Union, these very "events" become part of the third-party endorsement of the product being sold.

PR helps "package" a political product for sale, often in subtle ways. When former New York governor Hugh Carey went to

*Another American legend, say Cutlip and Center, was Daniel Boone—"the creation of a landowner promoting settlement in Kentucky."

Washington in 1976 to get federal loan guarantees for a near-bankrupt New York City, he brought union and business leaders with him to show that the state and city were united in getting themselves out of trouble. "That was terrific PR," says Garth. "He wasn't just a governor with a city in trouble that wanted a handout; he went down as a group of the brightest leaders working on a problem but needing some help."

Likewise, a governor or other politician's tour of a flood area or disaster site serves a PR function. If the politician does not participate in this news cliché, it could generate negative publicity that implies the politician doesn't care. But more importantly, the extra publicity sets the stage for state or federal assistance for the affected area. Explains Garth: "Politicians don't have to lobby each other in private conversation. If they need assistance, they ask for it. But you might be asked to create a public climate of need to get support for congressional funding. A disaster no one knows about will have a difficult time getting aid." Even floods and tornados need their own PR representatives.

Examples of political PR disguised as real news abound.

☐ During the 1984 presidential campaign, President Reagan's own chief PR man, Michael Deaver, "admitted" in a press interview that Reagan sometimes naps during cabinet meetings. The press loved it, since it raised the "age issue" against Reagan. But the "age issue" never did develop into a big campaign problem, despite Deaver's remarks. Why not? Because Deaver's comment was apparently designed to defuse the issue by having the White House raise it before the Mondale campaign could. Having thus gotten Reagan's age into the open, the White House was then able to dismiss it, in part with Secretary of Defense Caspar Weinberger's comment that he too would like to doze during long, boring cabinet meetings.

☐ In January 1985, the *New York Times* ran a series of articles that accused the city's chief medical examiner, Dr. Elliot Gross, of producing a series of misleading or inaccurate autopsy reports on people who died while in police custody. Almost immediately after the series ran, the *New York Post* ran a front-page story trumpeting WHAT THE TIMES DIDN'T PRINT about Gross. The *Post* charged that the *Times* story was weak, unfair, and contradictory and that the story's primary sources were enemies of Gross.[7] The *Post* also hinted that the *Times* story was a PR campaign against the chief medical examiner by Michael Baden, Gross's predecessor who was ousted by New York mayor Koch in 1979. "Baden openly boasted he had so much clout with the *Times* he could get any story he wanted published," said the *Post,* quoting the widow of another former—and "legendary"— New York medical examiner, Dr. Milton Halpern.[8]

What the *Post* didn't print, however, was the fact that Gross's PR man, Howard Rubenstein, who had given the newspaper the story, was also the *Post*'s PR man.[9] According to the *Daily News, Post* executive editor Roger Wood would not comment on Gross's connections with the *Post.* [In April 1985, a mayoral investigatory body found that Gross had not been guilty of any wrongdoing.]

In the early eighties, stories about the business potential of outer space began appearing in the press. *Fortune* and *BusinessWeek* were two to cover the "news." Those stories were initiated by NASA, says David Garrett, the agency's public affairs officer, to help generate commercial customers for the space shuttle. Similarly, NASA placed stories in *Ebony* and *Jet* in 1983 "to get the black community interested in science and technology," says Garrett.

NASA, like the Pentagon, is always looking for the PR angle to justify its budget. Flybys of the space shuttle over Boston, New York, and Washington and the shuttle's visit to the Paris Air Show in spring 1983 are only the most overt publicity stunts to build public excitement and support. NASA also sends a "space mobile," films, and exhibits to schools around the country for educational—and PR—purposes aimed at the voters of tomorrow. NASA newsletters, detailing recent discoveries and successes, are sent to science teachers in 35,000 U.S. schools. The agency's protocol division handles influential guests (like opinion leaders in Congress, the Office of Management and Budget, and aerospace companies) at space launches and now at shuttle landings. "We invite people who can get support for the agency," admits Garrett. Most recently the influential people brought in to be influenced by the PR included Wall Street brokers and others from the financial community who will help invest in the commercialization of space.

One of the most spectacular political PR news stories, however, was one that a major news organization hyped for its own ratings. In early 1984, CBS News's *60 Minutes* and the short-lived *American Parade* aired interviews with former president Richard Nixon. CBS played to the last row: "You have never seen him less guarded, more direct, or more outspoken," said a CBS News advertisement. "I have never known a president to speak for the record as unguardedly as Nixon has," said *60 Minutes* executive producer Don Hewitt.[10]

The disturbing thing about this whole affair—aside from the fact that CBS News bought U.S broadcast rights to the interview for $500,000*—is that it was a clear political PR production. Nixon's interviewer was Frank Gannon, a friend of the former president who had done PR with Ron Ziegler for a time in the Nixon White House. The press made almost nothing of this matter. Gannon claimed the Nixon interview was the first of many celebrity interviews to come from Gannon's production company, Historic Video Productions. "For the first [interview] of what [Gannon] hopes will be a long series, with Cary Grant and Indira Gandhi as possible future subjects, he turned to his old boss," reported *People* magazine. Gannon admits Historic Video Productions' series of celebrity interviews has never materialized, and he is now occupied with being editor of *Saturday Review*. Nixon's New York office would not discuss the matter.

Gannon says the interview was his own idea, but that one of Nixon's motives was undoubtedly to boost his own image and put Watergate to rest once and for all. The effectiveness of the PR is frighteningly evident in the press that followed the event. AFTER DECADE, NIXON IS GAINING FAVOR, headlined the *New York Times* in August 1984, the ten-year anniversary of his resignation; "Richard Nixon is back," said a *USA Today* story around the same time; "[The CBS broadcast] will probably enhance Nixon's re-emergence," said *Newsweek*.[12]

Only *Parade* magazine put the whole affair into proper perspective. It quoted the August 1974 wonderings of George

---

*The money was paid to Historic Video Productions, Gannon's company, based thousands of miles away from his Greenwich Village home in—of all places—Curaçao. Amazingly, the press had no questions about that either.[11]

Frampton, one of the lawyers on Leon Jaworski's Watergate special prosecuting force. Said Frampton then: "I wonder if ten years from now history will endorse the notion that Mr. Nixon has 'suffered enough.' . . . The prospect of Mr. Nixon publishing his memoirs . . . should remind us that, unlike his aides who are convicted of crime, Mr. Nixon will have the 'last say' about his own role in Watergate if he is not prosecuted."[13]

Parade went on to quote a March 14, 1984, *Washington Post* account of a Nixon appearance: "The cream of America's business and industrial establishment welcomed Richard Nixon back into the fold. A sellout crowd of 1,600 at the Economic Club of New York . . . gave him three standing ovations. . . . Nobody mentioned Watergate."[14]

Despite great performances like that, however, in the world of political PR, the White House is generally regarded as the crème de la crème. No president has had a more sophisticated PR operation than Ronald Reagan's. And perhaps as no President before him, Reagan has depended heavily on professional public relations advice.

Former White House deputy chief of staff Michael Deaver is a public relations man and former partner in Haneford and Deaver, a California PR firm. Deaver, who left the White House for the real money of private sector PR after Reagan's re-election (though he continues to maintain close contact with the White House), is largely responsible for making Reagan the president he is. "Much of the success we've enjoyed in the first term is directly attributable to him," said President Reagan upon the January 1985 announcement of Deaver's spring departure.[15]

Other former Reagan White House operatives responsible for the smashing first-term success are also PR people. Former White House director of communications David Gergen did PR for the Nixon and Ford administrations; after leaving the administration, aide Lyn Nofziger formed Nofziger & Bragg Communications, an affiliate of Carl Byoir & Associates that brags about its "effective liaison with the executive branch."

Robert Gray, of Washington's Gray & Company, which handled PR work in the President's 1980 campaign, has extensive connections among White House staffers and regularly offers PR advice on his own and at the request of the White House.

White House people also have a nationwide network of PR contacts with whom they regularly consult. And when Ed Meese was chief of staff, he established two PR consulting groups which met regularly at the White House to discuss domestic and international affairs—groups made up of some of the nation's top PR minds, including AT&T PR man Jack Gertz and representatives of Burson-Marsteller and Hill & Knowlton. The groups meet every three months for dinner, with former Nixon communications director Herbert Klein and Ron Ziegler both also in attendance.

The PR apparatus set up by the White House is astounding. The Office of Communications is divided into three sections: the public affairs office deals with research and briefings to the President; the media relations office makes sure the out-of-Washington press is well taken care of; and the press office, headed by spokesman Larry Speakes, deals with the Washington press corps.

A fifteen-person speech unit does nothing but work on White House speeches. The advance office is responsible for setting up sites the President is to visit—right down to the TV camera angles that will be used—and even making sure that presidential motorcades arrive at a time when they won't affect rush-hour traffic, as was the case when Reagan visited New York to attend the Alfred E. Smith Memorial Dinner in 1984.[16] Yet another section produces videotaped addresses by the President to be used at hundreds of local gatherings around the country that do not warrant a personal appearance.

Most interesting is the office of public liaison, created during the Nixon administration. "That office brings in outside groups to get their support and to brief them," says Gergen. It is also an important communications link outward. "Mostly conservative groups come in, get a briefing, then go out and spread the word—proselytizing," explains Gergen. Key groups include those dealing with minorities, women, small business, Central America, and the antiabortion movement. "They need to be plugged in," says Gergen.

Across the Potomac, in McLean, Virginia, the polling firm Decision/Making/Information keeps a constant monitor on public opinion for the White House. Headed by pollster Richard Wirthlin, DMI can detect sudden shifts in the public view of what the White House says or does, or of what the White House wants to say or do. Wirthlin meets in person monthly with President Reagan; the opinion research information, however, flows in continuously.

During Reagan's re-election campaign, DMI conducted 250 computer-assisted telephone interviews per night, starting in summer 1984. Conducted from five interviewing centers—located in Detroit; Houston; Provo, Utah; Santa Ana, California; and McLean—from 5:30 P.M. to 12:30 A.M., the national opinion tracking survey was tallied, organized, analyzed, and in the White House by 6:00 the same morning. The pace of polling increased to 500 interviews a night in October, then to 1,000 every night for the crucial last two weeks leading up to Election Day.[17]

According to *Advertising Age,* the Reagan pollsters also conducted more than fifty focus groups in fifteen key states to develop strategy; extensive, in-depth interviews to discover the most effective imagery to use for TV commercials ("Leadership that's working"); and market-and viewer-response testing of commercials. "During the Reagan-Mondale debates, the Reagan-Bush research team used the TRACE copy-testing equipment/methodology of Market Facts to monitor, second by second, audience reaction to statements made by the candidates," reported *Advertising Age.* "One of the biggest negatives registered was Mr. Mondale's negative reaction to the President's comments about making a theoretical missile defense system available to the U.S.S.R. in return for some sort of disarmament agreement."[18]

Finally, the GOP's "Voices for Victory" program put Republican spokesmen in the 208 U.S. areas of dominant influence (ADIs, a marketing segmentation of the country used in advertising) to monitor local media coverage of the campaign, report nightly to Reagan-Bush '84 headquarters, and then issue "rapid response" press statements as needed.[19]

The latest wrinkle in the White House PR has to do with something that Reagan's—and other presidents'—public relations people have known for a long time now: the out-of-town press will give the President a much fairer deal in coverage and is much more respectful and awe-filled than is the Washington press corps. In the past, Presidents have gotten out-of-town coverage unadulterated by the Washington press "filter" by bringing in groups of newspaper editors for Oval Office chats with the President and by actually traveling around the country on publicity tours.

In January 1985, the Reagan White House took this one step further. It launched the White House News Service, a computer-based wire service that transmits White House press releases, official statements, and texts of speeches directly to newsrooms around the country via the ITT Dialcom network.[20] Thus, small newspapers that cannot afford a White House correspondent of their own and would otherwise have to depend on the Washington media can quickly get the same official material that the White House press corps gets in its unadulterated PR state.

The day after the White House News Service was announced, the Reagan administration announced a similar system for local television stations that would allow satellite interviews with President Reagan and high government officials.[21] There is already such a system in place for overseas broadcasters, available through USIA's WorldNet system. Reagan also has radio covered with his weekly address on that medium on Saturdays; according to a Cornell University study, conducted by Professor Joe Foote, the *Washington Post* covered 94 percent of the speeches, the *New York Times* 85 percent, CBS 71 percent, and NBC 60 percent.

What is the impact of this massive PR machinery? By gaining an intimate understanding of how the press works and thinks, its flaws and assets, its effect on the people and how the public absorbs the news, White House PR has been able to gain an almost unbelievable degree of control over the flow of information to the public. By so doing, obviously, it is able to control the public's perception of the administration, as demonstrated by its deft handling of the Grenada invasion.

There are numerous other examples of the effectiveness of this PR.

☐ Just before the spring 1983 international economic summit in Williamsburg, Virginia, Hedrick Smith, the *New York Times* chief Washington correspondent, was invited to lunch by Deaver. Several days later the *Times* ran a page-one story about Reagan's intense preparation. The real purpose of the article for Deaver, though, was that it set the tone for the ensuing television news coverage of the event; TV news portrayed Reagan as hard-working and firmly in charge.[22]

□ President Reagan's zero-zero option speech, in which he proposed a way for the Soviet Union and the U.S. to reduce nuclear weapons, was broadcast live in the U.S. in the afternoon, an unusual time. Actually, the speech was directed at another target public—Europe, where it was broadcast live via satellite in the Continent's prime time. As a result, some 200 million people in several countries crucial to U.S. arms policy saw a reasonable President Reagan willing to negotiate with the Russians to reduce, not just limit the growth of, nuclear arms.

□ After a Wirthlin poll showed Americans two-to-one opposed to the administration's federal cutbacks for education, White House PR blanketed the nation with speeches talking about merit pay for teachers, decreased class size and other inspirational messages about education. Wirthlin polls that followed showed public opinion had turned two-to-one in favor of the Reagan policies.[23]

Clearly the White House is exploiting the media's often flawed way of doing business. For example, the White House indulges its yen for television news coverage by embedding plenty of visual imagery in its events. When television news is courted with exactly what it wants—plenty of drama, pictures and excitement, and a minimum of complicated details that eat up a lot of air time—the White House can count on TV coverage for events it wants to publicize.

"We construct events and craft photos that are designed for thirty seconds to a minute so that it can fit into that 'bite' on the evening news," defends Deaver. "We'd be crazy if we didn't think in those terms."[24]

Similarly, PR-placed news by leaks, backgrounders, and "high administration sources" gives print journalists the cachet of being privy to the inside workings of Washington. This, obviously, plays well to the readers.

Thus, the real success of the Reagan PR operation is that it has figured out how to involve the media as a knowing partner in the business of building favorable public opinion for the President—criticism and bias in reporting notwithstanding. "The

White House press served with unusual frequency during Reagan's first two years as a kind of *Pravda* of the Potomac, a conduit for White House utterances and official image-mongering intended to sell Reaganomics," says C. T. Hanson, of the *Columbia Journalism Review.*[25] Meanwhile, White House PR people profess to being quite happy about the President's press coverage—and they seem credible indeed.

Observes former Carter press secretary Jody Powell, "There are a lot of people going to school on this administration, and one of the lessons is that the press's bark is much worse than its bite. They'll huff and puff around, but in the end you can cut severely into the flow of information and manage it with a much firmer hand than we were able or willing to."[26]

But while the Reagan White House is by far the most advanced in PR, it is by no means the first to try to control the media.

Joseph C. Spear's book, *Presidents and the Press,* points out that "Franklin D. Roosevelt used the press as no President before him had." Roosevelt was the first to introduce "background" sessions with members of the press, and he banned direct quotation of his remarks by reporters covering him, unless he authorized use of the quote.[27]

Gergen, who much admires Dwight Eisenhower's PR man, James C. Hagerty, says, "Jim Hagerty actually told the networks which clips they could use" from the President's press conferences, which in those days were filmed, not broadcast live.

John F. Kennedy, of course, was as great a communicator as Ronald Reagan is. He was the first to recognize the drama of press conferences broadcast live and knew that his talent in sparring with the press made him look good.

Jimmy Carter had his television fireside chats (pirated from FDR's radio version of the same thing), town meetings, and highly publicized overnight visits to the homes of just-plain-folks. All of it helped create Carter's image as a populist President of the people.

And in 1978, according to a recent Harvard University study, the Carter administration approved a covert PR program "asking U.S. sympathizers and agents in the European press corps to give more favorable press coverage to the [neutron] bomb, either for money or for free." The report says that former secretary of state Cyrus Vance and national security adviser Zbigniew Brzezinski approved the program; Leslie Gelb, then director of the State Department's bureau of politico-military affairs (and now national security correspondent for the *New York Times*), was a leading advocate.[28]

Even Gerald Ford played the image game, at a time when control of the media was not as big an issue with the White House press corps as it is now. "When Gerald Ford was sworn in, he realized he had to act immediately to reassure the nation that he was not another Nixon," writes Spear. "He informed the Marine band that played at presidential functions to eschew 'Hail to the Chief' . . . Television crews were invited into the presidential kitchen to film Ford as he toasted his own breakfast muffin. Members of the President's staff and cabinet were asked to suggest the names of individuals with whom Ford could conduct well-publicized telephone chats. This public relations gimmick was formally known as the 'presidential telephone call recommendation program.'"[29]

Spear maintains that it was the Nixon administration that "brought PR out of the closet [and] put the seal of approval on television and imagery as political tools."[30] It is true that Nixon was responsible for installing much of the PR machinery now in place. Yet the Nixon White House was run primarily by advertising people, not PR people. Approaching PR from a Madison Avenue frame of mind, where the message is bought and paid for, and therefore controlled outright, they thus wielded the equipment awkwardly.

The Nixon people thought they could buy favorable news coverage the way you buy a thirty-second commercial slot on *All in the Family*. Says Ron Ziegler, now president of the Truck Stop Operators of America, "There were excessive attempts [by various White House officers] to overprogram stories."

Ziegler maintains the Nixon administration did almost nothing to mold a favorable Nixon image. He tells an interesting—and somewhat sad—story about his President and his lack of even the most rudimentary PR sense. "Photojournalists were demanding, 'Please let us get a photo of the President on the beach,'" remembers Ziegler. "I finally convinced the President that he should approve—and get that right—I convinced him that he should approve a photo of him walking on the beach. It wasn't to show him as a charismatic surf-walking figure; he knew he wasn't that. It was to please the press.

"So we got the press and set them up and he comes walking down the beach—wearing his black shoes! Is that PR? No. I know for a fact that he basically rebelled against presenting himself as anything but what he was. And he just didn't walk on the beach in public."

Gergen, who served in both the Nixon and Reagan administrations, believes that good political PR would have helped Nixon. "Had Nixon's people been more open early on, the whole form and outcome of Watergate might have been different. Nixon would have benefited from a more open public relations policy."

Suggests Sydney Morrell, of Jeffcoat, Schoen, & Morrell PR, "If President Nixon had just told the people involved to step aside while they were being investigated, with the understanding that they would be fired if wrongdoing was uncovered, the whole thing never would have happened the way it did."

But Ziegler cautions against using PR to project qualities a President simply cannot deliver. "A false image will always be found out. One reason President Carter lost his bid for re-election is that the American public realized that the image he was projecting was contrary to what apparently they felt he was. The President who probably presented the most honest image of himself is President Nixon. He shook his jowls. He was humorous in private but never tried to fake it publicly. He was what he was—even when he walked on the beach in shoes."

Ziegler, who describes himself as a PR person even though his background is with the J. Walter Thompson advertising agency, still apparently does not understand that PR does not create false images; it emphasizes—sometimes out of true proportion—positive, true images. PR uses the flaws of the press to help emphasize those images.

And good political PR gets attention focused away from the negative true aspects of an issue onto the positive, equally true aspects of an issue that the PR is better able to deal with. Their failure to understand this is evidence again that, while the Nixon team toyed with many of the modern tools of White House PR, it took the real PR people of Ford, Carter, and Reagan to properly implement and perfect them.

The press preoccupation with White House PR—complaining about it rather than doing something to counter it—creates the impression that Ronald Reagan is the only one pulling PR strings in politics. That, of course, is not true. The White House has some worthy PR opponents out there.

For example, former secretary of the interior James Watt was literally driven from office by a vigorous PR offensive by environmental activist groups led by the Wilderness Society. That Washington-based group put together a thick, two-volume loose-leaf compilation of hundreds of news clips detailing the environmental sins of Watt's regime. The general public never saw this sophisticated, highly organized PR tool called *The Watt Book*; it was circulated only to members of the press and Congress and to other opinion leaders as an "information source," says Gordon Roberts, director of the Wilderness Society's PR.

The Wilderness Society PR depended in large part on sympathetic Interior Department insiders who leaked reports and information about Watt. This information was analyzed by Wilderness experts who then disseminated a package of information with the interest group's own spin on it to the press. Wilderness sends press releases to some 1,200 newspapers with circulations above 25,000 and has developed a good rapport with usually sympathetic environmental writers on the nation's leading newspapers. Since the Interior Department wasn't releasing this information, Wilderness had the "first-strike" benefit throughout much of its PR campaign, and the steady stream of criticism kept the "Watt Is Evil" story alive in the media. The effect on the public, of course, was to create the impression that everywhere one looked Watt was raping the environment.

The cozy relationship worked for Wilderness in the opinion section of the newspaper too. Between February and April 1983, some 300 to 400 editorials on wilderness issues appeared throughout the country, "largely due to our work," says Roberts. Eighty percent of those editorials sided with Wilderness. "Based on those editorials, I'd say we are dealing with a friendly media, or, as Secretary Watt says, the media is a tool subject to our manipulation," Roberts adds caustically.

The Wilderness Society's influence goes back once again to

the way the media operate. The Wilderness Society has brand recognition, so it is one of the first environmental groups journalists turn to when they need help covering or interpreting an environmental story. Too, says Roberts, Wilderness does the legwork for the media: "Many of these papers do not have the people in Washington to unearth this information. The *San Francisco Chronicle* only has one reporter here to cover six different beats."

As is typical in these kinds of issues, there is no absolute right and wrong. There are valid environmentalist arguments and there are valid Interior Department arguments. Each tries to present its side as the truth. "I don't think we indulge in hyperbole," says Roberts, adding, however, that "Secretary Watt *is* the Darth Vader of the environment."

The eventual environmentalist victory seems to be partly the result of an imbalance of PR. Wilderness admits it ran an "intense" anti-Watt PR campaign from the time Watt took over. And the campaign ran right down to the grass roots. "The best way to influence a member of Congress or the Executive branch is through what they hear going on in the districts and states," says Roberts.

The Interior Department, on the other hand, did not do much PR for itself, says Doug Baldwin, Watt's PR man. The extent of the work Watt wanted to do overhauling the entire Interior Department infrastructure necessitated, for the first year and a half of his term, a "policy decision not to engage in public affairs, but to work on organizing the department," says Baldwin. "The other side had a field day, because they had no opposition from us. There was no counterweight."

The opinionated, outspoken Watt himself aided the environmentalists' cause by saying something damning for the media to run with, seemingly every chance he could get. Finally, in April 1983, Baldwin launched his own PR offensive, getting Interior Department people to give speeches to local groups outside Washington and having Watt travel around the country to appear on "uneditable" talk shows. Learning this, anti-Watt factions in the Interior Department leaked a memo concerning the PR defense to Wilderness, which spread the word in the media. WATT OPENS PR BLITZ TO DEFEND HIS RECORD,[31] is how the *Los Angeles Times* played the story.

But talk to Dave Gergen, and one wonders if the White House PR did not in fact know exactly what it was doing with Watt all along. "This administration wanted to change the status quo," says Gergen. "On occasion, Jim would say, 'Maybe I went too far and said too much.' Watt knew, 'Someday you'll have to let me go.'"

Controversial Watt was there to deflect attention away from President Reagan's part in Interior Department policies. "As controversial as Watt was, it was better to have Watt out there talking than the President," Gergen told the *Village Voice*. "Watt became the lightning rod, and he knew that when he came in. It was a conscious policy in terms of shaping the news."[32]

Another hot political PR war—this one still being fought—involves the abortion issue. It is tailor-made for PR and also demonstrates clearly the danger of PR's muddling an issue. For despite all the complicated arguments, abortion is really an issue whose crucial "fact" has not yet been conclusively established: is the unborn human fetus a human being? If society decides that it is a human life, then, antiabortionists argue, its life and rights should be protected as with all other humans. If society decides that it is not a human life, then, proabortionists contend, its life and rights need not be protected.

Viewed in that context, it is apparent that the aim of PR on both sides will be to sway public opinion into "believing"—more correctly, "deciding"—the human fetus either is or is not human.

In one corner, PR for the antiabortionists is primarily headed by the National Right to Life Committee. In the other corner, the proabortionists' PR has been primarily headed by Planned Parenthood. Note carefully that neither of those organizations has the word "abortion" in its title.

Right-to-Lifers have been at a PR disadvantage for years now. "When you compare us to Planned Parenthood, you are comparing apples to apples as far as the two main PR forces," says Dan Donehey, the National Right to Life Committee's director of public relations, "but in terms of resources to fund our respective PR, you're comparing apples to oranges."

There are several reasons antiabortionists have been out-PRed. Being a confederation of some 2,000 organizations in 50 states, each grass-roots NRLC group has done its own PR. That ragtag nature disperses the kind of cumulative effect a single, concerted, efficient PR program—like Planned Parenthood's—can have in gaining support.

That also means the media, in covering the issue with the grass-roots image well entrenched, has chosen various spokesmen—like the Reverend Jerry Falwell—for the movement, rather than allowing the NRLC to choose one. Consequently, says Donehey, the lack of a single good voice discouraged public opinion from solidifying around NRLC, and a lot of fringe extremists that the public has trouble relating to or sympathizing with have been out representing the cause.

That the NRLC has hewn to the real issue of this debate—is a human fetus a human life?—shows how unsophisticated they are about PR. Proving that human fetuses are human beings has been a mighty tough job, since science cannot confirm a collective social opinion or moral belief. (Can one conclude scientifically that capital punishment is morally correct or incorrect?)

Finally, Right-to-Lifers have chosen the worst possible group to represent in a PR war, since there are no members of the oppressed group to get publicity with a march on Washington, nor has it been easy until recently to get network television cameras into the womb to show the terrible living conditions of an abortion in progress.

The proabortionists have been successful by moving the debate off the central issue. After dismissing the human question as something that can never be proven, proabortionists have muddled the debate with these often emotional issues:

□ *Women's rights:* women have the right to do what they want with their bodies.
□ *Sexism:* men, who have never experienced the pain of childbirth, should not mandate that women go through it.
□ *Freedom of religion:* the Catholic Church should not impose its own moral vision on everyone.
□ *Quality of life:* antiabortion laws should not prevent people from choosing *not* to bring a deformed, retarded, or otherwise imperfect child—including those of the "wrong" sex—into this world because those children would not experience the quality of life normal people enjoy.

- *Poor vs. rich:* if there are laws against abortion, poor people will not be able to get an abortion, but the rich will.
- *Public health needs:* despite the law, people will find back-alley butchers to provide unsafe illegal abortions if they really need one.
- *Unenforceability of the law:* if people really want an abortion they will find someone to perform one.
- *Rape and incest:* all women should not be barred from having abortions because some unwanted pregnancies are the result of rape and incest.
- *Medical need:* some abortions are necessary because the mother's life is in danger from pregnancy or childbirth.
- *Family planning:* people should have abortion as an option, because they either do not want an unplanned child or they cannot afford one.
- *Freedom of choice:* antiabortionists are not forced by law to have abortions; therefore, proabortionists should not be barred from having abortions.

This last issue—"pro-choice"—is the proabortionists' fallback position, now that the tide of public opinion is flowing in favor of the antiabortionists. According to a January 1985 *Newsweek* poll, 58 percent of the public favors a ban on abortions, except in the case of rape or incest or if the mother's life is in danger.

The pro-choice stance was established by PR back in 1979, says Kent McKamy, of McKamy & Partners Public Relations. At that time, McKamy says, the proabortion movement shifted the primary PR front organization from the National Abortion Rights League to Planned Parenthood. The idea was to push the word "abortion"—which antiabortionists were successfully starting to associate with the word "murder"—into the background of debate.

McKamy says the aim of his PR work was "to espouse the idea that choice was the central issue of the debate. We wanted to stress that with fence sitters, and get people not to defend their position with an untenable theme—abortion is a right—but rather that abortion is a matter of choice.

"It's easy to say the whole issue is 'abortion is murder,' but that is an inflammatory issue that puts the argument on an emotional level. Good PR says, 'Let's step back from the emotions and look at the issue: abortion is a matter of choice.'"

What McKamy is really saying there is that good PR moves the debate to where it can be more easily fought. "That's basic. If you've got an opponent who is gaining currency, the first thing you do is change the battlefield," he says.

The pro-choice argument had been around proabortionist circles for years, but it was not a big public issue. "If you asked someone on the street before 1979 which group supports pro-choice, they'd probably have said, 'Pepsi,'" says McKamy. "We were hired to give the idea legs."

To spread the pro-choice idea, McKamy says he talked with some 500 newspaper editors and 200–300 television producers to get them talking about the issue and to do stories on it. To dramatize the abstract thought of freedom of choice and to raise the specter of a "threatened right," McKamy talked about all the underprivileged people who would no longer be able to have an abortion if the right were taken away, about the low quality of life that would be suffered by those born deformed,* and about those victims of rape and incest.

McKamy also wanted to marshal significant numbers of authoritative opinion leaders in medicine, law, education, and religion, "as many people not attached to the movement as possible to support it," he says. This so-called ally program centered on direct mailings. It also involved getting favorable editorials in the handful of about forty-five members of the media that influence the rest of the media—"gatekeeper publications and broadcasters" like the *New York Times*, the *Los Angeles Times*, the *Washington Post*, the *Chicago Tribune, Harpers, Atlantic*, the *Nation*, the *New Republic, CBS Morning News* and *Today*.

Regular polling at three-month intervals during McKamy's one-year campaign for Planned Parenthood was another effective tool. "That can be a very powerful weapon," he says. "You can show the tides of belief, and that persuades fence sitters."

But McKamy seems to think the antiabortionists have been

---

*Some antiabortionists also see abortion-on-demand as a first step toward infanticide; euthanasia; and elimination of the retarded, deformed, and handicapped from society, an opposing attempt to divert attention from the central issue.

very effective with their "highly emotional campaign, including pictures of dead fetuses, dead fetuses in jars, and now this new film they have, *The Silent Scream*. It's all very emotional stuff."

Indeed the tide does seem to have turned in favor of antiabortionists. The NRLC's Donehey attributes it to several factors, most relating to better PR. Science, medicine, and technology, of course, are coming up with more and better evidence about when life begins and have been pushing the earliest time frame in which a premature fetus can survive outside the womb back to before the last trimester of pregnancy.

But much media attention is also now being focused on a single spokesman, Dr. Bernard Nathanson, an atheist and a former proabortionist who performed 60,000 abortions at his New York clinic, and who has turned antiabortion.

Nathanson's film, *The Silent Scream,* which uses ultrasound videography to show a fetus being torn apart in an actual abortion, has gotten wide media coverage. "We are running hard and fast with that latest weapon," says Donehey. But the NRLC PR man adds that one reason the film is so effective is that it is a dramatic, visual argument that plays well for television.

Perhaps one of the most potent weapons, however, is President Reagan. Right-to-Lifers are benefiting from some of the most sophisticated political PR advice available, which comes to them from the White House office of public liaison mentioned earlier in this chapter. President Reagan himself brings up the abortion issue in speeches at every chance. Reagan's involvement has legitimized abortion as a "human rights issue, despite the fact that ABC, CBS, and NBC say it's a religious argument," says Donehey.

Political PR is a potent force. To continue to be a truly informed electorate, the American public must understand how it works and demand that the media work harder to counteract its deleterious effects on political debate.

While political PR is the ultimate trip, the United States is not the final battlefield. That lies between the United States and the Soviet Union, and the PR battle lines are already drawn.

Next, first report from the front.

eleven

The Commoditization of Thought

PR AND THE EVIL EMPIRE

WASHINGTON, SEPTEMBER 1983. We are in the midst of a secret war between the U.S. and the Soviet Union. This is not a test:

The Soviet Sukhoi-15 fighter pilot's voice crackles over the radio in Russian. "I see [the target], visually and on radar."

The Americans, hunched over their equipment, listen intently to more of the conversation.

"The air navigation lights are burning. The strobe light is flashing.

"I'm dropping back. Now I will try a rocket.

"I am closing on the target.

"I have executed the launch.

"The target is destroyed."

Korean Airlines flight 007 goes down, with 269 people aboard. Al Snyder, sitting in his war room in Washington, is now responsible for the U.S. counterattack on the Russians.

He will not be using a sword; his weapon will be the pen—or, more correctly, audio and video equipment located at the United States Information Agency's Washington headquarters on C Street. Snyder, director of USIA's television and film service, is a commander in the intensifying U.S./Soviet PR War. Snyder and his people are working day and night this Labor Day weekend on a top-secret key offensive—a ten-minute videotaped presentation of the Soviet radio transmissions documenting the fact that the Russians deliberately, coldly, and ruthlessly shot down an unarmed civilian aircraft.

By Monday, Snyder's people will have obtained an audiotape of the radio transmissions from Japanese intelligence listening posts on the edges of the Sea of Japan; they will have had State Department and USIA linguists carefully listen to the poor-quality tape and translate it; they will have had Defense Intelligence Agency and Central Intelligence Agency experts confirm times, locations, and flight paths of the aircraft involved, including the KC-135 U.S. reconnaissance plane the Russians claimed they mistook KAL 007 for; they will have located a special video character generator for the Russian Cyrillic alphabet to add authenticity to the visual translation of the Russian voices; and they will have gotten permission from the United Nations to place TV monitors in the Security Council chambers, shrewdly waiting until the Soviet duty officer was replaced at his post there Saturday so that a friendlier officer would allow placement of the monitors right behind the seat Soviet Ambassador Oleg Troyanovsky would occupy on Monday—providing a perfect photo opportunity for the media, a Reagan administration trademark.

The PR assault scored a direct hit. U.S. Ambassador Jeane Kirkpatrick delivered a speech excoriating the Soviet action before the U.N. Monday, then played the videotape. The tape, which greatly dramatized the KAL 007 terrorism for the TV generation, got extensive play on the network news programs. It was later played again in part by President Reagan in a television address to the nation. But perhaps the best shot was the picture that appeared on the wire services, on television, and on the September 19, 1983, cover of *Time*: the photo of Troyanovsky icily staring into the distance and ignoring the damning video screen over his shoulder. "A memorable image of Soviet stonewalling," commented *Time,* which, like every other news organization, apparently didn't realize that the picture had been carefully staged by USIA.

Within hours, Tass, the Soviet news agency, was forced to admit the Soviet military had "stopped" the plane.

As quickly as PR has advanced since World War II, and, particularly in the past fifteen years, the evolution is not yet complete. Where is the manipulative outreach of public relations going?

No one can predict with absolute certainty the future course of a beast so flexible, an entity so ready to adapt to change. But we can identify two major trends in public relations that do not bode well for the free flow of public opinion.

The first of these trends is that the Soviet Union—long the awkward, tight-lipped communications hermit—is beginning to learn the tricks of the PR trade, and the KAL 007 incident appears to have been a turning point of sorts.

"[Knight Ridder national security correspondent James] McCartney ranks the Soviet Embassy lowest in press sophistication," said an October 1983 *Washington Journalism Review* article. "'The Russians are totally incompetent. I suppose they think they're sophisticated, but they're so inept that it's beyond belief.' If his phone calls are answered, he says, the person answering frequently declines to give his name. Responses to his queries sound like something read from *Pravda,* McCartney complains, or worse, the person dealing with a correspondent often seems not even to have read *Pravda.* 'They're not worth much for regular input and they don't do their homework,' says McCartney, who travels throughout the Soviet Union as part of his assignment."[1]

"They're incredibly clumsy when it comes to public relations," said Princeton University Sovietologist Stephen Cohen after the KAL 007 action.[2]

But around the same time, the view of the Russians by a political PR genius was somewhat more sensitive to subtle changes taking place. Said David Gergen, relaxing in his office as Christmas 1983 festivities resounded through other parts of the White House, "The Soviets have been very ham-handed in PR in some big areas. During the recent German elections, they had a real opportunity to make gains, but they were so heavy-handed that they lost votes. That was a PR disaster. But they are much faster to respond now than they used to be, and they're much more deft. Within hours they're right back at you, and their answers are more incisive, less bureaucratic."

Starting with KAL 007, the Russians seem to have blossomed into the PR-eighties:

□ The Soviet response to the incident was without precedent for that country. Shortly after the KAL blasphemy, Marshal Nikolai

V. Ogarkov held a live, televised satellite press conference with foreign reporters—complete with a huge map indicating flight paths. At that conference, Ogarkov introduced his PR defense that the Korean plane had been on a spy mission. That may sound like boilerplate Soviet rhetoric, but it accomplished what it was designed to do: move debate and news coverage away from the real issue—in true crisis PR fashion. Ogarkov's relative openness managed to lend more credence to this than that given most Soviet rhetoric. To this day, the issue of what that plane was doing over Soviet airspace is a matter of contention—even though the brutal murder of 269 unarmed civilians would seem to make that a moot point.*

□ During the KAL 007 crisis, Soviet television carried an interview with the actual pilot who had shot down the jetliner—who insisted he tried to warn the plane to land. That is hardly *Nightline*, but it is certainly the closest the Soviets ever came to an equivalent, given the greater regulation of Soviet news.

□ In October 1984, the Kremlin allowed *Washington Post* reporter Dusko Doder to conduct a rare interview with Soviet president Konstantin Chernenko. The *Post* publicized and played up the interview concept of the story, talking about "Our man in the Kremlin,"[3] and publishing a front-page picture—compliments of Tass—of Chernenko being "interviewed" by the American journalist. Likewise, the *Post* played down the fact that the "interview" consisted, in large part, of prepared written responses to written questions submitted earlier, and that the "oral interview" was really a "brief conversation"—in which Chernenko referred the reporter to the written Q&A at least four times. Someone in Moscow understood how the usual dearth of opportunities for Western press contact with the Kremlin could lead a newspaper to glorify what amounted to errand running by a U.S. reporter.

□ In February 1985, Soviet Foreign Minister Andrei A. Gromyko held a *Meet the Press*-style televised interview with four Soviet journalists to "discuss" the U.S./Soviet arms control talks.

□ In an October 1, 1984, article, the *New York Times* happily reported on "A First on Moscow Beat: News With a Human Face"

*"KAL 007: After a year's investigation, the *Nation* magazine believes that the official U.S. version is not credible," read a full-page ad in the *New York Times*, October 25, 1984.

about new-style press briefings by Vladimir B. Lomeiko, who is described as "a tall and pleasant-mannered man with glasses [who] stands ready not only to describe the latest Soviet position, but also to answer questions." Completely missing the fact that the Russians had embarked on a new PR image, the *Times* quickly and generously explained away the sudden change in Soviet demeanor as "the latest sign of a slow rise of a less defensive generation of Soviet officials."[4]

□ Moscow is even working on its own version of "Dear Abby." According to a report in the April 7, 1984, issue of *Editor & Publisher*:

Call it the "Ask Ivan" column.

The Soviet Union is offering to respond to the questions of American newspaper readers—and it is suggesting that it might offer the *Moscow News* as a forum where American journalists and government officials can respond to letters from Russian citizens. . . .

The Soviet responses . . . would be prepared by the Novosti Press Agency. The agency operates the *Moscow News,* an English-and-Russian-language daily that circulates in the U.S. and U.S.S.R.

"Just to take a case, someone might say, 'What is an election campaign in the Soviet Union and how does it compare with an election in the United States?'" [Yuri Popov] said in a telephone interview. . . .

Popov said "many newspapers are already interested" in the idea as a result of the mass mailing from the [Soviet] Embassy.[5]

□ The Soviet Union has been accelerating its efforts at spreading damaging "disinformation" about the U.S. to the foreign press, reported the *Wall Street Journal.* Just one of many examples of PR-style disinformation (though we stress again that the most sophisticated and effective PR generally deals in truths) is this one, which was initiated by the Soviets and appeared in India, Egypt, Pakistan, and the Philippines: when astronaut Neil Armstrong was on the moon, he heard the chanting of the word *azan,* which he later found to be the Muslim call to prayer. Consequently Armstrong converted to the Muslim faith, for which NASA supposedly fired him. (USIA arranged a teleconference between Armstrong and foreign journalists to combat the untrue story with the facts that Armstrong was never a Muslim and that he left NASA voluntarily in 1971 to teach and set up his own business.)[6] Obviously, this story was intended to get Muslims angry at the U.S. by building the image that the U.S. discriminates against members of the religion.

□ For a while, the Soviet government's Vladimir Posner was virtually a regular on the ABC News program *Nightline*. Posner, points out James Billington, director of the Woodrow Wilson International Center for Scholars, is "a fourth-echelon disinformation specialist . . . [who] was given equal billing with higher-level Americans."[7]

□ "Exclusive" video footage of Russian political prisoner Andrei Sakharov was "obtained" by ABC News—another video was later obtained by NBC News—which aired it with much hype as the first "proof" that Sakharov was not dead or dying, as rumored. The tapes were "leaked" by the Soviets to the U.S. media through Russian journalist Victor Louis, who is often used to pass information from East to West, according to *Newsweek*.[8]

□ The supposed murderers of Polish Reverend Jerzy Popieluszko were put on an unusual public trial in Warsaw. The U.S. press often covered it, and the final guilty verdict against the four police officer "defendants," as though the trial were being held in the U.S. rather than in a totalitarian Soviet-bloc country, where legal concepts like "rights," "innocent until proven guilty," and "fair trial" are literally foreign. The *New York Times* designated the trial "a landmark" but failed to recognize that it was really a landmark in Soviet-bloc attempts at PR. Warsaw attempted to manipulate its own citizens and world opinion by making it appear that the Polish government was not involved and would bring the "real" murderers to justice. Not until the third-from-last paragraph of its story on the verdict did the *Times* mention—in one sentence—"But as [the trial] ended, complaints were heard that the revelations about the crime itself, its motives and its circumstances, were incomplete."[9] The trial and the press coverage were incomplete, for example, in that they did not answer the question of whether the order for the execution of Popieluszko came from anyone higher in government than the four defendants, or, perhaps, from another, nearby country.

□ In late 1984, the Soviet Union seemed to open its doors wide to American television crews from NBC News, KCBS-TV in Los

Angeles, Metromedia's flagship station WNEW-TV in New York, PBS's *Inside Story*, and KOMO-TV Seattle. "Somebody in the Soviet bureaucracy may have said, 'This is a wonderful propaganda opportunity,' but I don't think they succeeded," says Paul Smirnoff, WNEW-TV news director.

"They wanted access to an American audience, and they were willing to take the risk," says Ron Bonn, NBC special segment producer. "The newer Russians coming into power—and particularly into PR areas—know about TV; they know about our effect." Both Smirnoff and Bonn deny the Russians actually scored a PR coup.

But Billington, in a *Washington Journalism Review* critique of NBC's *Today* and NBC *Nightly News* coverage, pointed out: "[NBC] had done better than before in covering . . . the U.S.-Soviet rivalry," but the American audience probably did not learn much about Soviet life from the program and may have even been somewhat misled at times. He concluded the program had been used somewhat by Soviet propagandists:

> NBC, for example, failed to focus on the continuing chasm that exists between the Russian people as a whole and the privileged party oligarchy. . . . Recurrent chitchat about the cars in Moscow never explained that cars are a recent perquisite of power there, that there are fewer cars in other cities and that roads everywhere are inadequate and spare parts almost nonexistent. NBC stressed the large number of women doctors but never made clear the relatively low quality of health care. The point was made that telephone calls cost very little but not that it is often nearly impossible to use the Soviet telephone system, and that there are no telephone books.[10]

□ And now Soviet leader Mikhail Gorbachev is acting like—and is being received by the United States press as—a charming media star; his wife has even been compared to former First Lady Jacqueline Kennedy.

At the same time that the Soviets are becoming better at PR and the Western media are joyously welcoming this new PR spirit with open arms, a second major trend is taking place within the U.S.

When the *Washington Post* or the *New York Times* breaks some legitimate exclusive story, it will often be picked up by the wire services, television, and other leading newspapers, thus validating the importance of the original story and making it into a big issue. A similar phenomenon is going on with PR news. The PR news network that works behind the legitimate U.S. journalism infrastructure is now beginning to respond with an odd synergism to its own hype, with PR from one source, such as government, validating the importance of the PR coming from another source, such as public advocacy groups or business.

For example, when leading environmentalist groups found they were treading water in their attempts to mobilize public opinion against the policies of former secretary of the interior James Watt—since the effects of such policies are often difficult to concretize for the public at large—they benefited greatly by stirring up public debate over a more emotional, more easily labeled issue: Watt's personality as revealed in his famous foot-in-the-mouth episodes. Politicians could not reasonably expect to defend Watt's record without seeming to defend his apparent bigotry, since environmental PR had managed to merge the two issues in the public mind. By the end of more than a year of PR-induced hysteria, even Republican congressmen were tripping over themselves to call for Watt's resignation. Environmental groups helped create the issue and sold it to a generally sympathetic press. The press lost no time describing the "hornets' nests" Watt had stirred up, then reported politicians' PR responses to the original PR controversy. This validated the incredible suggestion that a bureaucrat's public gaffes are single-handedly enough cause for his removal—even in the absence of true scandal or incompetence. (If that were cause, Washington would be a ghost town by now.)

Those dedicated to the elimination of nuclear weapons have generated a huge clip-book of publicity the last several years. But because the Soviet Union does not allow demonstrations against nuclear weapons in their country, nor does it bow to public opinion in the area of defense, the effect of the freeze movement has been to put pressure almost entirely on one side of the armament fence.

Capitalizing on that PR movement, the entertainment industry came out with the movie *WarGames*. As we saw in Chapter

6, part of that movie's PR campaign involved getting antinuclear politicians like Massachusetts congressman Ed Markey involved in PR for the movie. Obviously, Markey was using the movie to validate his own antinuke stand, too.

Then the news media got on the PR bandwagon, and, piggybacking on the movie PR, ABC News *Nightline* did a program on the movie and its premise. ABC got an interesting program, *WarGames* got publicity, and everybody was happy.

Next ABC's business side sniffed ratings and put some real publicity muscle behind *The Day After,* a made-for-TV movie about a nuclear attack on the U.S. This came in November 1983, as the U.S. began deploying new intermediate-range nuclear missiles in Western Europe and as demonstrators there protested violently against the U.S. move. While the network insisted it was performing a public service, ABC made sure it performed that service during the crucial "sweeps" week, when the sensationalist program graphically showing the horror of nuclear war could help boost ratings, which, in turn, boost ad rates. In the process, it validated the freeze movement PR.

The creators of the program admitted they wanted the program to scare the hell out of the public to spark debate about the arms race.[11] Obviously the program was not intended to scare people into demanding more horrible nuclear weaponry. "If this film could sober the world and slow the pace with which we seem determined to turn our planet into a nuclear porcupine, then I guess I'm signing up," said director Nicholas Meyer about his thoughts upon being asked to direct the film. "How often do you get the chance to put your work in the service of your beliefs?"[12]

Added one of the film's stars, Jason Robards, appearing in the film "beats signing petitions."[13] *Newsweek* actually devoted a cover story, inspired by ABC's mammoth PR campaign, says ABC PR man Tom Machin. "There's never been a movie like ABC's *The Day After,* nor any video event that has stirred so much ferment in so many quarters before it even arrives on the air waves," said *Newsweek,* as though it had never before been exposed to slick entertainment PR. *Newsweek* continued, "*The Day After* has already emerged as the single biggest mobilizing point for the antinuclear movement, roused thunder from nuclear-freeze opponents who regard the film as a two-hour commercial for disarmament and inspired a nationwide educational debate about how to talk to children about the horrors of nuclear war."[14]

One reason freeze opponents saw a two-hour commercial in *The Day After* is that antinuclear advocates were provided with supposedly bootlegged copies of the film in April 1983—a full seven months before the program was aired—allowing them to gear up their own publicity mechanisms which in turn helped promote the ABC program.[15]

ABC's PR also played up the angle "Should kids watch this horrifying show?" The network distributed 500,000 promotional vehicles called "viewing guides" to TV stations, schools, and libraries which were supposed to tell children how to carefully view the program.

The PR for *The Day After* was so good, even the Communications Elite at the White House had to sit up and take notice. The Reagan administration, after lengthy discussions about how to react to the film, launched a campaign to show that Reagan was pushing for arms control but that it is the Russians who are blocking such efforts.[16] Immediately after *The Day After* was broadcast, Secretary of State George Shultz agreed to be interviewed on ABC to drive home just that message.

The nuclear arms debate, major as it is, is only the start of the U.S.-Soviet PR war. Like the arms race, it can quickly and easily escalate into a situation where the U.S. believes it must fight Soviet propaganda with U.S. propaganda. Note: propaganda, not PR.

We see a frightening potential for the PR industry to evolve so completely that it crosses that line between PR—which generally deals in facts—and propaganda—which in large part deals with untruths. The merger of highly sophisticated modern PR and international propaganda could be disastrous. One can easily envision a scenario where the American government can rationalize the use of modern PR/propaganda for reasons of national security. In such a case, we would all lose, no matter how noble the surrounding causes may be.

Protection lies primarily in the hands of the press, which holds the key to public understanding of this issue and is always our first line of defense against exploitation.

Journalists must learn to carefully recognize, understand, and be wary of all forms of PR from the most "innocent" to the most sinister. Once understood, PR can be fought through a surprisingly simple principle—returning to the standards, ethics, and responsibilities of good journalism.

As witness the White House press corps, it is not enough to point to PR manipulation and wince about how hard it makes the journalist's job. Says NBC White House correspondent Andrea Mitchell, "Some of us have been very aggressively reporting the lack of access, the infrequency of news conferences, the degree of manipulation. Now if the public doesn't see that Ronald Reagan is doing these things, I don't think that Jody Powell or anyone can blame us."[17]

Fighting manipulation is not primarily the public's responsibility; it is the press's responsibility. If trained journalists, whose own hype is intended to create the image that the news you get is the best, most complete, most accurate, and savviest available, cannot figure out how to get around PR, how can the public be expected to get the "real story?"

PR is not an unbeatable beast. The trick in overcoming it is to see how it has become so powerful. As this book hopes to show, PR has gained strength by playing on the weaknesses of the press. If the press truly wants to combat PR as so many White House correspondents and others profess, the answer is to correct the flaws that PR is preying on.

1. Publications and broadcasters must strive for balance in straight-news stories and in advocacy stories. The media serve two basic functions: a) as a pipeline through which information is distributed; and b) as a force for pointing out the flaws in society and suggesting ways of righting them. In both cases, journalists must strive to give balanced, unbiased coverage to both sides of an issue. PR tricks the public by making the journalist an advocate for some special interest, knowing he will present this advocacy in the guise of trustworthy, unbiased, balanced journalism. The two kinds of journalism must not be confused.

2. Reporters should do their own legwork. Accepting handouts and allowing communications specialists to influence the news-gathering process taints the news with special concerns. PR people are meant to be used in a limited way as just one of many

information resources, not to be self-interested collaborators in the evolution of news. Reporters and editors must not take the easy way out of performing their job.

3. News that is not genuine should not be reported. There is no law that says there must be a story about the President or the White House every single day. If there is no news on the glamorous, high-profile White House beat one day or five days in a row, then reporters and editors should have the courage to say nothing significant happened.

4. News that consists mainly of staged performances should not even be covered. ABC News White House correspondent Sam Donaldson is fond of complaining that the White House press corps has to report whatever the Reagan administration dishes out to it.[18] If a photo opportunity is simply a staged media event to build the President's image, or if the White House forbids questioning the President, then the media should have the guts to not cover the nonnews event. The same goes for other staged news.

5. Newspeople must return to the time-honored tradition of digging, digging, digging for the facts. In today's PR-glutted media, every source has an ax to grind, a position to push. The facts as presented by any one source should not be considered as complete or accurate. Journalists should check accuracy before they rush into print or onto the airwaves.

6. Journalists must become savvier about the real and ulterior motives of a source, including a) what image he is trying to create, b) how he will benefit from this image; and c) whether the journalist is being manipulated. Once he or she understands those three things, it is the journalist's responsibility then to explain this appropriately in his or her reporting. If the reporter finds there is an ulterior motive, he should not simply report that fact as a disclaimer that merely interrupts the source's "story," he must strive to present the "real story." Thus the entire focus of the story may have to be changed—even if it means more work for the journalist.

7. The use of unnamed sources must be limited and ultimately reduced. As everyone both inside and outside of journalism should know by now, allowing sources to go unnamed often disguises the specific purpose or interest of the unscrutinized source. If reporters can't get the story playing by the rules, then

they should not do the story. Unnamed sources should be the choice of last resort.

8. The press should not report an incomplete story to meet a deadline. A major weapon in the PR person's arsenal is getting reporters to rush into print with only half a story—the PR person's half. In the interest of fairness to opposing viewpoints and in the interest of quality journalism, reporters should take a reasonable amount of time to carefully examine and analyze the particulars of the story. Better for a news organization to run fewer stories but know that each one is worthy of the public's confidence.

9. Journalists must recognize imbalances in communications ability and set the scales right. If one interest group is represented by Communications Elite from the likes of Burson-Marsteller or Gray & Company, and the other side is represented by several inarticulate, nonprofessional spokespeople, the reporter should go out of his way to put both sides on equal footing. If the PR representative of one side has all the facts at his fingertips and speaks in nicely polished quotes, while the representative of the other side mutters a few muddled platitudes, all that means is that the journalist must work harder to investigate the merits of each case independently. The best communicator is not necessarily presenting the best, truest story.

10. PR must not be allowed to set the press's agenda; the press must set its own agenda. The White House now actually generates and manufactures news to prevent the media from generating their own news, which, the White House PR people believe, will be invariably negative. PR people advise their clients to not be *re*active to the news, but *pro*-active; they must set the direction of news coverage. Journalists must take back the territory that is rightfully theirs.

11. Television and print reporting must give up their addiction to vacuousness. For years now, critics of journalism have been attacking the capsulated, shallow presentation of television news as well as the pop, flashy, entertainment-style shallowness of publications like *People* and *USA Today*. The reason is that this cheats the news. Cheating the news encourages PR people to lend a hand, presenting their "story" in bite-size chunks that sound digestible but have little substance.

Public relations, as a way of bringing an issue to public attention, is not by itself bad. The right to honest debate, and even to advocacy of causes, of course, is guaranteed by the First Amendment. But abuse of PR's sophisticated communications ability is a menace to the part of the First Amendment that mandates a free press. PR must be brought in line, and the only institution able to do that is its chief partner—the press itself.

Notes

1. The Communications Elite:
Public Relations' Rising New Influence and Power

1. James Feron, "Barbadian Leader Describes Disputes and Confusion in Arranging Invasion," *New York Times*, October 28, 1983.
2. Francis X. Clines, "A Reagan Press Official Resigns Over Grenada," *New York Times*, November 1, 1983.
3. Fay S. Joyce, "First Evacuees Arrive in U.S. From Grenada," *New York Times*, October 27, 1983.
4. Joanne Omang, "Americans in Grenada, Calling Home, Say They Were Safe Before Invasion," *Washington Post*, October 26, 1983.
5. Joyce, op. cit.
6. Philip Taubman, "U.S. Reports Evidence of Island Hostage Plan," *New York Times*, October 28, 1983.
7. "Auditing the IRS," *BusinessWeek*, April 16, 1984.
8. Alex S. Jones, "New No. 1 in Public Relations," *New York Times*, March 26, 1984.
9. Lee Iacocca with William Novak, *Iacocca, An Autobiography* (New York: Bantam, 1984), pp. 71–72.
10. Jones, op. cit.
11. "The Media in the Dock," *Newsweek*, October 22, 1984.

2. Imitation News:
The Press and PR, Part I

1. William A Henry III, "Journalism Under Fire," *Time*, December 12, 1983.

---

2. Francis X. Clines, "TV Spots Begin the Selling of the President," *New York Times,* May 18, 1984.
3. Phil McCombs, "A Frustrated Press Waits in Barbados," *Washington Post,* October 29, 1983.
4. Phillip Knightley, *The First Casualty. From the Crimea to Vietnam: The War Correspondent as Hero, Propagandist, and Myth Maker,* (New York and London: A Harvest Book, Harcourt Brace Jovanovich, 1975), p. 315.
5. Knightley, op. cit., pp. 272–274.
6. Knightley, op. cit., p. 333.
7. Rod Townley, "The Wars TV Doesn't Show You—And Why," *TV Guide,* August 18, 1984.
8. Bernard Weinraub, "U.S. Press Curbs: The Unanswered Questions," *New York Times,* October 29, 1983.

3. The Remote-Controlled Journalist:
The Press and PR, Part II

1. Walter V. Carty, "The New Era in Business-Financial Media Relations," *Critical Issues in Public Relations* (Englewood Cliffs, N.J.: Prentice Hall, 1975), p. 96.
2. Joanne Angela Ambrosio, "It's in the Journal. But This Is Reporting?" *Columbia Journalism Review,* March/April 1980.
3. Adam Osborne and John Dvorak, *Hypergrowth: The Rise and Fall of Osborne Computer Corporation,* (Berkeley, Calif.: Idthekkethan Publishing Company, 1984), p. 118.
4. Erik Larson, "Snags in Introducing New Computer Sidetrack Osborne's Stock Offering," *Wall Street Journal,* July 13, 1983.
5. Henry Post, "Useful, Using, Used: Roy Cohn and the New York Press," *Columbia Journalism Review,* May/June 1980.
6. "The Carefree Life in Fla.," *New York Daily News,* August 24, 1984.
7. "Homes Selling Like Hotcakes," *New York Post,* August 24, 1984.
8. Thomas Hartman, "Reporting For Service. The Big Guns of the Military Press," *Washington Journalism Review,* July/August 1984.
9. "Boom in the Business Press," *Newsweek,* January 7, 1985.
10. Carty, op. cit., p. 98.
11. "Judge Rules Publisher Acted As Investment Adviser," *Dow Jones News Service,* July 16, 1984.
12. James Deakin, *Straight Stuff. The Reporters, The White House and The Truth,* (New York: William Morrow and Co., 1984), pp. 102–103.
13. Jane Mayer, "Jackson's Media Skills Boost Candidacy During Dramatic Success in Diplomacy," *Wall Street Journal,* January 6, 1984.
14. Post, op. cit.
15. Jody Powell, *The Other Side of the Story* (New York: William Morrow and Co., 1984), p. 139.
16. Post, op. cit.

4. Dramamine Screamers:
How PR Works

1. David Hoffman, "How Reagan Controls His Coverage. At Home: The Candidate, Packaged and Protected," *Washington Journalism Review*, September 1984.
2. John Koten, marketing column, *Wall Street Journal*, March 8, 1984.
3. Edward L. Bernays, *Public Relations* (University of Oklahoma Press, 1952), p. 159.
4. Don Sherman, "The Classy Chassis," *Car & Driver*, March 1983.
5. Michael Kramer, "Dear Fritz," *New York*, October 8, 1984.
6. Alexander M. Haig, Jr., *Caveat* (New York: Macmillan, 1984), pp. 17–19.
7. Thomas Griffith, "Proving Lincoln Was Right," *Time*, October 22, 1984.
8. Michael J. Robinson and Maura E. Clancey, "King of the Hill. When It Comes to News, Congress Turns to the *Washington Post*," *Washington Journalism Review*, July/August 1983.

5. Who Are These Guys:
The People and Their Tools

1. *China Syndrome*, Columbia Pictures Industries Inc., 1978.
2. Stanley Penn, "Unwanted Publicity. Role of Ruder & Finn in Iran-Javits Contract Shows PR's Influence," *Wall Street Journal*, March 25, 1976.
3. John E. Cooney, "Vox Unpopular. Public-Relations Firms Draw Fire for Aiding Repressive Countries," *Wall Street Journal*, January 31, 1979.
4. Clayton Haswell (AP) "At 91, He's the Father of Hype," *Staten Island Sunday Advance*, November 27, 1983.
5. Mark Hertsgaard, "How Reagan Seduced Us. Inside the President's Propaganda Factory," *Village Voice*, September 18, 1984.

6. Lights, Camera, Hype!
Entertainment PR

1. Edward L. Bernays, *Public Relations* (University of Oklahoma Press, 1952), p. 39.
2. Joanmarie Kalter, "News That Isn't (Really)," *TV Guide*, September 22, 1984.
3. Ibid.
4. Kurt Anderson and Janice C. Simpson, "A Puerto Rican Pop Music Machine," *Time*, June 27, 1983.
5. Alan Thicke, "Why I Took the Country by Drizzle—Instead of by Storm," *TV Guide*, November 3, 1984.
6. Joseph Deitch, "Books as News," *Publishers Weekly*, October 14, 1983.
7. Ibid.
8. J. Tevere MacFadyen, "The Future: A Walt Disney Production," *Next*, July/August 1980.

7. PR in the Cabbage Patch:
Product PR

1. William M. Bulkeley, "Toy Warrior Robots Seen Uprooting Cabbage Patch Dolls' Record for Sales," *Wall Street Journal*, July 23, 1984.
2. Stuart Diamond, "Now, Pay Phones on Jetliners," *New York Times*, October 15, 1984.
3. "Anise and Cardamom Spice up These Fruit Desserts," *Orlando Sentinel*, September 6, 1984.

8. Raising the Stakes:
Business PR

1. Thomas J. Lueck, "Crisis Management at Carbide," *New York Times*, December 14, 1984.
2. James Sterngold, "ITT Inquiry on Liquidation Reports," *New York Times*, December 13, 1984.
3. UPI, "Phillips says Pickens' PR Blitz is Violation," *New York Post*, December 14, 1984.
4. Nicholas Pileggi, "That New Flack Magic," *New York*, September 3, 1979.
5. "Cigarette Etiquette," *New York Times*, May 1, 1984.
6. Document provided by and created by Walt Disney public relations department describing the functions of the department.

9. The Battle for Corporate Survival:
Crisis PR

1. Sharon Begley, Mary Hager, Linda Brenners-Stulberg, and John Carey, "Dioxin: How Great a Threat?" *Newsweek*, July 11, 1983.
2. Jeremy Main, "Dow vs. the Dioxin Monster," *Fortune*, May 30, 1983.
3. Ibid.
4. Ibid.
5. David Pauly, Richard Manning, and Hope Lampert, "Dow's Bad Chemistry," *Newsweek*, July 18, 1983.
6. Bill Abrams, "Fierce Public-Relations Fight Is Preceding Westmoreland's Court Battle With CBS," *Wall Street Journal*, May 13, 1984.
7. Bill Abrams, "CBS Inc. Attacks Book That Criticizes its Vietnam Program," *Wall Street Journal*, April 24, 1984.
8. Maureen Dowd, "Most of Westmoreland Jury Seemed to Favor CBS, but Doubts Remained," *New York Times*, February 20, 1985.
9. Peter McGrath and Nancy Stadtman, "Absence of Malice," *Newsweek*, February 4, 1985.
10. John Greenwald, Marcia Gauger, and Christopher Redman, "The Talk of the Money World," *Time*, April 16, 1984.
11. Jonathan Friendly, "Editor Tells of 'Nightmare' at Wall Street Journal," *New York Times*, May 11, 1984.
12. Harry Anderson and Nancy Stadtman, "The Journal Bares its Soul," *Newsweek*, April 16, 1984.
13. Friendly, op. cit.

14. Richard Phalon, *The Takeover Barons of Wall Street, Inside the Billion-Dollar Merger Game* (New York: G.P. Putnam's Sons, 1981), p. 193.
15. "The Last Great Battle?" *Forbes,* April 15, 1969.

10. The Ultimate Trip:
Political PR

1. Scott M. Cutlip and Allen H. Center, *Effective Public Relations,* revised 5th ed. (Englewood Cliffs, N.J.: Prentice-Hall, 1982), p. 509.
2. Stephen Hess, *The Government/Press Connection* (Washington, D.C.: The Brookings Institution), p. 3.
3. Cutlip and Center, op. cit., p. 511.
4. Nicholas Pileggi, "That New Flack Magic," *New York,* September 3, 1979.
5. Edward L. Bernays, *Public Relations* (University of Oklahoma Press, 1952), p. 33.
6. Cutlip and Center, op. cit., p. 70.
7. Guy Hawtin, Jeff Wells, and Ransdell Pierson, "What the Times Didn't Print," *New York Post,* February 1, 1985.
8. Guy Hawtin and Jeff Wells, "M.E. Widow Bares Baden's Close Links to Times," *New York Post,* February 7, 1985.
9. Don Singleton, "Anatomy of a News Story. The Big Guns Boom for Gross," *New York Daily News,* February 8, 1985.
10. David M. Alpern and John J. Lindsay, "Nixon in Prime Time," *Newsweek,* April 16, 1984.
11. Ibid.
12. Ibid.
13. Lloyd Shearer, "George Frampton's Prophecy," *Parade,* May 6, 1984.
14. Ibid.
15. Bernard Weinraub, "Deaver to Leave White House Post for Private Life," *New York Times,* January 4, 1985.
16. Niles Latham, "Reagan's 'Gift' to the City," *New York Post,* October 19, 1984.
17. Jack Honomichl, "Research Acts as Reagan's Eyes, Ears," *Advertising Age,* November 5, 1984.
18. Ibid.
19. Ibid.
20. AP, "White House Computer Line to Provide 'Unfiltered' News," *New York Times,* January 7, 1985.
21. Gerald M. Boyd, "White House Planning Direct Link to TV Stations," *New York Times,* January 8, 1985.
22. Rich Jaroslovsky, "Manipulating the Media is a Specialty for the White House's Michael Deaver," *Wall Street Journal,* January 5, 1984.
23. Ibid.
24. Thomas M. DeFrank, "Michael Deaver Rates the President's Press," *Washington Journalism Review,* April 1984.
25. Joseph C. Spear, *Presidents and the Press. The Nixon Legacy,* (Cambridge, Mass., London: The MIT Press, 1984), p. 27

26. Mark Hertsgaard, "How Reagan Seduced Us. Inside the President's Propaganda Factory," *Village Voice,* September 18, 1984.
27. Spear, op. cit., pp. 37–38.
28. Philip Taubman, "1978 U.S. Bid to Plant Press Articles Reported," *New York Times,* October 25, 1984.
29. Spear, op. cit., p. 276.
30. Spear, op. cit., p. 237.
31. Eleanor Randolph, "Watt Opens PR Blitz to Defend His Record," *Los Angeles Times,* May 1, 1983.
32. Hertsgaard, op. cit.

11. The Commoditization of Thought:
PR and the Evil Empire

1. James Buie et al., "Foreign Governments Are Playing our Press," *Washington Journalism Review,* October 1983.
2. Fay Willey, Robert B. Cullen and Steve Shabad, "The Stonewall," *Newsweek,* September 19, 1983.
3. Dusko Doder, "Our Man in the Kremlin. A Visit With Comrade Chernenko," *Washington Post National Weekly Edition,* October 29, 1984.
4. Seth Mydans, "A First on Moscow Beat: News With a Human Face," *New York Times,* October 1, 1984.
5. "Soviets Seek News Exchange," *Editor & Publisher,* April 7, 1984.
6. John J. Fialka, "Tales of Imagination in the Foreign Press Give U.S. Headaches," *Wall Street Journal,* December 15, 1983.
7. James H. Billington, "From Russia With NBC," *Washington Journalism Review,* November 1984.
8. "A KGB Home Movie," *Newsweek,* September 3, 1984.
9. Michael T. Kaufman, "The Verdict in Poland," *New York Times,* February 9, 1985.
10. Billington, op. cit.
11. Harry F. Waters et al., "TV's Nuclear Nightmare," *Newsweek,* November 21, 1983.
12. Nicholas Meyer, "'The Day After.' Bringing the Unwatchable to TV," *TV Guide,* November 19, 1983.
13. Ibid.
14. Waters, op. cit.
15. Ibid.
16. Robert S. Greenberger, "White House Moves to Counter Fallout of 'The Day After,'" *Wall Street Journal,* November 21, 1983.
17. Mark Hertsgaard, "How Reagan Seduced Us. Inside the President's Propaganda Factory," *Village Voice,* September 18, 1984.
18. Jane Mayer, "Reagan, in China, Focuses on TV," *Wall Street Journal,* April 27, 1984.

Index

229

Berger, Fred, 134
Bernays, Edward L., 68, 85–86, 101–102, 119–120, 190
Beutel, Bill, 102
B. F. Goodrich, attempted takeover of 183–184
Bhopal, India, gas leak disaster at, 91, 140, 168
Bishop, Maurice, 11, 12, 13, 19
Bogart, Judith, 85, 127
Bohning, Don, 17
Books. *See* Publishing industry
Borman, Frank, 159–160
Boston Globe, 78, 88, 185
Brennan, Robert, 36–37
Breseman, Al, 129–130
Brinkley, David, 63
Broderick, Matthew, 98, 100
Brosnahan, Timothy, 156, 157, 158
Brothers, Dr. Joyce, 120
Building industry, *ad hoc* public relations and, 144–145
Burch, Michael, U.S. invasion of Grenada and, 9–10, 16, 21, 25, 85
Burson, Harold, 31, 67, 83
Burson-Marsteller, 30, 31, 67, 84, 87, 155–156, 157, 195; corporate crises handled by, 168–170; Dramamine public relations and, 69–71; and impact of religion on business, 162
Burt, Dan, 30, 175, 176–177
Bush, George, 24, 196
Business magazines, growth of, 54; stock analysts and, 74–75
Business news, public relations and, 28, 54–59
Business public relations, 31–32, 140–163; categories of, 141–142; Congress and, 152–159; growth of, 141; interest groups and, 153. *See also Ad hoc* public relations; Crisis public relations; Image public relations
BusinessWeek, 54, 57, 75, 127, 172; advance publicity for, 135; articles on business potential of outer space, 192–193; product public relations and, 131; public relations sources and, 56–57

C

Cabbage Patch Kids, 115, 131, 141; product public relations for, 120–125
Callaghan, Jim, 73, 84; dioxin issue and, 165–166

Capital Legal Foundation, 176
Carl Byoir & Associates PR, 74, 84, 87, 135, 136, 144, 162–163, 194; corporate takeovers and, 183–184
Carson, Johnny, 111, 120
Carter administration, 40, 63, 64, 65, 128, 199; use of public relations by, 199–201
Casey, William, 106–107
Catto, Henry, 32
CBS, 30, 40, 79; Oberlin College public relations and, 133; Reagan's speeches and, 197
CBS Evening News, 28, 62, 79, 110
CBS Morning News, 23, 70, 116, 124, 127
CBS News, 193; product public relations and, 135; and Westmoreland, 173–178
Celebrities: FCC decisions and, 157–158; media "events" for, 187–189; new products and, 94, 95; public relations for, 103, 111, 115; video press releases and, 102
Censorship, U.S. invasion of Grenada and, 24, 38–39
Charles, Eugenia, 13, 15, 24
Cheney, Richard, 31, 163; corporate takeovers and, 181–185
Chicago Tribune, 53, 70, 176
China Syndrome, The, 81, 84
Claritas corporation, 93
Clines, Francis X., 34–35
Cohn, Roy, Hamilton Jordan cocaine case and, 64–65
Coleco. *See* Cabbage Patch Kids
Columbia Journalism Review, 199; critique of *Wall Street Journal* news sources, 48–49; on Hamilton Jordan cocaine case, 63–65
Commercials. *See* Advertising
Committee for Prudent Deregulation, 155–158
Communications Elite, 9–11; invasion of Grenada and, 11–25; members of, 11; role of, 31–32
Compton, John, 21, 23; U.S. invasion of Grenada and, 12–14
Computers: PR Newswire and, 89; use in football, product public relations as news on, 126–127
Concorde supersonic jet, opposition to landing at U.S. airports, 146
Congress: business public relations and, 146, 152–159; FCC decisions and, 157, 158; medium for reaching, 79; public relations staffs of, 189
Congressional hearings, public relations

Newspapers (*cont.*)
    musical groups and, 109; public
    relations stories in, 29–30;
    publishing public relations and,
    112; Reagan administration public
    relations and, 197; Wilderness
    Society's public relations and,
    202–203. *See also* Military trade
    press; Press; Press and public
    relations; Trade press; *and under*
    specific newspaper names
Newsweek, 29–30, 31, 38, 54, 79, 88, 110,
    114; abortion issue and, 206, 208; on
    Day After, 217–218; on dioxin issue,
    166; entertainment public relations
    and, 103, 104; FCC case and, 156; on
    Nixon interviews, 193; product
    public relations and, 132, 135;
    publishing public relations and, 113
Nicaragua, public relations news on, 51
Nightline, 51, 62, 107, 135, 214, 217
Nixon, Richard, 26, 193–195
Nixon administration: office of public
    liaison, 195; political public
    relations and, 66, 200–201
North American Air Defense Command
    (NORAD), 97–100
Norton, Jan, 70

O

Oberlin College, public relations for,
    133–134
Office of War Information, 108
Ogilvy & Mather Public Relations, 89, 161
Oil Industry: Mobil's attempted takeover
    of Marathon and, 181–183; public
    relations and news and, 58–59
Okun, Erwin, 116, 117, 118
Op-ed pieces, 153, 156
Opinion polls, 89–95; abortion issue and,
    206, 207; on confidence in press,
    33; new methods, 91–95; proposed
    ban on saccharin and, 91–92; public
    relations use of, 89–95; Reagan
    public relations and, 198; on
    Tylenol, 169. *See also* Public
    opinion
Organization of Eastern Caribbean States
    (OECS), 25; U.S. invasion of
    Grenada and, 12–15
Osborne, Adam, 49–50, 130, 131, 138
Osborne Computer Corporation, 49–50,
    138
Osgood, Peter, 74, 136, 144–145
Other Side of the Story, The (Powell), 64

P

Packard, Vance, 68
Pauley, Jane, 123, 124
PBS, 79; *Nightly Business Report*, 70; in
    Soviet Union, 215
Pearlman, Sy, 59, 60
Pearlstine, Norman, 180, 181
Pentagon public relations, 53–54, 189–190
People magazine, 70, 103, 110, 111;
    cheating the news and, 221; on
    Nixon interviews, 193; product
    public relations and, 135
Pet Rocks, 120
Planned Parenthood, 204, 205, 206, 207
Police, the (rock group), public relations
    and, 109
Political public relations, 32, 75–76,
    187–208; abortion issue and,
    204–208; differentiation from news,
    189, 190–193; disasters and, 191;
    disguised as real news, 191–193;
    extent of use, 189–190; federal
    government and, 189; history of,
    190; influence of, 208; and media
    "event" for Cook's arrival in U.S.,
    187–189; methods, 191, 201–202;
    Nixon and, 200–201; Nixon
    interviews and, 193–194;
    organizations using, 189–190;
    Reagan administration and,
    194–199; White House use of,
    194–202; Wilderness Society and,
    202–204
Politicians: independent endorsers of, 73;
    use of public relations by, 30, 67,
    75–76
Polls. *See* Opinion polls
Powell, Charles, 29, 104, 105, 106
Powell, Jody, 64, 199, 219
PR Newswire, 88–89
Presidents and the Press (Spear), 199, 200
Press: agenda-setting by, 221; attitudes
    toward public relations people,
    68–69; Iran-Iraq war and, 40; poll
    on confidence in, 33; public attitude
    toward, 33–34; rise and influence of
    public relations and, 32; Soviet
    invasion of Afghanistan and, 40;
    Wall Street Journal's public
    relations on stock tipping issue and,
    179–181; in wartime, 39–40; White
    House control of, 75–76. *See also*
    Media; Press and public relations
Press and public relations, 33–45; as
    adversary relationship, 57–59; Air

relations and, 85, 120
Snyder, Al, 209–210
Soap, product public relations and, 119–120
Somoza, Anastasio, 84, 85
Soviet public relations: American television newspeople in Soviet Union and, 215; changes in, 211–215; Korean Airlines flight 007 incident and, 210, 211–212. *See also* U.S.-Soviet public relations war
Space shuttle, and articles on business potential of outer space, 192–193
Speakes, Larry, 86, 195
Spielberg, Steven, 104, 105
Staebler, Charles, 47, 49
Standard and Poor's, 144
Stock analysts, public relations and, 74–75, 144
Stock prices, public relations manipulation of, 143–144
Stockholders, as target public of GM, 77
Studio 54, 51, 63–65, 114

T

Talk shows: book public relations and, 112; CBS News–Westmoreland matter and, 176; issues public relations and, 153; product public relations and, 135–136
Target public, 27, 28; business public relations and, 144; hijacking hoax and, 147–148; medium selection and, 78–80; public relations use of, 76–78
Taubman, Philip, 20, 64
Television: advertising and public relations on, 68; advertising problems, 68; business news on, 54–55, 58–59; CBS News–Westmoreland matter and, 176; compared with other media, 15–16; "Financial Interest and Syndication Rule" and, 154–158; Mobil's attempted takeover of Marathon and, 182; morning talk shows, 59–60; musical groups and, 110; news sources, 61; news timing of students arriving from Grenada and, 22; product public relations and, 126–127, 129; promotional news and, 60; public relations influence on, 35, 59–60; publishing public relations and, 113–114; Reagan administration public relations and, 198; Soviet, 212; Soviet representatives on, 214;

U.S. invasion of Grenada and, 15. *See also* Local television news; Television news
Television news, 31; public relations and, 51, 60; quality of, 221–222; video press releases and, 87
Tennyson, Christopher, 133, 134
Third-party endorsements, 71–74; abortion issue and, 207; corporate takeovers and, 184; entertainment public relations and, 106–107; hospitals and, 127; Knoxville World's Fair public relations and, 134; new products and, 94–95; product public relations and, 128; stock prices and, 144
Third Reich, public relations for, 85
Three Mile Island nuclear-power-plant accident, 121, 168
Time magazine, 16, 29–30, 31, 38, 76, 79, 103, 110, 152*n*, 157; entertainment public relations and, 103, 104; FCC case and, 156; Korean Airlines flight 007 incident and, 210; product public relations and, 135; on public attitude toward press, 33–34; public relations for Menudo and, 111; publishing public relations and, 112–113. See also *Ariel Sharon* v. *Time Inc.*
Today show, 19, 23, 103, 115, 216; Cabbage Patch Kids public relations and, 123–124
Topping, Seymour, 34, 46–47
Trade press, use of public relations by, 53–54
Trammel, Jeff, 154, 155, 159
Trombly, Susan, 103, 104
Turkheimer, Nathan, 96
TV Guide, 111; CBS–Westmoreland matter and, 174
20/20, 51, 60, 110, 111, 113, 114, 130, 135
Tylenol case, 168–170

U

Union Carbide, gas-leak disaster in India, 91, 140, 168
United States Committee on Public Information, 107–108, 119
United States Department of Defense: freedom of the press in wartime and, 40; public relations operation at, 9–25; released footage on U.S. invasion of Grenada, 24; U.S. invasion of Grenada and, 20. *See also* United States Government

relations and, 66, 86, 193, 194, 201
Watt, James, 216; political public relations and, 202–204
WCBS-TV, 88, 127
Weinberger, Caspar, 19, 22, 23, 191
Western Pacific railroad, attempted takeover of Houghton Mifflin by, 184–185
Westin, Av, 51, 58, 113, 130
Westmoreland, William, 30; CBS News and, 173–178
Westmoreland v. *CBS, Inc., et al.,* 173–178
White House: chief spokesman for, 26; control of press, 75–76; imitation news and, 220; political public relations against, 202–204; sources and insiders, 61–62; use of public relations by, 194–202
Wiener, Robert S., Cabbage Patch Kids public relations and, 120–125
Wilderness Society, 202–204
Winans, R. Foster, 178–181

Wire services: Cabbage Patch Kids and, 123; PR Newswire stories and, 89; White House News Service, 197
Wirthlin, Richard, Reagan public relations and, 195, 198
WNBC-TV, 59, 88, 127, 137
WNEW-TV, 127; in Soviet Union, 215
Women, public relations and cigarette smoking by, 85, 120
Women's Wear Daily, 51, 137
World Information News Service, 97–101
World News Tonight, 51, 58, 110
World War II, public relations during, 39–40, 108

Y

Young, Lew, 57

Z

Ziegler, Ron, 26, 193, 195, 200–201